Haymaking using horsepower to drive a mechanical elevator.

BREMHILL PARISH
THROUGH THE AGES

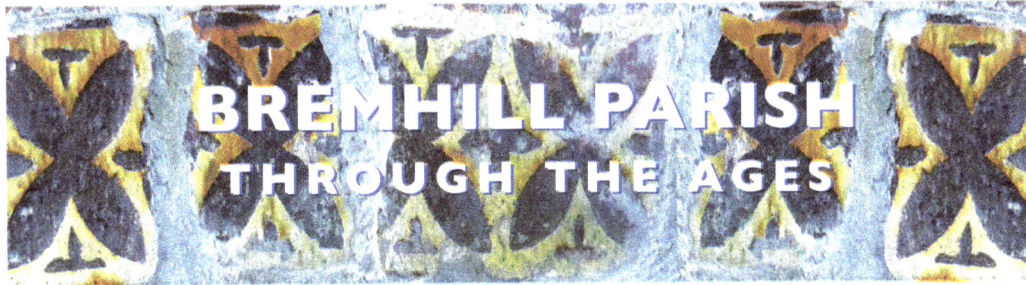

The Heritage of a Wiltshire Community

Louise Ryland-Epton

With contributions from Ewen Bird, John Harris, Christopher Kent, Isobel Moore, Jim Scott, Helen Stuckey, David Wood.

Designed and produced by John Harris.

THANKS TO OUR SUPPORTERS

Made possible with
Heritage Fund

VICTORIA COUNTY HISTORY

Calne Area Board
Wiltshire Council

'*Bryme*' (Bremhill) given by King Athelstan to the Abbey at Malmesbury. Also mentioned are '*Chedecotum*' (Charlcutt) and '*Speerful*' (Spirthill).

C 935

Edward the Confessor confirms Bremhill, together with Foxham, Charlcutt and Spirthill are possessions of the Abbey of Malmesbury. The parish has a value of £16.

1065

England is conquered by Norman invaders under Duke William. William is crowned King.

1066

Empress Matilda gives 'a singular and romantic spring on the summit of a hill in Pewsham Forest' to the Cistercian monks for an abbey. The site will become Stanley Abbey.

1151

King John signed the Magna Carta.

1215

A new chapel and refectory are built at Stanley Abbey.

1270

Bremhill is inherited by Sir Henry Bayntun (*d.*1616) who maintains close ties with the parish.

1593

The estates pass to Sir Edward Bayntun (*d.*1657) 'a man of arrogant and uncertain temper, often at odds with his neighbours, and his public career …was fraught with disputes.'

1616

Rev. John Tounson becomes vicar of Bremhill.

1639

English Civil War and Interregnum. Rev. John Tounson loses the benefice for contact with parliamentary forces. In *c.*1645 Bremhill Manor possession of Sir Edward Bayntun destroyed by parliamentary forces.

1642-1660

Rev. Tounson returns to take up his post as vicar and remains for a further 27 years. He harasses local Quakers and brings many lawsuits against his parishioners.

1660

The Dumb Post Inn is established. The name is a source of conjecture.

C 1675

A TIME LINE OF BREMHILL

A workhouse is created in Bremhill in the church house, probably now the site of the village hall.

1781

Moravians establish a school for girls at East Tytherton. Its first headmistress is Ann Grigg.

1794

Celebrated poet and eccentric Rev. William Lisle Bowles becomes vicar of Bremhill.

1804

Marchioness of Lansdowne establishes a school at Foxham.

C 1818

Queen Victoria ascends to the throne.

1837

A monument to Maud Heath is erected at the instigation of Rev. Bowles and the Marquess of Lansdowne.

1838

Reading Rooms are established at Bremhill, Charlcutt and Foxham by Lord Fitzmaurice with his brother the Marquess of Lansdowne.

1882-5

Major excavations take place at the Stanley Abbey site.

1905

World War I.

1914-1918

The Stanley Estate is sold to the Lansdownes of Bowood.

1919

A Celtic cross in the churchyard of St Martin Bremhill is dedicated to those local men who died in WWI. Other tablets are erected around the village.

1920

East Tytherton village hall is opened to great excitement after many years in the planning. The East Tytherton branch of the Women's Institute starts in the same year.

1924

1348
Black Death arrives and sweeps through the country. Between 25-50% of the population dies. Hazeland Mill becomes a woollen mill due to increase of woollen industry.

1455-1485
The War of the Roses. England is torn apart by civil war.

C 1474
Maud Heath's charity established to maintain a causeway from Bremhill through East Tytherton and Langley Burrell to Chippenham. Maud is painted as a humble woman but was a substantial property owner.

1536
Stanley Abbey is dissolved in Henry VIII's first wave of dissolution of the monasteries. However, in 1537 the Abbey site is sold to Sir Edward Bayntun (d.1544) of Bromham Hall.

1564
Agnes Mylles of Stanley is hanged as a witch for the murder of William Bayntun, the infant son of Sir Edward Bayntun (d.1593).

1566
Sir Edward Bayntun finally acquires Bremhill and Stanley after legal disputes over his brother's will and financial dealings.

C 1694
Joseph Haskins Stiles purchases Bremhill estate. In 1742, it is put up for sale by order of Chancery but remains on the market for years. Stanley remains owned by the Bayntun family.

1712
Sir George Hungerford of Cadenham Manor dies with his financial affairs 'much entangled' after a law suit with his son Walter. A Baroque marble monument was erected in St Martin's Church.

1745
A Moravian settlement is established at East Tytherton by John Cennick. The chapel and manse are re-built 1792-3.

C 1750
A bakery is established at Bremhill.

1753
Bremhill estate is purchased for £57,500 by William Petty, Earl Shelburne. He becomes Prime Minister and in 1784 the Marquess of Lansdowne. The family also acquire land at Spirthill and Foxham.

C 1770
The Dumb Post Friendly Society is created offering support to local working men.

ARISH THROUGH THE AGES

1846
Bremhill hosts an Anti-Corn Law Meeting. Local women Mary Ferris and Lucy Simpkins speak inspiring Charles Dickens to write the poem, *Hymn of the Wiltshire Labourer.* The vicar, Rev. Drury, is appalled.

1847
Bremhill School is built next to St Martin's Church.

1855
A second Wesleyan chapel is built at Foxham. The vicar feels more people attend chapel than the church.

1857
Bremhill Post Office is opened on 1st April.

1871
Moravians establish a new school in East Tytherton for local children which becomes the most popular in the parish. The Local Education Authority controls it in early twentieth century.

1880
The Church of St John the Baptist is opened at Foxham with building costs covered by subscriptions including from the Marquess of Lansdowne and the vicar, the Rev. Eddrup.

1930
Foxham School is closed.

1939-1945
World War II.

1947
The Bowood Estate sells off a large number of farms and property across the parish, including the Dumb Post Inn.

1959
The Spirthill and Charlcutt Women's Institute is formed, which becomes the Bremhill and District WI by 1969.

1969
Bremhill School is closed. The building becomes the village hall.

1972
Bakery at no. 24 in Bremhill is closed down.

Contents

First published in 2021
This paperback edition published in 2023

Published by Bremhilll Parish History Group
in association with *The Hobnob Press, 8 Lock Warehouse, Severn Road, Gloucester, GL1 2GA.*

www.bremhillparishhistory.com
www.hobnobpress.co.uk

ISBN 978-1-914407-58-1

British Library Cataloguing Data. A cataloguing record for this book is available from the British Library.

Typeset in Humanist 521 and Minion.

To the people

of Bremhill parish,

past, present

and future

Foreword

The Bremhill Parish History Project was started in 2018 to research, record and share the heritage of our parish in north Wiltshire and the story of the community over the last 1,000 years. We embarked on a broad programme of workshops, talks and field-trips, encouraging as many volunteers as possible to get involved, with the aim of making the resulting material widely accessible in a variety of formats. This book is one of the principal outputs of the project.

As there had been no attempt since the early nineteenth century to pull together a history of the parish, we did not know quite what we were going to find. We knew there was a lot of heritage around us, as there are 101 listed buildings and monuments in the parish.

This book - and the chapter for the Wiltshire Victoria County History volume that has been produced in parallel - certainly gives one a good understanding of these local landmarks and our cherished landscape. However, it is the fascinating human stories that have been uncovered that provide the most remarkable content, bringing the past to life through vivid personal and local perspectives on historic national events and social and economic trends.

Significant funding for the project came from the National Lottery Heritage Fund and a range of local grant-making organisations, including the Calne Area Board, the Wiltshire Victoria County History Trust, the Bradenstoke Solar Park Community Benefit Fund, Bremhill Parish Council, the Charlcutt Reading Room and Library Fund, the Friends of St Martins, the Friends of St Nicholas and the Chalke Valley History Trust. Our thanks to them all for their generosity and support.

The project has been very much a team effort, and I want to record my thanks and appreciation to the members of the steering group - John Harris, Sarah Jones and Helen Stuckey, who have contributed ideas, enthusiasm and research and helped keep the project on track.

We were most fortunate to be introduced to our professional historian, Louise Ryland-Epton, by the Wiltshire Victoria County History team. Louise has been a pleasure to work with, combining rigorous research with a fluent writing style, and has been highly encouraging to our volunteer researchers and writers.

Louise has been greatly assisted in this, her first book, by John Chandler, the eminent local historian of Wiltshire, and by Eleo Carson, who has bought a wealth of experience and energy to the task of editing.

The finished quality of the book is testament to the professionalism, high standards and dedication of John Harris who has kindly taken responsibility for the design and production, as well as personally contributing writing, illustrations and photographs. Steve Harris has also played a crucial role in producing the artwork for the book.

Our thanks also to the village co-ordinators - Ewen Bird, Craig Gingell, Tom King, Derek McCord and Isobel Moore - and to the many people of the parish who have participated in the project over the last couple of years in a wide variety of ways. The pandemic obviously caused significant disruption, as many events that had been planned had to be cancelled or went on-line. The Bremhill History Festival had to be reduced in scale, but we were able to launch our heritage trail app and a series of well-attended on-line seminars were organised. Indeed the project provided, for many, a welcome point of social contact and engagement during a difficult time.

For just as it is the people of the parish whose stories illuminate this book, it is their successors who have made the process of this project so engaging and enjoyable. Hence the dedication – to the people of Bremhill parish, past, present and future.

Martin Nye
Bremhill Parish History Group

Preface

Where in England would you find a parish which gave rise to a poem by Dickens and where a local gentlewoman (or indeed was she a gentlewoman?) made provision so that the people of the parish could keep their feet dry on an elevated causeway on the way to market?

This book is the history of that parish, Bremhill, in north Wiltshire. It is about the landscape, villages, and buildings of the parish, but for the most part, it is about its people. It illustrates the history of the community of Bremhill through the experience of those who lived there. There are the eccentrics, the possible villains, those who suffered or were oppressed, and those who stood up to injustice or broke the conventions of their time. Many of the most fascinating stories are about women and working people, who typically do not find their way into history books.

The book uses archival and online research of primary source material, oral history testimonies and written pieces from many volunteers within the community. Some of the lives which were uncovered proved too compelling to ignore. Some were rich in source material and ended by being explored at length. In contrast, others, although seemingly fascinating, proved elusive and have ended up as a sentence or two. The further back in time we went, the more complex these stories were to explore. However, in the twentieth century, the sources were very rich, while the recollections and information from those living within the community were invaluable, and one of the reasons why this era was examined in depth.

The book is presented as follows:-

Chapter 1: Landscape, Settlement and Buildings - looks at the landscape of the parish, considers its earliest history, how the settlements acquired their names and how the villages and buildings developed. The fascinating story of Stanley Abbey is revealed. From the possible location of a Neolithic standing stone to the creation of a Cistercian abbey to its development as a Tudor mansion set within a formal garden, the house was the likely setting of an alleged murder.

Chapter 2: Ways, Water and Steam - examines the history of the transport links between the parish of Bremhill and the wider world, the trackways and roads and later canal and railway developments which brought it into contact with the broader region. The history of Maud Heath's causeway which was originally created by the gift of a local widow in 1474, is discussed. Was Maud Heath a wealthy widow or a simple market trader? The route of the causeway is also explored.

Chapter 3: Agriculture, Trades and Emigration - looks at how the community made a living in the centuries up to 1911. Unsurprisingly, the importance of all forms of agriculture and food production such as brewing and cheese-making is revealed, but other aspects such as woollen cloth manufacture and even soap making feature. At times, the financial hardship endured by local people is exposed, but so too is their resilience and ingenuity. The tale of Lucy Simpkins portrays this very well. Lucy was a labourer's wife who stood up and made such a passionate and eloquent speech at Bremhill in 1846 about the difficulties of feeding her family that it inspired no less a writer than Charles Dickens to write a poem.

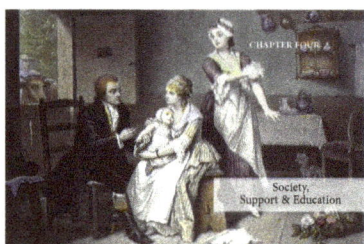

Chapter 4: Society, Support and Education - investigates the social history of the parish, its character and communal life. It includes consideration of how the community looked after each other or helped people look after themselves, through welfare, charity, friendly societies, and education. The account is sometimes surprising, such as the provision of medical care for the poor from the 1760s and occasionally nauseating, like the use of dog excrement in a Tytherton Lucas remedy for sore throats. The chapter also explores morality and gossip and includes a tale of a secret, probably forbidden, marriage.

Chapter 5: Folklore, Superstition and Witchcraft - describes the customs and superstitions the people of the parish practised in past centuries. This chapter is possibly the most unexpected. It includes tales of bizarre rites observed locally into the nineteenth century (one involving naked babies and a ritual performed on the pagan festival of Beltane) that may have origins in pre-Christian times, ghostly apparitions and an alleged case of witchcraft that ended in the hanging of Agnes Mylles, a woman from Stanley in 1564.

Chapter 6: Government, Crime and Punishment - explains how the parish of Bremhill managed its own affairs for much of its history, including some aspects of criminal justice. It examines some of the crimes (or possible crimes) which took place in the parish from the thirteenth century. From the occasion, Adam, son of Maud, was run over by a wagon, through to Robert Slade in the nineteenth century who the coroner decided 'accidentally' impaled himself to death on a pitchfork. It also investigates a seventeenth-century sex scandal in East Tytherton when the community administered its own brand of rough justice.

Government, Crime & Punishment

Chapter 7: Churches, Chapels and Religion - contemplates the influence of religion and religious intolerance in Bremhill parish through the centuries. The first parish historian, nineteenth-century vicar, and eccentric Rev. William Lisle Bowles looms large, but so too does his more problematic predecessor, Rev. John Tounson, who brought numerous lawsuits against his parishioners and in his persecution of one Charlcutt Quaker went as far as to rustle her cattle. This chapter also looks at the history of the churches at Bremhill, Foxham and Tytherton Lucas, considers the importance of local chapels, and the Moravian church's development in East Tytherton.

Churches, Chapels & Religion

Chapter 8: Wars, Change and the Parish Today - the final chapter brings the parish's story into the twentieth century, a period of war and huge socio-economic change. The experience of the parish during the World Wars is investigated in-depth, including the work done by local women in WWI and the role of the Home Guard in WWII. Again, the narrative highlights the resilience of local people, and is illuminated by the reminiscences and anecdotes of those currently living in the parish. The chapter ends by bringing the history of the community into the twenty-first century, and concludes that adaptability and a strong appreciation of a shared heritage will enable the parish to thrive in the future.

Wars, Change & The Parish Today

Dr Louise Ryland-Epton

December 2021

CHAPTER ONE

Landscape, Settlement & Buildings

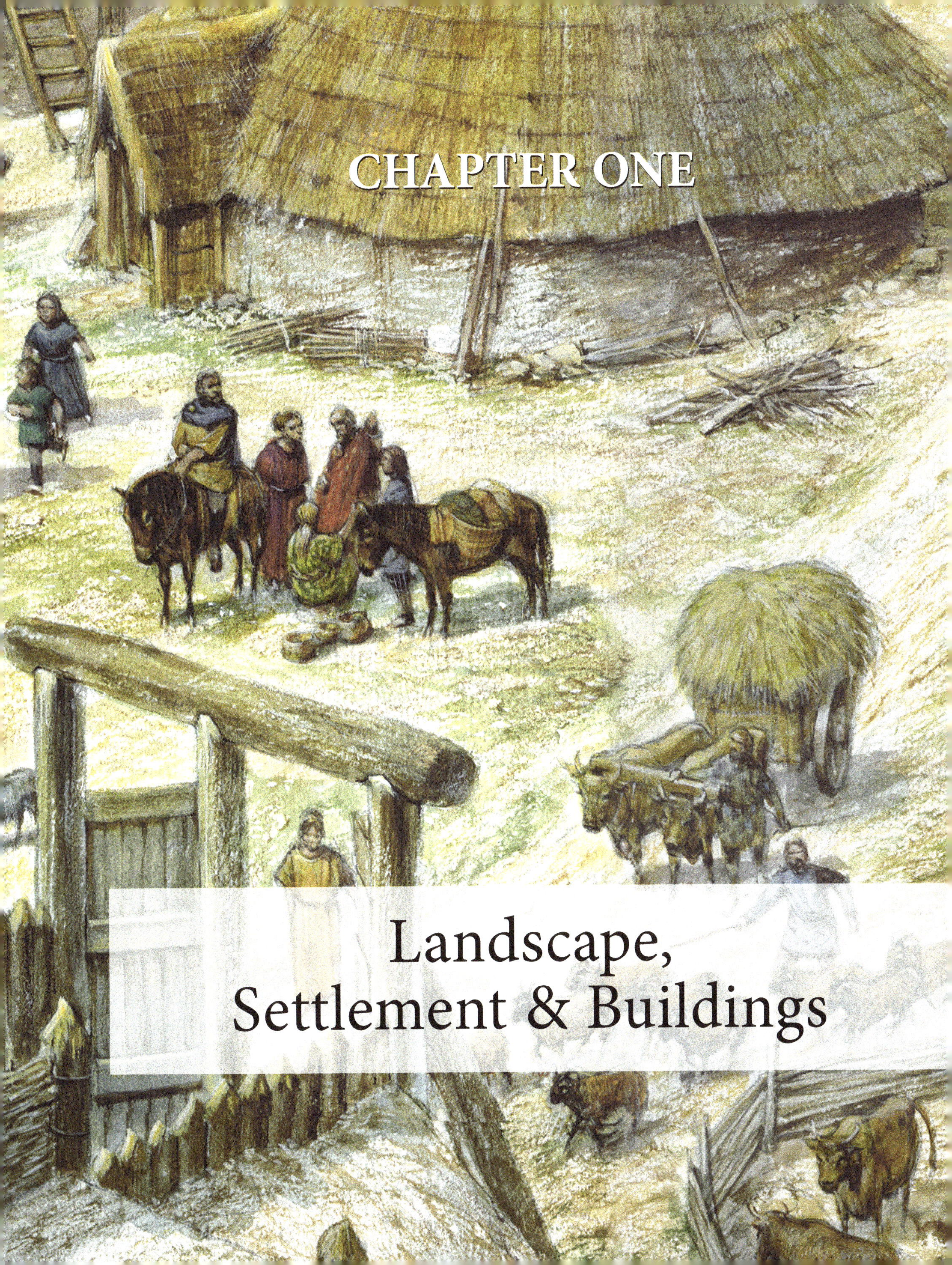

Chapter 1: Landscape, Settlement and Buildings

Today, Bremhill is a large scattered civil parish of 7,694 acres in north Wiltshire, lying between Calne and Chippenham. The first parish historian, the poet, Rev. William Lisle Bowles, described it in 1828 as 'situated partly on a commanding eminence and partly in a luxuriant and extensive vale.'[1] It is an apt description. However, it could be described more precisely. The western and north-western portions of Bremhill parish are Oxford clay, and the terrain is comparatively flat and low-lying. A Corallian Limestone ridge dominates the east and south-east of the parish. This forms steep escarpments, a high plateau and to the east, a far more broken, intimate landscape. The Cowage Brook flows south into the Marden River near Ratford at the southern tip of the parish, while the Marden flows north-west to join the Avon near Tytherton Lucas. Minor streams and watercourses rise along the escarpment and trend westward to the River Avon.[2]

1.1 Roman, Anglo-Saxon and Norman Bremhill

Fig. 1: Drawing from a Roman frieze depicting a family with their mode of transport (*carpentum*) during the 4th century AD.

Fig. 2: (previous page) A fortified enclosure around an Anglo-Saxon thegn's manor house provided protection for his work-force and their dwellings.

The Romans settled in Britain from AD43. In north Wiltshire, their Romano-British settlement patterns are primarily associated with villa estates alongside smaller dispersed farmsteads in the valleys. Near the present-day parish of Bremhill, there are two possible villas in the grounds of Bowood Park. A further villa was discovered and later excavated at Bromham in 1765.[3]

Additionally, an estate has been discovered at Lyneham. Rev. William Lisle Bowles, the vicar of Bremhill from 1804 to 1845, was fascinated by the possibility of Romano-British occupation of his parish and noted evidence of Roman settlements near Bremhill. He encouraged local people to look for finds and paid for coins dug up in one field, Red-hill at Studley, and noted 200 had been collected in twelve months, largely from the fourth-century reign of Emperor Constantine.[4] It is likely that these, and any other villa estates still to be discovered in and near Bremhill, were associated with and dependent on a small town, Verlucio, which straddled the Roman road from London to Bath close to the present village of Sandy Lane, some three miles south of Bremhill. Verlucio would have had an extensive territory around it that it administered, and after the Roman period had ended, this may have fragmented into smaller units. However, despite some Roman material found in recent years, a geophysical investigation in 2019 found no clear-cut evidence of Roman habitation at a test site in Foxham.[5]

By the middle Anglo-Saxon period, between the seventh and eighth centuries, Wiltshire had been carved up into great royal estates. Chippenham was one, complete with a royal residence. Although Bremhill may originally have been included in the Chippenham estate, by the Norman invasion in 1066, much of the area associated with the parish of Bremhill no longer belonged to the Crown. A charter in the possession of Malmesbury Abbey from 935 recorded a grant of sixty hides of land at Bremhill, or approximately 7,200 acres, from King Athelstan to the monks of Malmesbury Abbey.[6]

Fig. 3: Roman coins found at Red-hill, Studley.

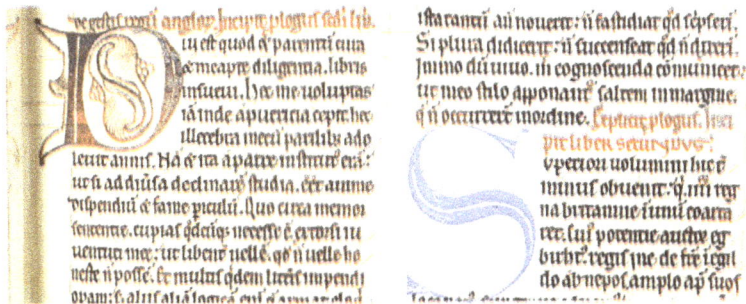

Fig. 4: William of Malmesbury's fraudulent 12th century charter, purported to date back to 935, recorded King Athelstan's gifts of land including a holding in Bremhill.

This document in the form that it has come down to us is probably a forgery, made later by the monks to try to establish their title to land which they knew they had owned for some time.[7] In 1065, King Edward the Confessor made a confirmation of Malmesbury Abbey's land, and this referenced an original gift by Athelstan. This charter assessed the holding at thirty-eight hides (or about 4,560 acres). As well as Bremhill, the charter also referred to land in Euridge (in Colerne), Spirthill, Charlcutt, Foxham and Avon. Like the earlier document it too is disputed, but it may have an authentic core.[8] Either way, by 1066, Bremhill, comprising thirty-eight hides including the settlements at Spirthill, Charlcutt, Foxham and Avon, was, indeed, in the possession of Malmesbury Abbey.

CHRISTIAN MALFORD

SAND PITS

THE GREAT TREE

THORNEND

AVON GROVE WOOD

CATCOMB WOOD

FOXHAM

AVON

CADENHAM

STOCKHAM MARSH

GOATACRE

CATCOMB

SPIRTHILL

RIVER AVON

CADE BURNA

CHARLCUTT

ASH BEDS

EAST TYTHERTON

TURNHAM WOOD

CURRICOMB

BREMHILL GROVE

HONEYBED WOOD

TYTHERTON LUCAS

COWAGE BROOK

STANLEY

HAZELAND WOOD

BREMHILL

RIVER MARDEN

RATFORD

Fig. 5

ARTIST'S IMPRESSION OF

THE ANGLO-SAXON ESTATE OF BREMHILL

(USING CURRENT PLACE NAMES)

Malmesbury Abbey also preserved a document which purported to describe the boundaries of their Anglo-Saxon estate of Bremhill. It is undated but was perhaps derived from one drawn up when the monks forged the Athelstan charter. It is written in Latin and Old English, and analysis of the landmarks listed to define the boundary suggests that it equated very closely to the parish as it existed right up until the nineteenth century, a correspondence which seems remarkable but is quite commonplace in documents of this kind. The landmarks have been translated into modern English, as follows:[9]

First from the place which is called marsh-harrier coomb to boundary valley.

And from boundary valley straight along the course (of the stream) to the street.

And from that street to Cat Brook, and from the head of that brook straight to the Avon.

And thus, straight along the Avon to Christian Malford, and from that place straight to huckeam [possibly Foxham].

And from that to the great tree, and from that place to the sand [or 'gravel'] pit, and thus to the steep slope, and thus along the steep slope to stile way, and from that way to black marsh, and from that marsh back to the starting-place, that is marsh-harrier coomb.

The first line of the description refers to the hamlet of Catcomb in Hilmarton. From there, the border passed to 'boundary valley', which lay to the south of Goatacre, and gave its name to the River Marden. The stream, in line two, refers to the Cowage Brook, and the bounds followed this for several miles south along 'boundary valley' passed Charlcutt and Spirthill to the Brook's junction with the River Marden, below Ratford and adjacent to Hazeland Wood. It then continued along the river to a point by Hazeland Mill. Then slightly south of the river for a stretch to re-join the River Marden and to Stanley. The 'street' may refer to what is now Stanley Lane, and from here, the bound went north towards East Tytherton and crossed the Cat Brook (Cade Burna). The boundary next ran north and west to connect to the Cade Burna at a junction of streams north of Curricomb Farm. It then followed the Cade Burna until it met the River Avon north-east of Tytherton Lucas. After that, it followed the line of the river passed the hamlet of Avon to the village of Christian Malford, and thereafter east to Foxham. It has been suggested that the 'great tree' mentioned in the last section of the description was probably at Thornend and the 'steep slope' was the hill on which RAF Lyneham was located. After skirting the summit of the hill, the parish boundary descended just to the west of Catcomb Wood, and then joined the road between Foxham and Catcomb, which may be the stile way referred to in the text.

Fig. 6: Watercolour of scribes in a *scriptorium*, a room set aside in a monastery for the preparation of manuscripts.

The area outlined in the charter encompassed the settlements of Bremhill, Foxham, Avon, Charlcutt, Spirthill and East Tytherton. Within these bounds also, but independent from it in 1066, was the small estate of Cadenham, which paid geld for two hides. In 1086, it was held by William (Malbank) tenant of Earl Hugh of Chester.[10] Cadenham, is likely to be derived from the name Cada, and thus means Cada's ham (homestead). The name Cada is also associated with Catcomb, a settlement to the east in Hilmarton, and the stream, the Cade Burna, which is mentioned in the charter.[11]

At the Norman invasion in 1066, Bremhill was the easternmost parish within the Chippenham hundred (the hundred broadly aligned with the original Chippenham royal estate). Although outside the forest of Chippenham, the area possessed a long strip of woodland, about three miles long and a quarter mile wide, within its extent. In the Domesday survey, ordered in 1085 to record the resources and taxable values of all the boroughs and manors in England, it is also recorded as having thirty-seven ploughlands, corresponding almost exactly to the thirty-eight hides referred to in the pre-Conquest charter. A ploughland was an imprecise measure but referred to the land that could be cultivated by one plough team in one year. In this instance, the manor possessed upwards of 3,000 acres of cultivatable land. Alongside this, there were twenty-two acres of meadow and three mills. The survey also recorded forty-five peasant households in Bremhill (this would have included settlements at Bremhill, Foxham, Avon, Charlcutt, Spirthill and possibly East Tytherton) and twelve slaves; a further eight households and two slaves were recorded for Cadenham. Using a multiplier of 4.5 for households but regarding slaves as individuals, the approximate total population of Bremhill was 220 and for Cadenham it was 45.[12]

The name given for Bremhill is 'Breme' and is derived from the old English word, *bremel*, meaning 'bramble, collection of thorns.'[13] The Domesday Book refers to four acres of *spinetum*, meaning 'thorns' or 'brambles', perhaps a local landmark from which the parish derived its name.[14] The suffix 'hill' came later.

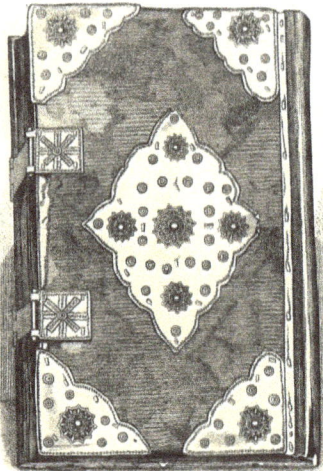

Fig. 7: Illustration of the clasped Domesday Book commissioned in 1085 by William the Conqueror.

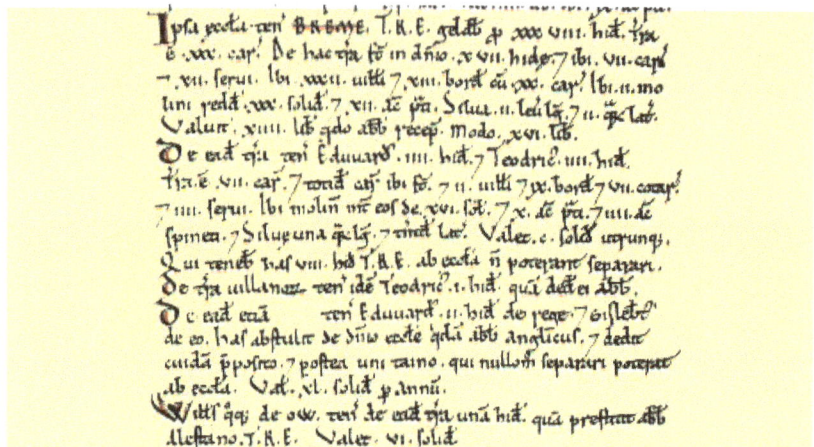

Fig. 8: The actual entry in the Domesday Book for Bremhill as 'Breme' in the Hundred of Chippenham.

During the same period, Stanley remained a tithing (a term for a sub-division of a manor or parish) of Chippenham, the only settlement within the royal forest of Chippenham (later known as the forest of Pewsham), and where generally habitations were likely to have been discouraged.[15] Although within the forest area, marshland lay between Stanley and Chippenham.[16] In 1086, the Stanley estate paid geld for one hide and three virgates of land. There was land for one plough and ten acres of meadow. Its population was small, probably around thirty and likely dispersed and concentrated on farmsteads on the higher ground.[17] In 1086, it was held by Azelin from Waleran the Hunter, who possessed a total of sixteen estates within Wiltshire. Stanley was worth 30s annually. Bremhill was, by comparison, valued at £23 in 1066.[18]

The name Stanley derived from 'leah', the Old English for 'forest, wood, glade, clearing.'[19] The first element indicated that it was a stone clearing (within a wooded area). There are a few stony outcrops visible in the landscape. Dr Graham Brown suggests a 'plausible interpretation' may be that there was a pre-historic standing stone here (a stone set upright into the ground probably between 4,000 and 1,500 BC).[20] As well as the possible site of a standing stone, it has been suggested that there was probably a medieval settlement area in Stanley, east of Hither Farm, where aerial photographs have revealed earthworks associated with ridge and furrow.[21]

Like Stanley, Tytherton Lucas (or West Tytherton), was recorded separately from Bremhill and was also a tithing of Chippenham. It was listed as two manors in Domesday Book, although one may have referred to East Tytherton. Between the two manors was one mill, five ploughlands and sixteen acres of meadow. The origin of the name Tytherton is uncertain. It may derive from a personal name or come from the Old English *tidre*, 'fragile, weak'. However, recently, it has also been suggested that Tytherton derives from the Old English verb *tydrian* 'to propagate' and - *tun* 'farm, village'.[22] An allusion perhaps to the settlement's agricultural fertility. In use from the thirteenth century, the suffix 'Lucas' may relate to Adam, son of Luke, who had a holding here in 1249.[23]

The other settlements of Bremhill did not have individual listings within the Domesday survey. However, their placenames indicate they are just as ancient. The name 'Charlcutt' is derived from cottages of the cheorls or free farmers.[24] It probably dates back to when Bremhill belonged to the king and this was where the peasants lived who were not slaves but worked partly on the royal estate.[25] The name is likely to refer to the use of the settlement at the time of the royal estate at Chippenham. The word Foxham refers to *ham* ('homestead') or *hamm* ('meadow') where foxes are common and Spirthill may be derived from the word *spirt*, referring to a jet of water.[26]

Fig. 9: A typical farmstead settlement at the time of Waleran the Hunter.

Fig. 10: Ceorls were peasant 'free' farmers connected to the vicinity of Charlcutt.

Fig. 11: Early engraving of St Martin's Church in Bremhill.

One of the most significant early buildings in Bremhill, and still an indelible part of the village, is St Martin's Church. The early history of St Martin's is open to debate. The structure retains elements of Anglo-Saxon origin. An exemption by the Pope in the mid-twelfth century records Bremhill church was possessed of chapels. An association with chapels at Foxham and Highway was clearly established in the following century.[27] It has led historians to conjecture that St Martin's may have had the status of a minster (mother church), possibly established when Malmesbury Abbey acquired Bremhill from the king.[28]

However, Dr Simon Draper suggests an alternative.[29] He submits that Malmesbury Abbey did not acquire Bremhill from the monarch but rather from an Anglo-Saxon thegn (lord) to whom the king had granted the estate in the 900s. When thegns obtained estates, they often built manors and founded churches next to them. The oval enclosures built around the manor houses and churches are often visible in the landscape. The area around St Martin's and Manor Farm (now Bremhill Manor) and including a nearby spring exhibit the same characteristic. The shape of the enclosure is clearly visible in the earliest maps of the village.[30] The Anglo-Saxon masonry in the church also supports this theory. The settlement of Bremhill, thereafter, developed next to the enclosure. While geophysical surveys carried out of the lawn and a field at Bremhill Manor in 2020 found no obvious features that could be associated with the Anglo-Saxon occupation of the site, it remains a viable hypothesis.[31]

Fig. 12: Illustration of how an oval enclosure might have looked in the area around what is now St Martin's Church and Bremhill Farm (now Bremhill Manor).

During the ownership of the estate of Bremhill by Malmesbury Abbey, an abbey grange or farm is known to have been located close to St Martin's.[32] The barn at nearby Bremhill Manor (formerly Manor Farm) may be a relic of this farm and one of the few reminders of the association between the parish and the abbey.[33]

Fig. 13: The roof timbers of the Grade II Listed medieval barn adjacent to Bremhill Manor.

Fig. 14: The late medieval barn by Bremhill Manor may be part of the original grange of Malmesbury Abbey.

Although the manor itself is dated about 1820, the rear of the structure includes stonework concurrent with the barn and is likely to have been built on the site of the grange.[34] The other possibility is that the grange was incorporated into what became the vicarage.[35] At the dissolution of the monasteries, the estate of Bremhill along with the grange was bought by Sir Edward Bayntun and was maintained as a secondary family residence.[36] In the early seventeenth century, a survey of the estate states their residence, a substantial twenty bay and two-storey building, lay to the south-west of St Martin's Church at Bremhill. In which case, the grange and Bayntun house are likely to be at Bremhill Manor (Manor Farm) and not at the old vicarage now named Bremhill Court.

Fig. 15: A medieval core with a crown post forms part of the roof structure in Bremhill Court.

Fig. 15a: Bremhill Court (Bremhill Parsonage) the residence of the Rev. William Lisle Bowles.

However, Bremhill Court itself contains a medieval core, consisting of a hall house. Analysis of the timbers shows that some of the trees were felled during the 1320s. The building is likely to have been constructed by a person of status. Who this was, and their association with Malmesbury Abbey, is open to conjecture.[37]

Fig. 16: Engraving showing the apparel of a Cistercian monk.

Stanley Abbey:
A monastic settlement by the River Marden

Stanley Abbey was established in 1154 within the environs of Chippenham forest (in the king's estate of Chippenham) on the south bank of the River Marden by Cistercian monks, who had moved from a nearby site at Loxwell.[38] The order sought to locate their monasteries in places which allowed for isolation from the secular world. Stanley Abbey was placed in an area of marshland that was used as common pasture. It has also been suggested that the area was the site of a standing stone, which may have made it particularly attractive to the monks.[39]

The abbey was described later as occupying 'very rich land' and 'by the river's side, but in a place in the wintertime altogether unpleasant.'[40] Dr Graham Brown suggests, as the only settlement within the royal forest, Stanley may also have been associated with hunting, possibly the site of a royal hunting lodge used by the king while at Chippenham or Calne.[41]

The new abbey was constructed in stone; nonetheless, within fifty years, and for reasons that are not clear, the structures began to be rebuilt. The abbey initially thrived, and monks left in 1204 to establish a daughter house in Ireland.[42] Due to the difficulty of finding a good supply of water, an aqueduct was completed in 1214 from the old supply at Loxwell to the new lodge of the abbot.[43]

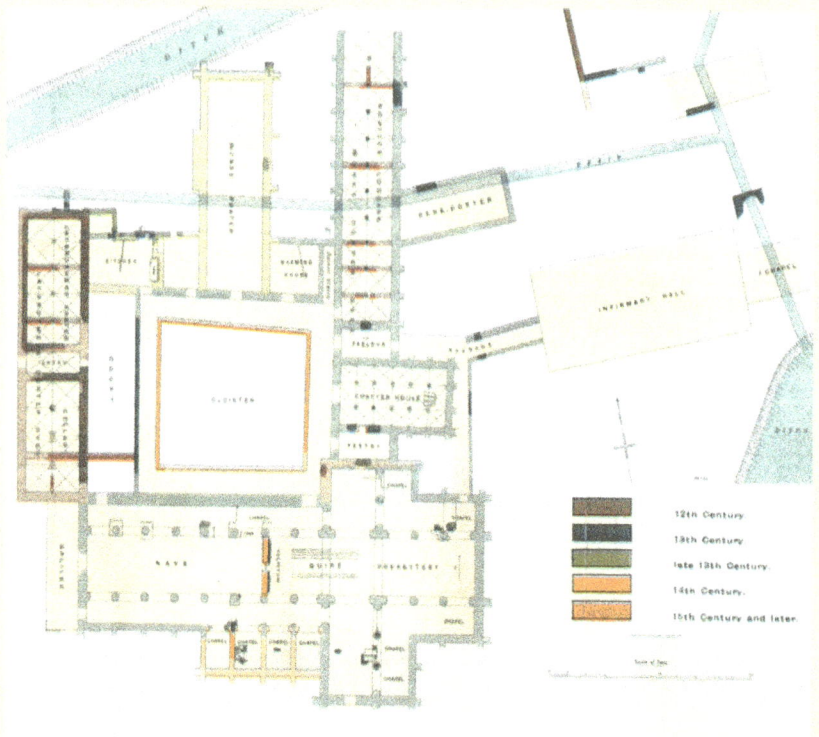

Fig. 17: The plan of Stanley Abbey's monastic complex drawn following Harold Brakspear's excavations in 1905-6.

In 1266, the Church of the Blessed Virgin Mary was completed, a new refectory was added in 1270, and in 1292, the monks were granted a licence 'to build houses of their abbey and a wall around them.[44] The repair and building of the structures likely continued, and even in 1535, some of the buildings were 'newe builded'.[45]

The thirteenth century was a period of relative prosperity for the abbey. In 1308, Edward II visited for two days. However, the monastery did not have a substantial benefactor, and from the early fourteenth to the mid-fifteenth century, it experienced some financial difficulties. This occasionally necessitated the sale of estate assets, while other property, such as a house in St Dunstan-in-the-West in London, were given up.[46] As the centuries passed, land and property were increasingly leased out by the abbey.

Fig. 18: The seal of Stanley Abbey.

Accounts survive of the abbey's granges (farms) from the reigns of Edward I, Henry V, and Henry VIII and suggest that their estates were mainly engaged in mixed farming. In 1303, Stanley Abbey held 211 acres of land, in separate parcels, converted from forest to either arable land or pasture for sheep and cattle. They also had a grant of a moorland and wood (possibly Close Woods) in lieu of the right to take timber from the forest itself.[47] As early as 1189, there is evidence of water meadows on the Stanley estate allowing an earlier growth of grass.[48] There is little indication that those living within the settlement of Stanley worshipped at the abbey, but the institution served as both employer and landlord.[49]

In 1535, Stanley Abbey was valued at £177 per annum.[50] Its assets included a church and estate at Stanley and parcels of land at Nash Hill (Lacock) and Nethermore, both part of Chippenham forest and at Loxwell, where it had been located before moving to Stanley. The monastery also possessed a block of land at Langley Burrell and some small parcels nearby.[51] It was dissolved in February 1536. At this time, there were nine monks in residence and one novice, along with forty-three servants of the monks, 'of honeste conversacion all desyringe contynynuance'.[52] The abbot, Thomas Calne (or Morley), received a pension, but the consequences of the closure of the abbey on the other monks and where they went after, are somewhat ambiguous.[53]

Fig. 19: Glazed decorated tiles from the Abbey now in the collection at Wiltshire Museum.

At the time of its dissolution, the buildings at Stanley were strong and in good repair. Edward Seymour, 1st Duke of Somerset, purchased much of the abbey's holdings from the Crown, but Edward Bayntun brought the abbey itself and the estate at Stanley of around 450 acres for £1,200.[54]

After that the Bayntuns converted the abbot's lodging (the west bay) into a mansion house. It was described in leases as a ten-bay building. Later works at the house suggest the Bayntuns created a network of decorative canals fed from the River Marden and several gardens, although these may not have been completed.[55] Evidence suggests that the tenants on the estate used the unutilised Stanley Abbey buildings as materials.[56]

Fig. 20: Graphic showing the garden canals fed from the River Marden with an overlay plan of the Abbey layout (see aerial map opposite).

However ornate and spectacular, the Stanley mansion and gardens were a secondary residence of the Bayntuns, whose main house was at Bromham, eight miles south. The family association may have been closest with Sir Andrew Bayntun, who died in 1564, and who was styled of both Bromham and Stanley. Later, the mansion may also have been the site of the alleged murder of William Bayntun by Agnes Mylles, a widow of Stanley (described in chapter 5). As a secondary residence, the house was sometimes leased to relatives or other tenants. Around the mid-seventeenth century, it became a farmhouse.[57] By the time John Aubrey made his commentary on the site of the former Stanley Abbey around 1670, he observed 'here is now scarce left any vestigium of Church or house.'[58]

Fig. 21: Airborne survey in 1947 showing evidence of the garden canals and building foundations of Stanley Abbey.

Fig. 21a: The gatehouse at Spye Park reputed to be the original entrance to Stanley Abbey, moved and rebuilt in the 17th century.

The original abbey gatehouse is reputed to have been moved to Spye Park, Wiltshire, a later seat of the Bayntun family. However, the Historic England listing of the gatehouse suggests it is sixteenth century and was remodelled in the eighteenth century and does not refer to the fact it was moved from elsewhere.[59] All that remains of Stanley Abbey today are the medieval abbey farm buildings and raised areas of grass.

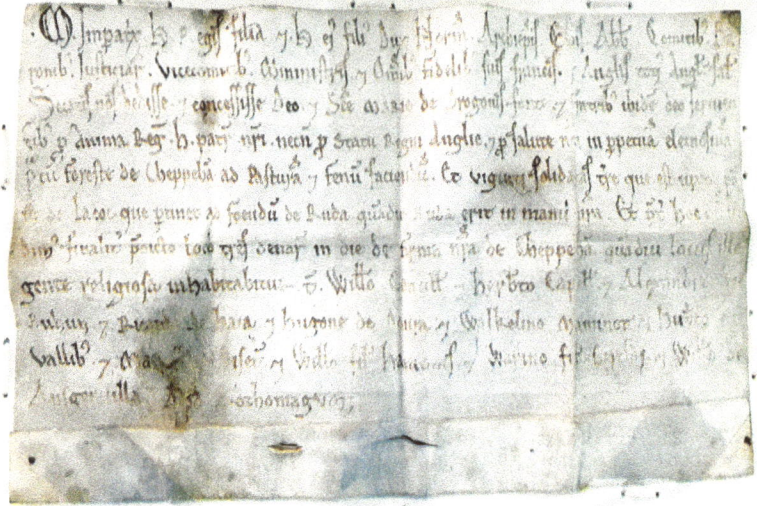

Fig. 21b: Stanley Abbey Charter of c.1151 from Empress Matilda.

Fig. 21c: St Edmund's Church, Calne, has a font made from the stone from the ruins of the Abbey.

1.2 Medieval to Early Modern

The ancient parish formed a rough rectangle four miles long from north to south and three miles wide east to west. For much of its history, the parish was exemplified by small hamlets, dispersed farmsteads, and mills spread over about 6,000 acres. In 1249, legal documents referred to the townships of Bremhill and Tytherton Lucas and mention a separate settlement at Stanley.[60] Bremhill was the largest. In 1332, there were seventy-six taxpayers in Bremhill compared to fourteen in Stanley and nineteen at Tytherton.[61] However, a better indicator of the local population came in 1377, when every person over the age of fourteen (and not a beggar or a clergyman) was obliged to pay a poll tax to the Crown to help fund a war with France. In Bremhill, there were 176 taxpayers, separate numbers were given for Foxham (126), Stanley (66), Avon, (21) and Tytherton Lucas (45). It is likely, therefore, the population across these communities equated to about 750.[62] In 1676, a total of 635 adult conformists and Nonconformists were reported in Bremhill, suggesting that the total population had grown and was probably in excess of 1,000.[63]

The principal landowners (and taxpayers) within the parish after the dissolution of the monasteries in the 1530s and 1540s were the owners of the manors. Their mansion houses were a feature of the landscape throughout the sixteenth and seventeenth centuries at Stanley, Bremhill, Cadenham and Tytherton Lucas. Only those at Cadenham and Tytherton Lucas remain.

Bremhill Manor, owned by the Bayntun family, was burned by royalist forces during the Civil Wars in 1645.[64] Edward Bayntun's behaviour during the war may have contributed to these circumstances. He had begun the conflict a parliamentarian, but had been accused of cowardice, 'exquisite tyranny' and was imprisoned in the Tower of London. He had made overtures to the king and ended being distrusted on both sides.[65]

The Hungerford family had a seat at Cadenham was built in the late seventeenth century, although it may incorporate elements of the original moated manor house which adjoined its current location. The moat and dovecote survive from the original structure.

Fig. 22: John of Gaunt, son of King Edward III of England, was largely responsible for persuading parliament to legislate for the Poll Tax to help fund war with France.

Fig. 23: Part of the original interior of the Cadenham dovecote showing a smooth lower section to prevent rats from climbing the structure.

Fig. 24: Window architrave at Cadenham depicting the Hungerford and Seymour crests.

Fig. 25: Cadenham Manor was built in the late 17th century by the site of the original moated manor house.

The Hungerford family owned Cadenham from 1468 and were thus established in the community decades before the Bayntuns acquired Bremhill and Stanley from the Crown, after the closure of the abbeys of Malmesbury and Stanley.

John Evelyn stayed with his wife's uncle, Edward Hungerford, at Cadenham in 1654, where 'we did nothing but feast and make good cheer.' He also visited the Bayntuns at their principal seat, Spye Park. He noted, with evident disapproval, 'in the meantime our coachman was made so exceedingly drunk that in returning home we escaped great danger. This it seems was by order of the Knight [Bayntun] that all gentlemen's servants be so treated: but the custom is barbarous and unbecoming a Knight.'[66]

Fig. 26: Spye Park, twice destroyed by fire, was planned to be rebuilt as a Palladian manor.

The other mansion house still standing in the parish is the Manor Farm in Tytherton Lucas, a manor house built in the sixteenth and seventeenth century, and which was altered around 1700.[67] Manor Farm, Tytherton Lucas is the only secular building within the parish of Grade II* listed status.

Fig. 27: Grade II* Listed Manor Farm in Tytherton Lucas with a wing dating back to the 16th century.

During the 1940s, aerial photographs taken of the village showed a variety of earthworks in the landscape, it included three concentric curving banks and ditches to the west of St Nicholas' Church. While it suggested an earlier manor house, there is no corroborating enclosure as there is at Bremhill (see chapter 1.1). However, these and earthworks to the south-east of the church may be evidence of settlement shrinkage during the medieval period or later.[68]

The Stokes family owned the manor at Tytherton Lucas from the late sixteenth until the early eighteenth century. Probably the most infamous owner was Abjohn Stokes.[69] In his will, which was proved in 1712, Abjohn left one shilling to his son, also called Abjohn, bequeathing the estate to his son-in-law, John Mereweather.[70] Thereafter it was subject to a long lawsuit between the two men.[71] It was later sold to John Townsend, a soap-maker from London.[72]

Cadenham remained in the Hungerford family until the death of Sir George Hungerford in 1712, by which time the Bayntuns had moved from the parish. After that the major estate-owners within Bremhill were not resident in the community.

The major construction of St Martin's Church at Bremhill took place in the thirteenth century, during which time the tower is likely to have been built. Two centuries later the tower was buttressed and re-fronted.[73] A chapel existed at Foxham by the early thirteenth century and possibly by the late twelfth.[74] During the nineteenth century the chapel was demolished and rebuilt, unfortunately we cannot know when the structure, as it then existed, was constructed with certainty. Although rebuilt in 1802, St Nicholas' Church at Tytherton Lucas was originally created in the thirteenth century.[75]

Fig. 28: St Martin's Church, Bremhill.

Fig. 29: St Nicholas' Church in Tytherton Lucas which may have been built over an earlier Saxon settlement during the 13th Century.

Fig. 30: Watercolour of the old Chapel at Foxham prior to the rebuilding in the 19th century.

Several watermills were also a feature of the parish during this period, although they too have been rebuilt. Stanley Mill belonged to Stanley Abbey in 1189 and was used for fulling cloth. It is likely to be the oldest such mill in Wiltshire.[76] The surviving mill structure is Grade II listed and late eighteenth or early nineteenth century.[77] During the seventeenth century, it was used both to grind grain and in cloth production.[78] By 1924 it was disused.[79] A mill at West Tytherton (Tytherton Lucas) was mentioned in the Domesday survey.

Fig. 31: The ruin of Scott's Mill demolished in 1987.

This was likely the mill later named Scott's Mill, which was originally part of the Stanley Abbey. Formerly a fulling-mill, it too was later used for grinding grain.[80] It stood on the opposing side of the River Marden from Scott's Mill Farmhouse, but after being in a dire condition in the 1970s, it was demolished in 1987.[81]

The structure of Hazeland Mill (now a house) is eighteenth century, but it was also originally the property of a monastic institution, as part of the Bremhill estate of Malmesbury Abbey. In 1534, it was listed as a grist and tucking (fulling) mill.[82] It later came into the possession of the Bayntun family. By 1643, it was leased out by the Bayntun family to Robert Tayler, a clothier [83]. It remained in Bayntun possession and appeared on the manor rent roll in 1659–79.[84]

Fig. 32: The imposing Hazeland Mill, now a private residence.

The seventeenth century Bayntun manor rent roll also lists other property let out by the Stanley and Bremhill estates. Unsurprisingly these were land holdings, cottages, and farms such as Bencroft, which still exist and reflect the importance of agriculture to the local economy. Many farmhouses within the parish today were originally constructed during the seventeenth century.[85]

These include: Scott's Mill Farm (originally part of the Stanley Abbey estate), Chesterman's Farmhouse at East Tytherton, Middle Farmhouse at Stanley Lane and Bosmere at Tytherton Lucas. These buildings have been adapted as needs and fashions have changed. At Foxham, Elm Farm whose main range is painted rubble and has a timber-framed cross wing which has been re-fronted in brick, dates from the sixteenth and eighteenth century. Stockham Marsh Farm dates from the early seventeenth and early to mid-eighteenth century, originally timber framed and rebuilt in red-brick.[86]

Top left: Fig. 33: Scott's Mill Farm, East Tytherton.
Top right: Fig. 34: Chesterman's Farm, East Tytherton.

Middle left: Fig. 35: Middle Farm, Stanley.
Middle right: Fig. 36: Bosmere Farm, Tytherton Lucas.

Bottom left: Fig. 37: Elm Farm, Foxham
Bottom right: Fig. 38: Stockham Marsh Farm, Foxham

The detail on the Bayntun rent roll suggests that at the time hops were being extensively grown, stone was being quarried and some of the parish remained marsh land. Physical evidence left in the landscape and reference in seventeenth century manor court records suggests a collective system of strip cultivation (ridge and furrow) was used in at least part of the parish until the seventeenth century. Several belts of less productive land were used as common land, including at Foxham and Stockham Marsh, where residents grazed their livestock. Later the marshes were drained, and the open spaces disappeared, instead, enclosed and improved as agriculture was transformed.

1.3 Eighteenth to Twentieth Century

Nonconformity had made an impact on Bremhill since the mid-seventeenth century, but their meetings had generally taken place within domestic spaces or in the open-air. One of the most significant developments in the eighteenth century within the parish was probably the construction of the red-brick Moravian church, manse, and church cottage.[87]

The Moravian community was founded at East Tytherton in 1745. The original chapel and manse were replaced in 1792–3, by which time a house for single sisters had been added. In 1793-4, the site was further developed when a girls' boarding school was also adjoined.[88]

Fig. 39: Moravian church and cottage at East Tytherton.

However, for most visitors to the village it was St Martin's Church at Bremhill which drew most comment. *The Gentleman's Magazine* described Bremhill village thus in 1814:

> *It is a village situated on a hill, about two miles north of Calne in Wiltshire. The church, a venerable structure with a tower, stands just south-west of the village, and the rectory, a stone house of the same character, is exactly south of that on a small terrace, commanding a most beautiful view, the hill immediately sloping from it to the south.*[89]

Developments of a more secular nature included the opening of a number of drinking establishments, these included the Dumb Post Inn and the Bell and Organ near the church at Bremhill, but also those of a less reputable nature. These changes, alongside the growth of a small retail sector, were aided in no small measure by an increase in the local population and developments in local transport links. By 1801 and 1811 the population of Bremhill had risen to 1,303, and this rose to 1,535 in 1831 and 1,550 in 1841.[90] At the latter date the total included thirty labourers working on the Great Western Railway, constructed between London and Bristol, locally completed in 1841 and which clipped the parish.[91]

Fig. 40: The Dumb Post Inn, Bremhill.

Fig. 42: Independent English farmers supporting local agricultural labourers became a way of life in the parish.

Earlier in the century, Bremhill had been bisected by the development of the Wilts & Berks Canal which was completed in 1810.[92] Wharfs had been built at Stanley and Foxham, helping to support some growing sophistication of the local economy, although for the Bremhill vicar, Rev. William Lisle Bowles, in 1828 the canal provided no more than a picturesque intrusion into village life. The parish remained, in his assessment, made up of some 'independent English freeholders farming their own estates - some renting tenants - all supporting numerous agricultural labourers and their families'.[93]

Rev. William Lisle Bowles, himself, contributed to the visual aesthetic of the parish through his gothic embellishment of the vicarage (which he called his parsonage) using 'the ideas of consonance and picturesque propriety'.[94] The monument to Maud Heath at Wick Hill was erected in 1838, paid for and organised through his collaboration with the 3rd Marquess of Lansdowne of Bowood. The monument depicts a seated statue of Maud Heath on a high column and has a verse penned by Bowles. The Pevsner building guide for Wiltshire notes that 'the quality of the poetry matches that of the statue.'[95]

Fig. 43: Maud Heath's monument and statue erected on Wick Hill in 1838.

Fig. 44: The Bremhill Parsonage, home of Rev. William Lisle Bowles.

In the mid-to-late nineteenth century, reflecting certain pre-occupations of the Victorian age, a number of communal buildings were constructed (or renovated) across the parish for religious worship and education. Chapels were built at Spirthill in 1828, Foxham in 1855 and Stanley in 1865, while the churches at Tytherton Lucas and Bremhill were renovated (see chapter 7).

St John the Baptist Chapel at Foxham was re-built following money raised by public subscription 1878–81, although it was financed, for the most part, by money provided by the 5th Marquess of Lansdowne, whose family had owned much of the parish since the mid-eighteenth century.[96]

Fig. 45: Charlcutt Reading Room and Library converted in 1888.

The Lansdownes also paid for the construction of the three parish reading rooms during the 1880s, at Foxham, Charlcutt and Bremhill. The construction of local schools also typified this period, they included Bremhill School (now the village hall) in 1846 and East Tytherton in 1870-1.[97]

Agricultural property continued to be created including several farmhouses such as Harden's at Tytherton Lucas and Pound Farmhouse at Stanley.[98] During the nineteenth century (particularly the 1870s), the Bowood estate built a number of estate cottages across the parish, many of which are now Grade II listed.[99]

However, after 1841, and in common with most rural communities in Wiltshire, the population fell, to 1,163 in 1881 and further to 1,090 in 1891, despite a boundary alteration in 1885 which brought 125 residents of Christian Malford into Bremhill parish.[100] By 1931, depopulation had continued such that the total, 793, was little more than half of that a century earlier. At the time of the 2011 census, the population was 942.

Top left: Fig. 46: Spirthill Chapel built 1825.
Top right: Fig. 47: Wesleyan Chapel, Foxham, dated 1855, now a private house.

Middle left: Fig. 48: East Tytherton School built 1870-1.
Middle right: Fig. 49: Bremhill School erected in 1846.

Bottom left: Fig. 50: Harden's Farm at Tytherton Lucas.
Bottom right: Fig. 51: Pound Farmhouse at Stanley.

Fig. 52: Bowood Estate cottages at West End, Foxham.

SALESBVRY

The forme of the Counsel House

A S. Edmonds
B Winchester Gate
C S. Martins
D S. Thomas
E The minster
F The Dorehouse
G Bedles stret
H S. Cathren stret
I Dragon stret
K High stret
L Raglen stret
M Love stret
N The Market
O Salt Lane
P Gremresse stret
Q Castle stret
R Fisheries stret

ASCALE OF PASES

WILSHIRE

PART OF

THE ARMES of the Earles of wilshyre & Salesburye

Will. Scrope.

Iam. Butler.

John. Stafford.

Hen. Stafford.

Tho. Bollen.

Will. Paulet.

Patrik.Fitzwater.

Wil. longespey.

Henry. Lacye.

Tho. E. of Lancas.

Wil. Montacute.

Ric. Neuil.

Georg. D. of Clarence.

Robert. Cecill.

WEST

PART OF

GLOCES:

Tetburye

Rodmerton
Kemble
Pole Canes
Cuckerton
Crudwell
Ashlay MALMESBURY Oksey
Hankerton
Longnewton Brokenborow Myntne
Westonbric Shipton
Oldbury
Malmes Whitchurch Charleton Garesden Brad
burye
Eastongray Bradle
Duddeston Brinkworth
Sapwerth Shar Foxley Brenkworth
Badminton litle ton Norton Colepark
Luckinton Aston
Badmanton great Alderton
Turfeld Rodborow Somerset
Grittleton Hullavington Sapery
Nettleshe DAMERHAM Stanton quints HUNDRED Clack
worth Sutton Christ Malford
West Kyneton Dracet Michaels Kyneton Cadnam howse
Castecombe Langley Auen HUND.
Wraxhall CHIPPENHAM HUND. Calneuse house
Littlecot Bireton West Tetherton
SHIRE Slaugtenford Chipnam Bramble Whit
Marsfeld Colerne Bowden CAN Comp
Coldaston The Shyre stones Stanley Pewsill Caln
Caterne Cosham Lekham Co
Swansvick Dichbridge PEWSHAM FOREST NTGS
Bancaston Box Hasselburye Bewdery Whethampton
Walcot The Chappell of playst parke Spye
Hamton Bathford Lacok Haldin
BATHE Bathweke Asford Brunham mil. Bapdist
Wraxhall Broughton The Cleare Roudon
Witcomb Clanerton Hanketon forley BRADFORD Milsham Sene The
Combe Chalfeilds Holt BLAKEMORE FOREST Part
Stoke Winsley HUND. Lincceton Stro
Freshforde Bradford Stauer whaddon Poulsholt Potern
Westwood ten MELKESAM Buckkum
South Stoke Iford Hilberto Servington Potern
Wellow Henton Winfall TRUBRIDGE Knayll Maston Worton
Farly castle. HUND. Steplaston Stoke Paterne Hundred
Phillips Norton H WHORWELSDOWNE Esse
Wuluerton North Bradley Eddington HUNDR. Gregt Chuerell
Lanerton Rede Bratten Little Cheuerell
Lullington Beckinton Baynton Coulston Wesf Lauen
Brackley Brett Westburye
WESTBURY HUNDRED.
Dilton
Frome Imber
Costy Upton SALESBU
WAR MISTER Warmister BRANCHE
Clayhill HUND. Dyl
Selwood Bushnystraw Haresbury HARESBURY HUNI
forest Kunke Chilterne THE B
Long Lear Great Sutton Upton HU
Charter Deueri bridge Thchington Caffenle Fisher
house Korynsham Hill Deuerell Corington Shering stn.
Brixton Boyton Stokton Wily
The Fearye Maden Bradley Monkston Deuerell Part of Warmister Hund. Bapton
Kingston Deuerell Pertwood Wily
DAMERHAM south Chiklet Chicklet Ridge Over Teffn
Kilmanton The Beacon West Knahill Berwick Leonard Chilmarke DAUWORTH
Bruham hill HUND Bisheps Faithill Nether Teffant
Funthill Gifford HUND.
Sturton MERE HUND. Hyndon Tilburye Sutton
Mere EastKnahill East Hatch Swalowchff
Penn Longlane teneley Castle Anfle
Stoke Square Mill. Sedachill
Cucklington HUND. Nether Donet Norryntn
Gillingham CHAL KE South Berwick
Bngley Motcombe Over Donet Ludwell Sutton
Gillingham Forest Semley Charleton Tollard Ryall HUNDR
Shaftesbury Cranbom
Fernham

PART OF DORSET SHIRE

SOMERSET

SHIRE

PART OF

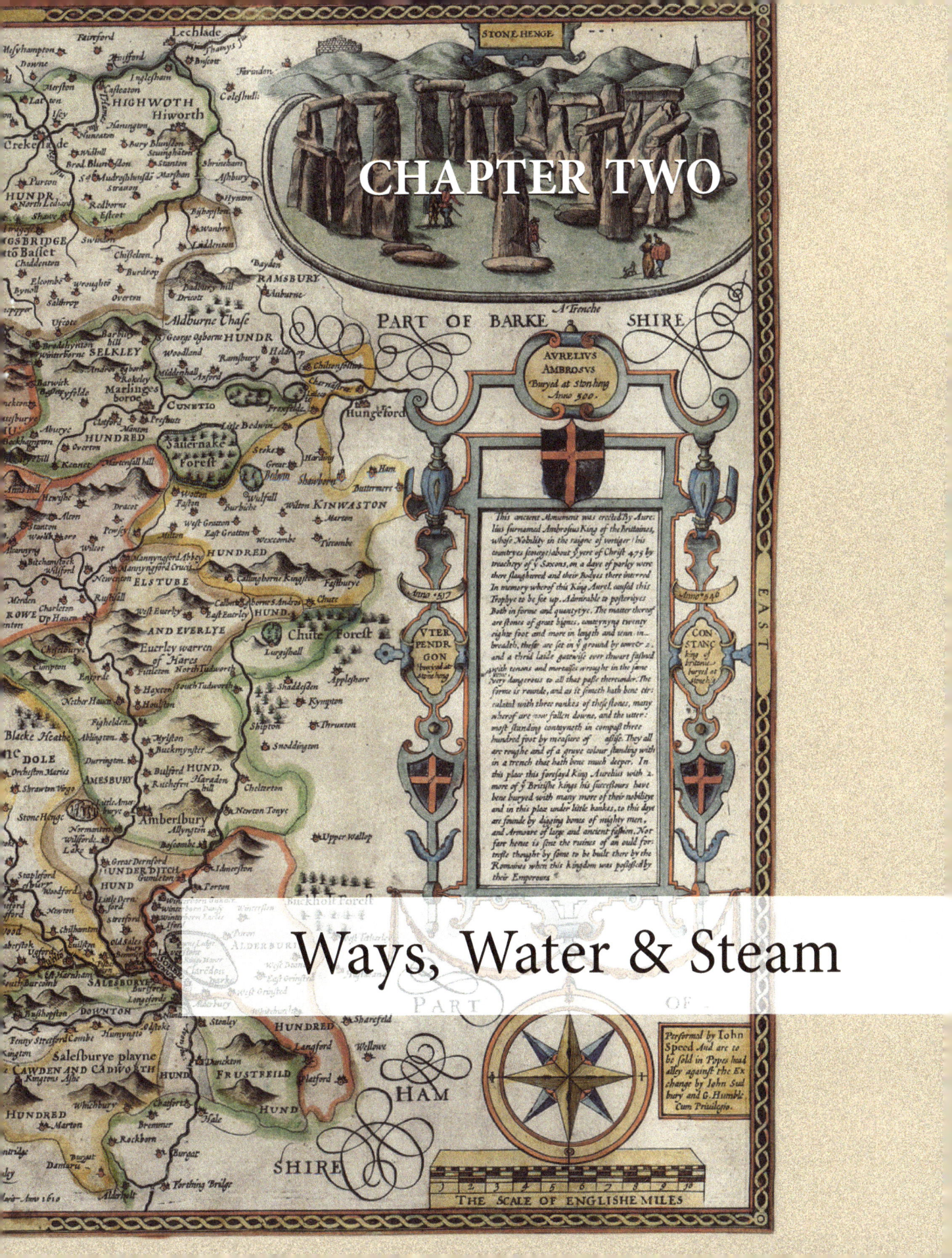

CHAPTER TWO

Ways, Water & Steam

Fig. 53: Impression of a Roman cohort on the march to *Verlucio* (A Roman fortified station at Sandy Lane).

2.1 Ways

Roads have provided the main lines of communication throughout history. After the Roman conquest, the focus of major new road construction in Wiltshire was the link to London and, within the county, the 'lesser junctions' of Old Sarum (*Sorviodunum*) and Mildenhall (*Cunetio*). Bremhill was bypassed by such road development and, thus, significant traffic.

However, quite apart from these major Roman routes were the networks of minor roads connecting farms and settlements, much as today. These likely crisscrossed what became the parish of Bremhill. In the Anglo-Saxon period, such roads, if they had any semblance of solid paving or metalling, were referred to as 'streets' (from the Latin word *stratum*). The lane coming south from the Dauntsey direction to Foxham is referred to in a Saxon charter as *Elde Strete* ('the old made-up road'), and one stretch of it is still called Friday Street. After it leaves Foxham on its way to Charlcutt, it is Hare Street, and that may be a significant name, as Hare Streets, and Hare Paths (our modern word 'warpath') usually denote a road along which a Saxon army might, or did once, pass.[101] An early routeway, running north-south across the parish, probably incorporated these stretches of the modern lanes.

Fig. 54: For two thousand years and more oxen (or bullocks) were the main beasts of burden on farms and roads up to the middle of the 19th century.

In the Middle Ages, monasteries administered large and widespread estates and needed roads to connect them to the outside world. The nearby abbeys of Stanley, Malmesbury and Bradenstoke, required roads that approached them across the parish. From a later map of 1675 (long after the monasteries had been dissolved), a road ran from Calne to Malmesbury; it may have followed the Friday Street and Hare Street line.[102]

Fig. 55: (previous page) Map by John Speed (1552-1629) the best known English map maker of the Stewart period. 'The Theatre of the Empire of Great Britaine' started solely with counties and grew into an impressive Atlas of the World.

One scholar of early roads suggested that Hare Street would have been used in summer, when it was easy to cross the Cade Burna by Hare Street Farm, but in winter a long detour may have been necessary, past Cadenham and up to Spirthill, to reach Charlcutt.

The map of 1675 also refers to 'The Plow Road to Chippenham'. This left the present A4 road near Studley.[103] A 'plow road' was a road made serviceable each spring by a large heavy plough used to cast furrows up into the centre which were then harrowed level, perhaps the equivalent of modern top-dressing. It must refer to Norley Lane, which passes by Stanley Abbey and continues as Stanley Lane, to rejoin the main A4 road east of Chippenham. It had been Stanley Abbey's access to the outside world, from 1300 if not before, and provided residents in the southern part of Bremhill parish with an easy route to Calne and Chippenham.[104] Later, when under the turnpike system tolls were introduced on main roads, a gate and gatehouse were placed at the Chippenham end of Stanley Lane to prevent travellers, drovers particularly, from using it as an alternative to paying the toll.

From the northern part of Bremhill parish, Maud Heath's causeway would take a traveller to Chippenham. It is described in full in the next section. However, it may be worth considering whether Maud's real intention, not stated in the foundation deed, was, by making a solid route between Chippenham and Bremhill Wick, to create an alternative to what became the main Bath road, further south, since that became notoriously boggy and difficult to traverse during a wet winter. If so, by funding an all-weather crossing of the Avon at Kellaways, Maud would have diverted traffic through Bremhill parish, and thereby present business opportunities to residents.

The turnpike trusts created in the eighteenth and early nineteenth centuries to improve main roads by charging travellers to use them, chose routes that skirted around the parish and left Bremhill in relative peace. The building of the canal and later the branch railway to Calne (both described below) also meant that, unlike many less well-connected places, there was little need for a village horse-and-cart carrier to take people and goods into town on market day. Indeed, none are recorded in local trade directories.[105]

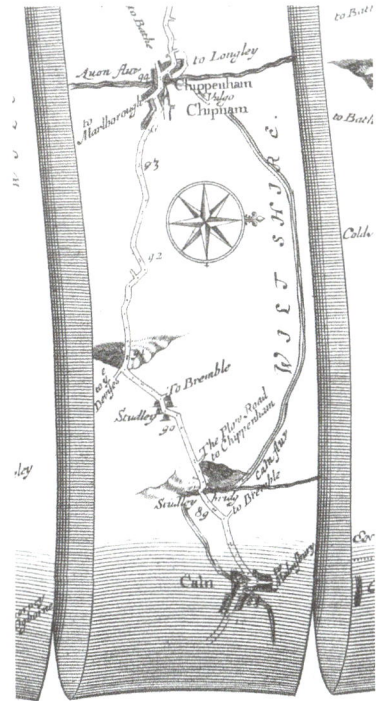

Fig. 56: John Ogilby (1600-1676) was a Scottish cartographer best known for publishing the first British road atlas. This map section clearly shows the 'Plow Road' to Chippenham starting at Studley.

Fig. 57: Watercolour (1850) of the turnpike gate near the end of Maud Heath's causeway in Chippenham.

Rev. William Lisle Bowles described how, in the 1820s, from the churchyard at Bremhill, 'on a still summer's evening, the distant sound of hurrying coaches on the Great London Road are heard, as they pass to and from the metropolis.'[106] But the village itself was quiet.

However, while Bowles revelled in the serene beauty of his village, he too took advantage of the new development. One of the many stories of his eccentricity refers to a journey he made riding his pony on a turnpike road towards Derry Hill from Calne on a hot summer day. Bowles was riding while reading a book, the pony taking advantaage of his lack of concentration by straying to the roadside and grazing. At length, Bowles dismounted and tied the animal while sitting himself at the roadside to continue reading. On the completion of his passage, Bowles 'rose, pondered on it and argued it out loud with himself, opened the book again . . . and forgetting the pony altogether sauntered leisurely up the hill, reading. On reaching the turnpike gate, he readied the money to pay the toll master. The toll master asked him why he was trying to pay. "Why for my pony, you goose", came the reply, whereupon the man pointed out he had no pony. Bowles looked down 'as if he expected to see it between his legs: then he became strangely confused, and only through the suggestion of the man, was enabled to remember where he had left the animal'.[107]

2.2 Ways: Maud Heath's Causeway

In 1474 a wealthy widow named Maud Heath gifted a number of properties and land in Chippenham into a trust fund so that the income from them could be used to create and maintain a causeway.[108] It enabled people from in and around Bremhill to travel to and from Chippenham by foot or packhorse without getting bogged down in the mud or wading through flooded fields at a time when foot apparel may have only been wooden clogs, pattens (protective overshoes), or sandal-like shoes made from cloth. The pathway, some four-and-a-half miles long, which includes a section elevated on stone arches, starts with a stone marker at the top of Wick Hill, descending to the river meadows at Kellaways before crossing through Langley Burrell and ending at Chippenham Clift.

Fig. 58: Example of a 15th Century Patten, which is an overshoe to keep the wearer's feet above muddy pathways.

Maud and her husband John would have been well aware of the difficulties of travelling to the marketplace in winter. They owned property nearby in St Mary Street, which ultimately became part of the deed of gift.

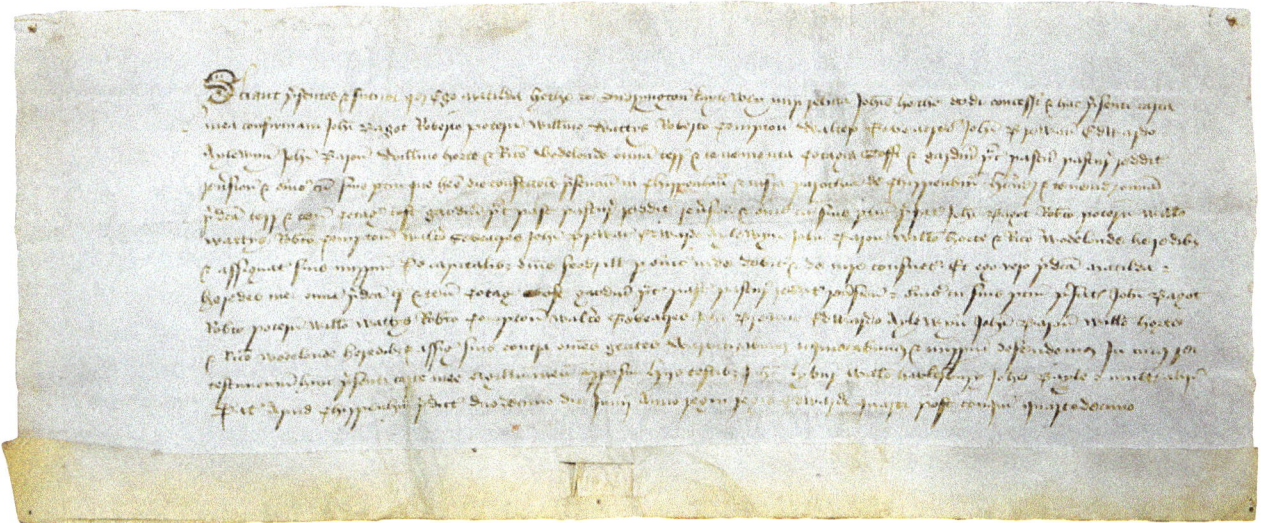

If the deed were translated in its original form, it would read:

Know those present and to come that I Matilda Hethe of Tudryngton Kayleway lately by the widow of John Hethe have conceded and by this my present charter confirmed to John Bagot Robert Poteru William Wattys Robert Compton Walter Gobeacres John Brewar Edward Aylewyn John Baron William Hozte and Richard Wodelonde all lands and tenements cottages tofts[109] and gardens meadows grazings pastures rents reversions and all their appurtenances which I have on the day on which these presents were made in Chippenham and in the parish of Chippenham to have and to hold all aforesaid lands and tenements cottages toft gardens meadows pastures grazings rent reversions and all of their appurtenances to the aforesaid John Bagot [and others] their heirs and assigns for ever saving to the chief lord of those fees all the service thence due and by right accustomed And I the said Matilda and my heirs will warrant acquit and for ever defend against all people all the aforesaid lands tenements cottages toft gardens meadows pastures grazings rent reversions and all of their appurtenances to the aforesaid John Bagot Robert Poteru William Wattys Robert Compton Walter Gobeacres John Brewar Edward Aylewyn John Baron William Hozte and Richard Wodelonde their heirs and assigns In testimony whereof I set my seal to this present charter. By these witnesses John Lybur William Hawkesbury John Bayle and many others. Given at Chippenham aforesaid on the fourteenth year of the reign of King Edward the fourth after the Conquest (12 June 1474) (Seal).

Fig. 59: The original 1474 Deed of Gift (8" x 2.5" on parchment) was discovered by Sir Gabriel Goldney MP among papers stored at Spye Park.

Interestingly, the deed was created during her lifetime (it is not Maud Heath's will). The deed itself was discovered among others when Sir Gabriel Goldney purchased the Stanley estate in 1871. After Maud had been widowed, she would have been entitled to own freehold property in her own right, as at that time, the law prevented married women from doing this.

Fig. 60: The Kellaways Sundial Pillar monument was erected in 1698 by the Trustees to mark the mid-point of the causeway.

Fig. 61: Artist's impression of young market trader dressed in the apparel of the late 15th century.

Their property automatically became that of the husband until his death, and then it was usually passed to a son. As a childless widow, her status would have been greatly enhanced by the situation. While the original trustee document and deed box are now stored at the Wiltshire and Swindon History Centre in Chippenham, the absence of a surviving will or parish record means that it is impossible to verify the details of her inheritance or her circumstances when she made her gift.

The first known public declaration of Maud Heath's intentions were made by the Maud Heath Trustees in 1698 when they set up a memorial pillar by Kellaways Bridge with an inscription that reads:

To the memory of the worthy MAUD HEATH of Langley Burrell Widow Who in the year of Grace 1474 for the good of Travellers did in Charity bestow land and houses about Eight Pounds a year forever to be laid out on the Highways and Causey leading from Wick Hill to Chippenham Clift. This Piller [sic] was Set up by the feoffes in 1698
Injure me not

Maud's pathway or causeway has been in constant use for more than five centuries. Numerous trustees have been responsible for the financing and maintenance of it, overseeing the erection of monuments to celebrate the lady and her gift. Oral tradition paints a picture of Maud as a market trader who bought eggs, butter, cheese and other produce from local farms, selling them at markets, most likely held near or at the site of Yelde Hall in the centre of Chippenham, not far from the properties that she and her husband John had owned. John Aubrey, writing in the period 1659-70, informs us that in the south aisle of St Martin's Church, Bremhill, in the top panel of the east window, there is an inscription 'Orate pro anima Johannis Heth' which translates as 'Pray for the soul of John Heath'. He is portrayed kneeling with a woman by him and with his coat of arms, giving an insight into the family name, which clearly had some standing in the local area.

Other, more fanciful accounts give a far different insight: 'By common report a market woman, who having felt by sad experience the inconvenience of a swampy walk, especially in the conveyance of such perishable wares as butter and eggs, devoted her life savings to the laudable purpose of providing a good footing for her successors in all time to come.' On the one hand, she is depicted as a wealthy trader. On the other, a higgler, floundering about in the mud and getting frustrated at constantly breaking her eggs on the way to market, a champion of the people who diligently saved her money to endow a pathway for future generations. Either way, Maud Heath's generosity lives on to this day, providing the means for trustees to maintain the causeway. It is reputed to be one of the oldest running trusts in the world and is also one of the longest privately owned paths maintained by any trust in the UK.

The Route of the Causeway

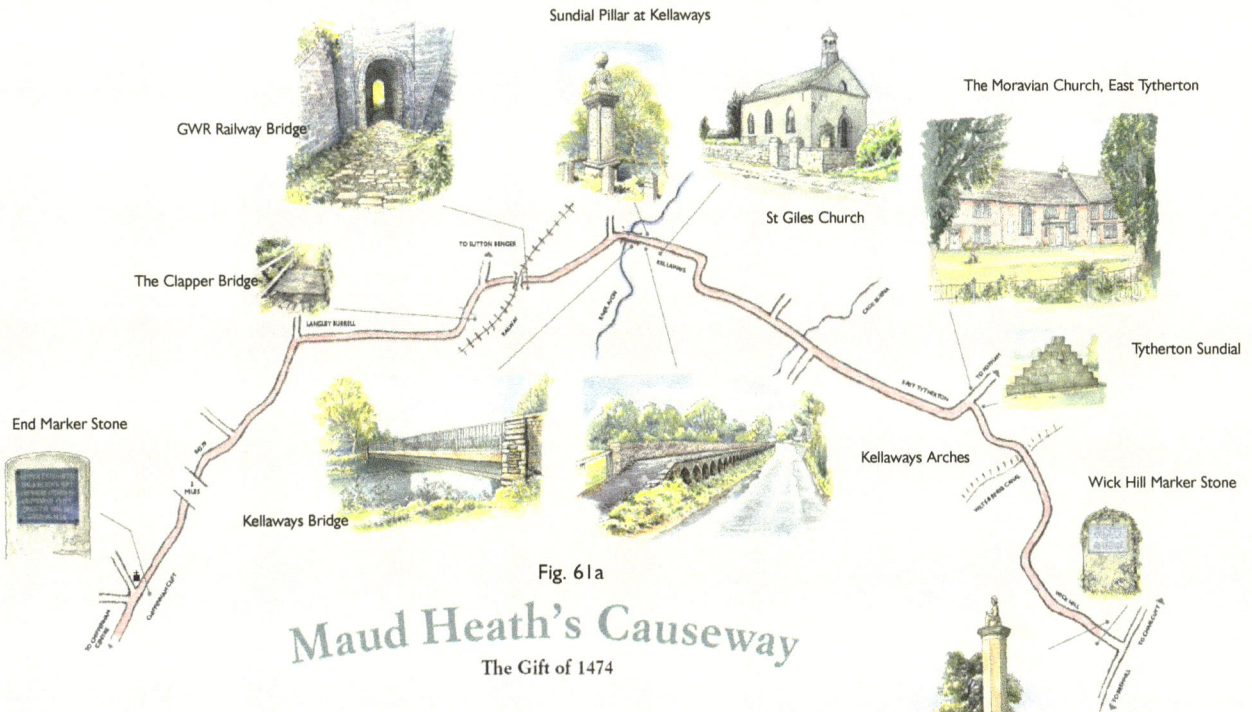

GWR Railway Bridge

Sundial Pillar at Kellaways

The Moravian Church, East Tytherton

The Clapper Bridge

St Giles Church

End Marker Stone

Tytherton Sundial

Kellaways Arches

Wick Hill Marker Stone

Kellaways Bridge

Fig. 61a

Maud Heath's Causeway
The Gift of 1474

Maud Heath's Monument and Statue, Wick Hill

The causeway runs for four-and-a-half miles through the parish of Bremhill from the top of Wick Hill down through East Tytherton, across Kellaways Bridge and the River Avon, under the railway line through Langley Burrell and into Chippenham. Along the causeway, there are a number of monuments and historical sites within the parish of Bremhill, which all have historical interest.

Wick Hill Marker Stone

At the top of Wick Hill, within sight of Maud Heath's monument, there is a simple stone pillar that is opposite Monument Farm. It was originally put in place in 1698 and has a companion marker stone at Chippenham Clift at the other end of the causeway. Its original inscription is lost, but, in rhyme, it informed the traveller that this was indeed the starting point of the causeway.

A subsequent cast iron plaque affixed to the pillar denotes the start of the causeway and attributes the translation of Latin verse into English to the Rev. Bowles, vicar of Bremhill, in 1827.

Maud Heath's Monument and Statue, Wick Hill

The imposing monument with a statue of Maud Heath was erected in 1838 by the 3rd Marquess of Lansdowne and the Rev. Bowles to commemorate the life of Maud Heath. The myth had grown by this stage that Maud Heath, rather than a wealthy widow, was, in fact, a local market woman. This was perpetuated by Lady Lansdowne, who researched the style of clothing and bonnet of a peasant trader in the fifteenth century for the sculptor of the statue. Accordingly, Maud is depicted as wearing a plain plebeian bonnet and simple clothes, by her side a basket of eggs and a staff. The monument is inscribed with:

> Thou, who dos't pause on this aerial height,
> Where Maud Heath's pathway winds in shade or light,
> Christian wayfarer in a world of strife
> Be still, and ponder on the path of life.

In January of 1990 severe storms beheaded the statue of Maud Heath and her head fell from the monument, rolling down the hill into a bramble patch. Fortunately, it was recovered and stored in a barn at Monument Farm by the Pocock family. James Long of Trowbridge repaired damage to the bonnet and the head was returned to its rightful place during repairs and restorations undertaken in 1990 and 1991.

Tytherton Sundial

Travelling down the hill and after crossing the now disused Wilts & Berks Canal, the causeway arrives in East Tytherton. In 1974, to commemorate the 500th anniversary of Maud Heath's bequest, a modern pyramid-like sundial was erected on East Tytherton's green by the trustees. Later on, in 1979, the Old Girls' Society of Tytherton School (former pupils of the Moravian Girls' School) dedicated a bench. This remains in front of the sundial adjacent to a memorial to the fallen of the parish in World War I.

The Moravian Church, East Tytherton

The causeway continues in East Tytherton past the Moravian church. A red-brick building, the centre of which remains the Moravian church, is dated 1792.

The Quakers' Burial Ground

As the causeway winds its way through East Tytherton, it passes Pinniger's House. Within the grounds, tucked behind an ancient yew tree, lies the Quakers' burial ground, which was established in 1659. Here it is reported that as many as 110 Quakers are buried.

Barnbridge

After leaving the outskirts of East Tytherton the causeway continues towards Kellaways. At Barnbridge, the causeway crosses a bridge over the Cade Burna.

St Giles Church

St Giles Church is one of the oldest churches on the causeway. It was originally erected in the early fourteenth century by the River Avon, adjacent to Kellaways Mill. It was plagued by frequent flooding from the Avon and rats that used to infest the area. Local parishioners frequently protested about the crumbling, damp state of the church as a health hazard. In 1802 Thomas Crook(e), churchwarden and a trustee of the Maud Heath charity helped lobby the bishop of Salisbury for a new church. This was eventually built on higher ground on the south side of the causeway. The old edifice was taken down and the stone used to build a retaining wall around the new church. St Giles Church was finally consecrated on 21 July 1808.

Kellaways Arches

Early problems of crossing flooded fields by the River Avon were overcome with wood piles and foot boards. These required constant upkeep by the trustees. The current Kellaways arches were constructed in 1812. They consist of sixty-four spans that raise the footpath well above the floodplain of the Avon. The stone arches were built forming a more permanent solution, allowing horses and carts to cross when it was widened five years later. The Kellaways arches are in two sections separated by Kellaways Bridge as it crosses the main section of the River Avon.

Sundial Pillar at Kellaways

The limestone pillar was erected to mark the mid-point of the causeway. It carries a Latin inscription to the worthy Maud Heath. This was subsequently translated and paraphrased by Rev. Bowles and added to the pillar in 1827. It includes a sundial which had Latin inscriptions on each face. These included (translated) 'time flies', 'let us do good while there is time' 'and I will return you never'.

Kellaways Bridge

A bridge was known to exist across the River Avon in the mid-fifteenth century. Approximately two centuries later, the royal cartographer mapping the route from London to Bristol recorded an alternative route to Chippenham, noting a bridge with sixteen arches over the Avon at Kellaways.[120] The minute book of the trustees records many instances of queries for their liability to repair the bridge.

In 1825, they requested that the county surveyor examine the bridge so it could be designated as a county bridge (and therefore funded by county rates). Matters dragged on, and in 1853 it was finally agreed that a new section of the bridge would be erected with the trustees paying half the cost.

Contractors replaced the central span with an iron structure which later needed attention, reviving old arguments about who should pay. The current pre-stressed beam bridge was erected in 1961 due to increasing and heavy vehicles using the road.

GWR Railway Bridge

The Great Western Railway line connecting London to Bristol and running past Chippenham needed to cross over the causeway. GWR set about purchasing land to span the road and causeway and they initially proposed a single spanned arch over both.

Such was the influence of the trustees at this time, they would only allow GWR to construct a bridge that had a separate arch forming a tunnel fifteen metres long to enable the causeway to run under the bridge unhindered.

The Clapper Bridge

This ancient form of bridge over a small stream derives from the word 'cleaca' meaning 'bridging the stepping stones' and was usually formed from one piece of natural stone.

End Marker Stone

The causeway continues through Langley Burrell and into Chippenham where it finishes adjacent to St Paul's Church. The end of the causeway is marked by a wayside stone, erected in 1698, with a metal plate attached bearing the inscription:

> Hither extendeth Maud Heath's gift
> For where I stand is Chippenham Clift
> Erected 1698 but given 1474.

This plaque is the companion of the one at Wick Hill that marks the beginning and end of the causeway. The original inscribed stone is kept by Chippenham Museum and Heritage Centre. It has been the subject of some conjecture. Firstly, the inscription refers to the word 'clift', a by-form of cliff, where was the cliff? Canon Jackson in his booklet on the 'causey' (causeway) written in 1854 wrote a footnote 'had the causey been carried onto the left (still keeping within the same parish), so as to follow the old road towards the town, it would have presently arrived at something more like a cliff.' This plausible opinion refers to the steep bank at Monkton Park.

Secondly, the original stone was discovered in 1968 when excavations for the new Barclays Bank in the market square at Chippenham uncovered the inscribed stone covering a drain in the cellar. One story suggests that the stone was torn down by a group of lads during the 1822 Langley riots, who, fearing transportation for their demeanours, hid it in a local cellar.[111]

Much of the original surface of the causeway has been overlaid with modern materials, but evidence of the original cobbles and stone can be found in the more remote rural areas and in field gateways where harder wearing granite sets were used. The sets were initially laid at right angles to the pathway to enable packhorses to gain a foothold in wet conditions, but this did not always meet with approval. Over time this prompted them to be re-laid in line as a solution. As a result, some stones sunk and became disarranged. Consequently, one commentator penned several verses to the trustees published in the Wiltshire Gazette in 1876.

Since then various representations have resulted in the pathway being covered in gravel, tarmac or paving slabs according to the location and pedestrian usage. From the original deed of gift, the Maud Heath Trustees have looked after the causeway and properties with which it was endowed. They have provided voluntary service through the Civil Wars, religious persecution, foreign wars and political unrest. This, in addition to complying with statutory regulations, working as landlords and surveyors, overseeing building works, and raising funds through financial investments to maintain the upkeep of this unique and ancient pathway through charitable involvement.

They call on the Trustees
To pity their groans
To give them a dry path
Of smooth even stones.

The side stones are falling
The puddles soak through
The foundation is going
It really is true.

Then raise up the
sunk stones
And level the walk
No more let this Causey
Be cause of sad talk.[112]

Horsepower in the parish

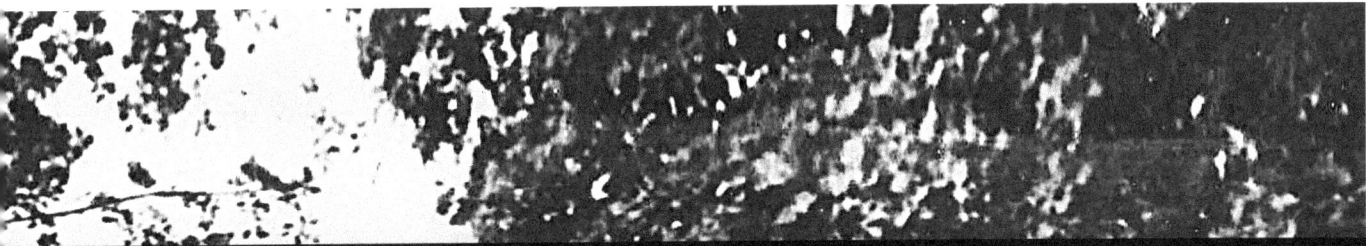

Fig. 62: Herbert Matthews (left) and James Matthews (centre) with the waggons and horses at their haulage business in Spirthill.

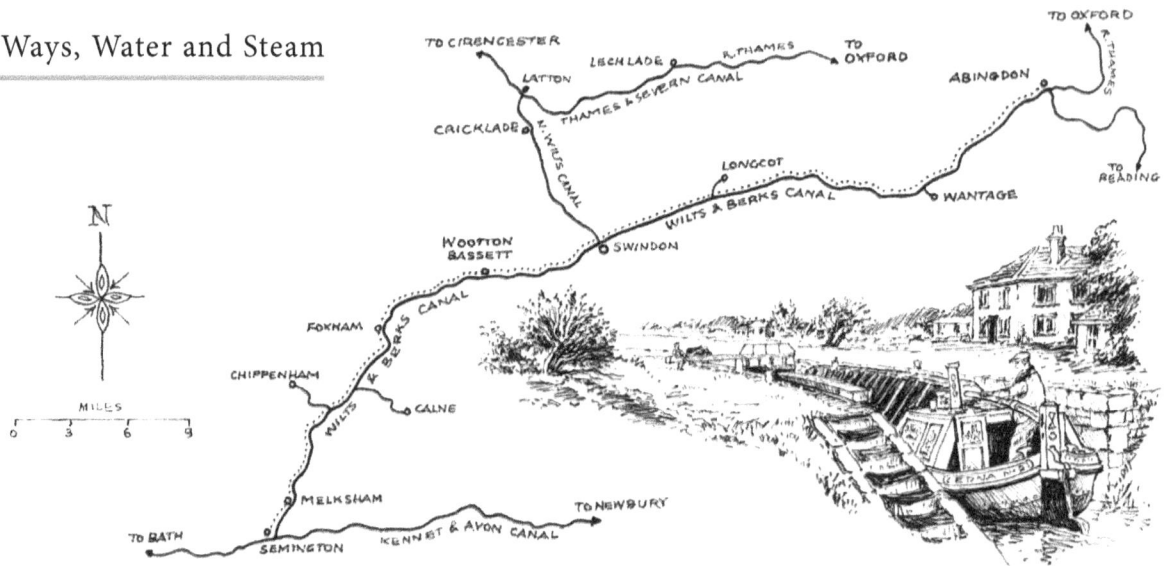

2.3 Water: Wilts & Berks Canal

At the end of the eighteenth century, the demand for raw materials to feed the Industrial Revolution rose rapidly.[113] These materials could easily be carried by water transport where canals existed. However, north Wiltshire and west Berkshire were little served by navigable waterways, and so these circumstances provided an incentive to expand the canal network in the area. In January 1793, a meeting was held to promote a new canal from Abingdon to Bristol. Many further discussions ensued with shareholders of the venture agreeing to the appointment of Robert Whitworth, as chief engineer, and his son William, to survey the landscape and draw plans. The Bill to allow work to begin was granted in 1795. It incorporated plans for navigable cuts from Bremhill to Calne and Pewsham to Chippenham.

The most significant engineering project on the canal line was at the main canal section near Stanley, which required a brick and stone aqueduct across the River Marden. Whitworth designed the structure with two twelve-foot arches built on dry land on one side of the river, the waterway was then diverted through one arch while the other was made.

Fig. 63: Illustration of how the viaduct over the River Marden might have looked before a hole developed in the canal bed.

Whitworth also created brickworks at strategic points along the canal route, including ones at Stanley and Foxham. These utilised the Kimmeridge clay prevalent in the Marden Vale. As the canal progressed, one brick kiln was closed, and another built nearer to the construction site and so on. The work of building the canal was done by 'navvies', a term which was an abridgement of the less poetical word 'navigator'.

The southern approach to the canal enters the parish from the direction of Forest Gate, where the A4 road crosses the canal. It then follows the line to Studley, under a minor road bridge passing under the disused Calne Branch railway, now a Sustrans cycleway and footpath. It continues to the site of the largest engineering work on the mainline, the aqueduct over the River Marden with two arches, now non-existent. Two deep locks, Stanley top and bottom, lifted the canal, passing the entrance to the Calne branch and onto Stanley Bridge and Stanley Wharf, site of the wharfinger's (manager's) house, now a private home. Beyond that, the Wick arched bridge featured along with a drawbridge at Bremhill Grove.

Fig. 64: Illustration of a fully laden 50ft. narrowboat carrying roadstone having navigated the lift bridge at Foxham.

Fig. 65: Foxham Top Lock restored by the Wilts & Berks Canal Trust and 'in water' by 2010.

Fig. 66: Locks awaiting restoration north of the River Marden at Studley.

Fig. 67: Canal viaduct over the River Marden photographed in the 1970s prior to its total collapse.

The next road intersection is at the bottom of Charlcutt hill by a small cut which was for overnight mooring and loading. During World War II, many locks and other canal structures were used for the army and damaged by explosives, including the Charlcutt canal bridge.

Between the Charlcutt canal bridge and Foxham, the canal ran in open fields under two drawbridges and over a substantial culvert spanning the Cade Burna stream. The canal passed east of Cadenham Manor under a bridge on the Foxham to Hilmarton road to 'climb' the hill via Foxham bottom and top locks. The latter is now restored, and the canal is in water for a mile. As it leaves the parish, there are two restored lift bridges and evidence of another. The Calne cut was entered at Stanley just north of the former aqueduct and continued through open fields until it ran beside Hazeland Mill. The canal then left the parish running beside the River Marden before entering a tunnel under what is now the A4 road and on to the centre of Calne.

When in 1810, the canal opened, it provided new business opportunities for Bremhill parish. The canal traded satisfactorily for a few years with Stanley Wharf and Foxham Wharf dealing with an average of 4,000 tons of coal per annum during the heydays of the 1840s. While the Great Western Railway became a significant threat to its eventual survival, the building of the railway provided a huge boost in income as a massive tonnage of stone, metal and equipment was carried by the canal infrastructure. However, in 1901 Wiltshire County Council agreed that it was in such a state of disrepair that it was of no use for waterway traffic.

In 1901, the canal was practically rendered impassable at the southern end when the Stanley aqueduct developed a large hole in the canal bed, and all the water drained into the River Marden. The 'death knell' came when one of the arches collapsed in 1906. The canal was abandoned in 1914.

2.4 Steam: Stanley Bridge Halt and the Branch Line to Calne and Chippenham

The Great Western Railway linking London to Bristol was completed in 1841.[114] The new line included a station at Chippenham. The town was, thereby, given an immediate economic boost. Nearby towns, such as Calne, were at a disadvantage, something which Calne tried to remedy during the following decade by promoting a branch line between themselves and Chippenham. By October 1859, the idea had been promoted twice with no success, but the *Devizes and Wiltshire Gazette* happily reported that circumstances were much more conducive to the plan due to 'the abundance of money at the present moment and the fact that both engineers and contractors have considerably reduced their estimates'. The only obstacle was the need to get the support of local landowners.[115] A public meeting in Calne Town Hall took place on 8 November 1859. After which, there was sufficient support for plans to begin apace for presenting a bill to parliament, necessary to gain the legal authority.[116] It was anticipated from the outset that the line would pass through the settlements of Bremhill, Tytherton Lucas and Stanley.[117]

The first sod of the Calne Railway was turned in J. Angell's field at Studley on 25 June 1861. The five-and-a-half mile branch line followed the valley of the River Marden to the south of the parish, passed the site of Stanley Abbey. Only after three inspections for the Board of Trade by Captain Tyler of the Royal Engineers was the line deemed fit for safe public transport. It opened on 29 October 1863 for goods traffic and for passengers on 3 November following.

Fig. 67a & 68: Stanley Bridge Halt and the single track from the Halt to Chippenham through open fields.

Fig. 69: GWR publicity photograph taken at the opening of Stanley Bridge Halt in 1905.

Fig. 70: Goods Train in 1952 heading towards Chippenham with Studley Hill in the background.

Fig. 71: The road bridge before the Halt looking west.

The new line was built with no intermediate stations. However, in March 1888, the GWR proposed a station and goods facilities at Hazeland, Bremhill. The MP for Chippenham, Sir Gabriel Goldney, also offered to finance similar facilities at Stanley. Although these plans had come to nought, on the proposed introduction of steam 'motor rail cars', a halt at Stanley Bridge had been mooted. However, by January 1905, it was reported no construction had yet started.[118] Nonetheless, on 3 April the same year, Stanley Bridge Halt was opened. Ever publicity conscious, the GWR issued a publicity photograph. It pictured a clientele of smartly attired Edwardians waiting to board a train.

Stanley Bridge Halt served both freight and passenger traffic. It was unstaffed and comprised a corrugated iron pagoda-style shelter and a timber shed, through the rear of which milk churns were unloaded from farm carts arriving from Tytherton, Bremhill and Stanley. This facility was removed in the late 1940s with the advent of road transport directly to the Nestlé factory in Chippenham. The platform was constructed on a timber frame, later infilled with ballast. Lighting was provided from three copper oil lamps supplied from a corrugated store shed at the Calne end of the platform. A fourth lamp inside the pagoda was unused and provided a regular nesting place for blackbirds.

By 1932 the steam rail cars had been succeeded by 'push and pull' trains comprising one or two ample carriages powered by a smart 0-4-2 tank locomotive evolved from an earlier design. On the journey from Chippenham to Calne, a driver and fireman controlled the engine from the footplate as usual, but for the return journey, the driver controlled the locomotive from a compartment in the leading carriage via a remote control system of rods and levers, while the fireman remained in charge of the needs of the locomotive. For this reason, they became known as 'push and pull' auto cars. For some return journeys, the locomotive was in the centre of a mixed train after vans containing Harris's pork products destined for many distant locations were attached at Calne.

Not all the passenger services began and concluded their journeys at Chippenham. There were also services to Calne from Westbury, Melksham, Trowbridge and Bath. During the summer months, a Saturdays only direct service to Weston-Super-Mare left Calne at 1.12 p.m. The line provided more than a local personal and commercial service during the 1939-45 conflict, serving the needs of the RAF camp at Yatesbury and transporting army vehicles and equipment from Salisbury Plain. Post-war, with the closure of the Yatesbury camp and the increasing use of road transport, the revenue generated by the branch line was significantly reduced. Notwithstanding the introduction of diesel multiple units for most of the passenger services in 1959, heavy snowfalls during the severe winter of 1962–3 saw periods of a return to steam-hauled trains.

The Marples-Beeching rationalisation of British railways followed in the mid-1960s and led to a calculated running down of the line, leading to its total closure on 18 September 1965, despite considerable local protests. It was convenient that the statistics of passenger numbers relied on data from a summer period when the regular commuters to the Westinghouse factory in Chippenham were on holiday. The last train left Calne to a fusillade of 101 detonators, one for each year of the line's existence. A final act of defiance was the temporary immobilisation of the train by an activation of the emergency communication cord at the junction with the mainline at Chippenham. The track was not lifted until 1967. Apart from an unfortunate gap on the very site of Stanley Bridge Halt, the trackbed first became a nature trail and subsequently a facility for cyclists, runners, walkers and dog owners.

Top left: Fig. 72: View from the cab of a diesel multiple unit arriving at Stanley.

Bottom left: Fig. 73: The Halt shortly before closure.

Below: Fig. 74: Token collection from East Chippenham signal box during the severe winter of 1962-3.

CHAPTER THREE

Agriculture, Trades & Emigration

3.1 Agriculture

Fig. 75: Village folk collectively harvest arable fields in the 17th century.

Fig. 75: Village folk collectively harvest arable fields in the 17th century.

Bremhill is, in many respects, a quintessential rural community. It is unsurprising, therefore, that for centuries the economy of the parish was dependent on agriculture. In the 1650s, the people of Foxham farmed the land collectively. Several large fields were given over to arable. Tenants had strips, which they were expected to keep drained and ditched, their plots marked by merestones. Common land provided grazing for cows, oxen, sheep and even geese. The community worked as one, so all the village cattle were sometimes driven onto the arable fields when the land lay fallow.

Reflecting a pattern that had probably persisted since the time of Henry VIII, in 1821, there were 286 local families 'chiefly employed' in agriculture, compared with thirty-seven in 'trade, manufacture or handicraft,' and a handful living from 'independent' means.[119] In 1827, Rev. Bowles described his 'agricultural parishioners', observing 'there are scarce any others.'[120] Until the early twentieth century, around 85 per cent of households across the parish were dependent on agriculture for their livelihoods.

Fig. 76: (previous page) The Anglo-Saxon heavy plough, pulled by a team of oxen, utilised a coulter which cuts through the soil ahead of a plough share to create the familiar 'ridge and furrow' characteristic of soil cultivation.

Throughout much of its history, the village was made up of separate 'manors', mainly in possession of two great monastic houses, the Benedictine order at Malmesbury and the Cistercians at Stanley Abbey. After the dissolution of the monasteries, in the reign of Henry VIII, these were acquired by Sir Edward Bayntun. Over the centuries, the Bayntun family sold off the manors of Foxham, Spirthill, and in the eighteenth century, Bremhill to the Petty family, who were to become Lansdowne of Bowood.[121] The Bayntuns kept Stanley Manor until the nineteenth century, when that too was sold. There were separate manors at Cadenham and Tytherton Lucas. Local farms, both large and small, were generally leased from these manors. Thus, within the bounds of Bremhill and Foxham in the early seventeenth century, there were just four freeholders who owned their property outright compared to over ninety leaseholders and tenants of various descriptions.[122]

A Humble Life:

The Story of John Harding[123]

For centuries a significant proportion of the adult male population of Bremhill was employed as agricultural labourers on tenanted farms. Wages were little more than subsistence level. The work was long and physically demanding. According to one Wiltshire account in 1811, the working day in the winter was 'from day-light till dark; in summer usually from six to six except in hay-making and harvest, when they are expected to work early and late'.[123]

One person who spent his working life of over sixty years as a local labourer was John Harding.[124] His story demonstrates the hard economic reality of village life through much of its history. John was born in the early 1750s, one of twelve children. He was the younger son of Charlcutt tenant farmer Richard Harding. Richard was, according to a later account, 'a kind and affectionate father'. The household was hardworking, modest and religious. John carried this grounding with him throughout his life. He received some education growing up but was working as a carter on his father's farm by his teenage years. Miraculously, at least eight of John's siblings also survived to adulthood and were, like him, employed on the farm, 'each having his different portion of work'.

His father, Richard, endured a long debilitating illness, perhaps resulting from a life of hard physical work. On his deathbed in 1772, after leaving John's mother well provided for, Richard left small legacies to four of his children but divided up the rest among his sons, Thomas, Robert, John and Abraham and daughter, Mary. They were no doubt his favourites. John was eighteen and a serious young man. He chose not to use the money but to save it and continue to work the family farm, now run by his older brother. John worked for this brother for the next twenty-three years until his brother died.

In his twenties, he married Mary King at the Church in Bremhill. The courtship had been long. The frugal couple had saved for years until they were reasonably financially secure. Mary was in domestic service but gave it up on getting married. They rented a cottage near to the farm. In the somewhat flowery language of Mrs Bowles 'it was situated in a beautiful part of the village: the sight of its white walls lighted up by the southern sun, gave it an air of warmth and comfort; and it stood in the midst of a neat garden well stocked with vegetables.' While Mrs Bowles makes their early life sound idyllic, money was extremely tight, and they went to great lengths to make ends meet.

Along with many working families, they grew vegetables which supplemented their staple diet of bread and potatoes. Mary span wool into yarn, much of which their children gathered off local hedgerows. It had the benefit of being free, but the children had to collect large quantities to fulfil the family's requirements, let alone provide an income.

Fig. 77: Country folk had to draw water from a well right up to the middle of the 20th century.

Fig. 78: Engraving of a mother and child greeting father after a hard day in the fields.

Fig. 79: The type of Spinning wheel that Mary would have used.

The household grew rapidly with as many as fourteen children who put considerable pressure on the family purse strings. For many families of the period, the burden of young children pushed them temporarily, at least, onto poor relief or to seek charity. This does not appear to have been the case with the Harding family, perhaps due to the success of Mary's spinning or other strategies which raised extra money. The children were employed too, as soon as they were old enough. Perhaps predictably, unlike their father, whose own childhood was in less straitened circumstances, they did not receive an education. This also contrasted with John's siblings, as many as half his children predeceased their father. It may have been related to poor diet or disease, such as smallpox, endemic in the eighteenth century, but it remains conjecture. For those who survived to adulthood, evidence suggests some became labourers and continued the cycle of poverty. At least one sought parish relief as an adult.

After his brother's death, the farm seems to have passed out of the family. John then worked for the Crook family on their small farm for around thirty-seven years. It is likely to be one listed in 1830 comprising just forty acres in Stanley. During this period, John entrusted the nest egg from his father to a lawyer who later fled with his money. It was never recovered. It left him approaching late old age working and with nothing to fall back on. According to the Bowles's accounts he was likely to have ended up in the parish poorhouse. It was at that point that John asked Rev. Bowles for help. Through Bowles's encouragement of the Marquess of Lansdowne, he was provided with two tenements for life which, at last, gave him financial security.

John died in 1835. One newspaper recorded his death: 'March 23, at Stanley near Chippenham, John Harding aged 86. This old man was sitting at his afternoon meal with his wife, when he fell from his seat, and expired before medical assistance could be obtained.'[125] He left everything to Mary. On her death, his small estate was divided between their surviving children, William, Robert, Richard, James, George, Rebecca and Harriet.

And future sons taught in their strength to save

The same sure path, to the same resting place

May future fathers of the village trace

Learn that first lesson from a POOR MAN'S GRAVE.

John drew attention in his last years. He had lived without recourse to parish welfare despite bringing up so many children, no mean feat. It earned him an award for 'industry and good behaviour' by the Bath and West of England Agricultural Society.[126] He had lived through tumultuous years of bad harvests and high food prices, war, social and technological change. He was hardworking, humble and suitably deferential to his social betters, which helped draw the admiration and support of Rev. and Mrs Bowles. His economic position was precarious, dependent on his good health and the availability of manual work, supplemented by good household management and secondary income. His refusal to use welfare meant he had to work into late old age. As the younger son, he did not inherit the family farm and, in an age of limited social mobility, could not climb out of a cycle of poverty. However, uniquely among the hundreds or thousands of local labourers throughout the centuries, he is eulogised in poetry. *The Epitaph on John Harding* by Rev. Bowles.

In the nineteenth century, there were around sixty local farms, some of which were very small. In 1830 three men, Walter Chivers, Bryan Rumbold and John Crook farmed twelve acres or fewer. Only a handful of farms within the parish were identified as being over 200 acres. The number of farmers and the mix of landholdings remained relatively constant until the twentieth century. The Ministry of Food National Farm Survey of Bremhill in 1941-3 does not paint a wholly different picture to 1830 with local 'farms' as small as eight acres. The ministry was not, however, impressed with the management of all local farmers. Arthur James at Siderow was a 'poor manager of labourers'. While Mr Kane at Charlcutt Hill, a 'poor manager of labourers and inefficient himself'.[127]

The presence in many probate inventories of the utensils of cheese making, such as cheese presses, tubs, vats and racks, indicates its local importance to farming. By the nineteenth century, Wiltshire had achieved some recognition as a cheese producer. In 1796, William Marshall reckoned the 'narrow loaf cheese' of north Wiltshire was 'high in fashion'.[128] Among the local producers of this delicacy was 'Mr Rich, of Foxham . . . a skilful and attentive dairyman, whose cheese has long been held in the highest estimation, and which is, in reality (this year at least), the most uniform, and the most highly flavoured dairy of cheese I have anywhere tasted.'[129] While Marshall praised Mr Rich, cheese making was the preserve of women, usually either the farmer's wife or under her direct management. North Wiltshire dairy women had 'superior skills' and exhibited 'best practice' but, thought Marshall 'the art is evidently destitute of principles . . . It may be said to be at present, a knack involved in mystery.'[130] Marshall encouraged men to take more notice of what the women were doing. However, little changed and according to a government report in the 1840s, cheese making in the parish remained the preserve of farmers' wives. It also noted dairy farms within the village were generally small.[131] Local cheese making centred on farm production until the last quarter of the nineteenth century.[132]

Fig. 80: 19th century Wiltshire cheese mould.

Production took place in dairies, locally called a 'white house'. The white house was originally a room in the farmhouse, but by the eighteenth century, extensions or separate accommodation was being built. Marshall describes the rooms as 'spacious and commodious. Set round with presses and whey leads: no shelves, the area being left free for the cowls and churns. The floors are of stone.'[133] It was usually on the north side of the house to keep it as cool as possible but still close to the kitchen to allow easy access for heating water.[134]

The finished product was ripened and stored on racks in the cheese loft. Although this could be above the dairy, it was more likely to be over the kitchen or later over the cows' stalls, 'the warmth of either' noted some communications made to the Board of Agriculture in 1797 'being thought greatly to forward the ripening process'. The order of rooms in the probate inventory of Spirthill farmer, Richard Bayley, in 1709 suggests his loft was over his brewhouse, in a room over a furnace.[136]

Fig. 81: Illustration from The Story of Cheese Making in Britain, (1959).

Storing cheese in this way also improved its security, as it could be of great value. In 1712, the contents of Thomas Mansell's cheese loft was worth more than twenty acres of barley and almost three times as much as his ten pigs.[137] In 1826, Robert Star was imprisoned for three months 'for stealing 2 cheeses at Bremhill'.[138] The cheese, thus stored, was generally brought up by factors and sold mostly to the London market.[139]

Local agriculture was generally mixed. Dairy production went hand in hand with arable by providing bedding and feed and was recognised as 'a circumstance favourable to a dairy.'[140] In the eighteenth century, Foxham yeoman Richard Bayley was typical. He had a small dairy herd of nine cows and arable of five and a half acres each of oats and barley and three acres of wheat.[141] He also had four pigs used locally for manure and meat.

As the local economy was based on farming, agricultural depressions hit the village particularly hard, but local people tried to mitigate unemployment and underemployment by pulling together. In winter 1816, just after the Napoleonic Wars ended, unemployment was high and distress acute. The parish vestry, a parish committee that served as its government, took the step of working in collaboration with farmers to provide work to local labourers. Each farmer was asked to employ one man for every £10 of the rateable value of their property. The parish then paid 10d in wages to the labourers and the farmer 6d per day. If the employer offered work 'by the lump', the parish paid half. If he could not provide employment, then the labourer moved on to the next farm. The parish was aware that some labourers might go out of the village for employment when work was plentiful at harvest.

Fig. 82: Wood engraving depicting the harvest being cut by sickle.

So they attempted to discourage this from happening by warning labourers that they would get less help if they had found work outside of the village during the summer.[142] A note on the back cover of the vestry book stated that if any man was 'unsatisfied by this statement of payment', they were 'to be given to Mr Bowles'.[143] What happened to them if they were 'given to Mr Bowles' was not elaborated. The arrangement may have been a great boon, as 1816 was a challenging year with 'one of the worst harvests known' and temperatures running five degrees Fahrenheit below normal. It even snowed in the south of England during September.[144] A similar system was used during winter 1828.[145]

Fig. 83: Collecting winter fuel in the snow.

It was not just agricultural unemployment that proved a challenge. The problem of low wages was another. In 1811, Wiltshire commentator, Thomas Davis, observed 'although the wages of labourers have been considerably increased within these few years, yet they are now barely sufficient for their subsistence'.[146]

Agricultural wages were low, and if harvests were bad and food prices went up, local people would struggle to eat. Many turned to the parish to provide them with relief, which for those in work in the early nineteenth century included supplements to wages and subsidies on rents.[147]

Bread formed their staple diet, and wage supplements were generally tied to its cost. Consequently, in the early 1830s, the cost of looking after the local poor rose and fell with the wheat price. In 1831, the wheat price hit a high of 66s a quart; the cost of Bremhill's welfare likewise hit £2,852, and when wheat prices plummeted to 46s in 1834, the value of relief fell to £1,930.[148] The situation did not improve to a significant degree for the rest of the century. In 1830 many farmers approached the Marquess of Lansdowne for a rent reduction which they could pass on to labourers in the form of higher wages. There is evidence to suggest that Lansdowne complied. In this, he was possibly influenced by Rev. Bowles, who increased the wages he paid workers on the glebe lands to 10s in the summer and 12s in the winter for able-bodied men.[149] As early as 1820, Bowles had argued for the necessity 'to raise the price of labour'.[150] In 1830, Bowles's efforts were applauded in the press, but then according to local accounts, the philanthropic churchman only employed one able-bodied man anyway.[151]

Fig. 84: 3rd Marquess of Lansdowne.

Relations between the estate holders and their tenants from the outside seem mostly cordial. In the late eighteenth century, Marshall observed of north Wiltshire: 'little of that oppression, which has manifested itself in many districts, has taken in this place. The good opinion and confidence, which ought ever to exist between landlords and their tenants, appear to be still sufficiently maintained.'[152] The 3rd Marquess of Lansdowne, as 'proprietor of the greater part of the parish', had a considerable influence over the livelihoods of many local people.[153] In many respects, he was a good landlord. As we have seen before, Lansdowne let the elderly labourer, John Harding and his wife live in his cottage rent-free.[154]

Fig. 85: Rev. William Lisle Bowles (1762-1850).

Bowles noted: 'much of the land, from feelings of benevolence in the noble owner [Lansdowne], is let out in small portions, so that there are few of the poorer inhabitants without a garden to their cottages in the whole parish.'[155] A further development was the provision of allotments throughout Bremhill parish which allowed local people to grow more of their own produce. Lansdowne also supported projects such as employing the unemployed on road improvements. [156]

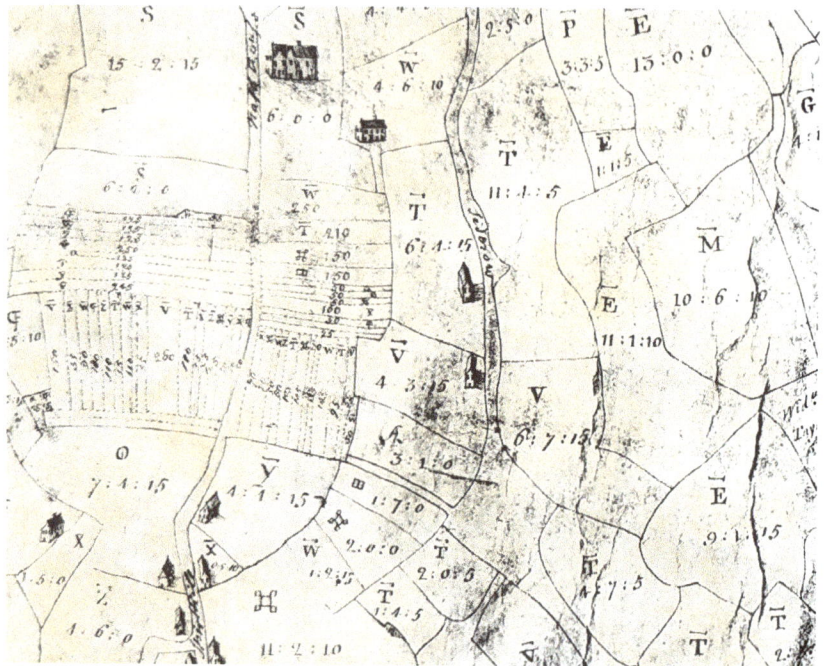

Fig. 86: Section of a Bowood Estate map showing narrow strips of land and allotments at Spirthill.

His philanthropy was particularly important. Unlike some other parishes, there were no local charities to call on during times of distress.[157] However, one reason why local people were economically vulnerable was that they no longer had access to some local common land because it had been enclosed. Traditionally local people could graze animals, collect firewood and enjoy all the benefits access to the commons provided. However, legislation sponsored by the Marquess meant these open spaces were going.[158] Labourers now relied more than ever on their wages. Lansdowne had a vast estate, and he did not live in the village, which meant he did not personally see the deprivations of his tenants. It meant other parishes might have benefited more from his generosity. In 1846, one visitor observed that while Bremhill 'was in deepest degradation' other villages within his estate were not.[159]

Fig. 87: If a local labourer became ill his family may have needed poor relief to avoid hardship.

Rev. Bowles saw first-hand the hardships of his flock. As a magistrate, he sometimes ordered welfare to be given to the local poor, at times against the wishes of parish officials.[160] However, he worried that the local labourer was turning to poor relief too readily: 'Instead of feeling the proud and conscious comfort that he is bringing up his children, humbly but honestly with the fruits of his own toil.'

The result, he feared, would be to 'deteriorate his character'. Welfare, he observed, 'operates even as a bounty on idleness, paralyses all the better affections of the heart, treads down all consciousness of humble and contented worth, and spreads on every side immorality and cheerless poverty'.[161] The reason he supported measures to introduce a fair working wage is probably related to the local 'appalling' system of supplementing local wages out of poor rates. He argued 'wages are thus kept as low as possible.'[162]

Throughout its history, the parish tried to look after its own, even if it was unclear what to do. That independence was probably the reason why there was resistance to pressure to relinquish control over local welfare. The parish had been responsible for looking after its own poor for centuries. In 1836, demand that it adopt the new workhouse system (made infamous by Charles Dickens's *Oliver Twist*) was opposed as 'an injury rather than a benefit'. While Bremhill ultimately succumbed and joined the Calne Poor Law Union, parish officials sometimes ordered local families out of Calne Workhouse.

In 1842, William Burgess, an unemployed agricultural labourer, his wife and four small children were removed from the workhouse. The vestry wanted William and his family to be supported back in the village until a new job could be found. William was successful in finding employment, and at the next census, he was living in Bremhill working as an agricultural labourer with his wife, children and a lodger.[163]

However, collective action was usually only successful in the short-term. While some farmers did manage to increase wages in 1830, it was only a temporary measure. The mid-1830s saw good harvests and lower-priced food, which reduced pressure on wages. So, payments began to drop. However, in the 1840s, things became progressively difficult again as the government started to add higher tariffs to imported wheat to safeguard home producers. It pushed up the cost of food.

The Bowood land agent reported to a Royal Commission in 1843 that local people in Bremhill ate 'bread, potatoes, with a very small quantity of bacon; sometimes cabbages from their allotments'. 'Butchers meat' was 'rarely eaten; hardly ever, unless it is given to them'. This inadequate sounding fare sustained labourers who worked from six in the morning until six at night.[164]

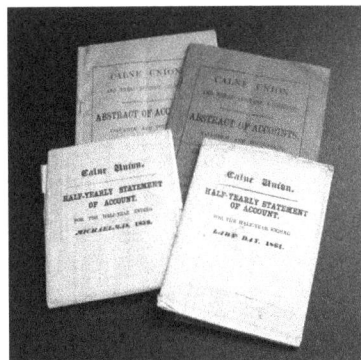

Fig. 88: Calne Poor Law Union account books archived at the Wiltshire Museum.

Fig. 89: Calne Workhouse in 1760 at the corner of Patford Lane (later New Road) and Silver Street.

Hymn of the Wiltshire Labourer:
Lucy Simpkins and the Anti Corn-Law League

Fig. 90: Post card of the village cross at Bremhill.

Given the economic hardships of local agricultural labourers, it is unsurprising their condition eventually catapulted Bremhill into the national consciousness. On an intensely cold and clear night in February 1846, in front of the stone cross at the centre of the village, crowds of men, women and children began to gather. The women generally wore coats and bonnets. The men appeared a gaunt and raw-boned set, the women pinched and careworn. According to an observer present that night, 'Some of them had trudged ten or twelve miles, and this after a hard day in the fields. It was curious to see the groups - the men with their smock frocks showing like white moving patches in the moonlight - making their way from all sides - appearing from the narrow streets - gliding across the churchyard - to the place of meeting.'[165]

The Corn Laws were probably the most debated political issue of the 1840s. By January 1846, it was 'obsessing the whole nation'.[166] To protect home producers, the government had increasingly added duties onto imported food-stuffs; this had peaked 1838–46. This action had raised the cost of food. In 1844 and 1845, there were terrible harvests which further drove up prices, worsening an already bad situation for the working classes. The Anti-Corn Law League was created in the 1830s and agitated in favour of free trade, largely in urban areas. But by 1842, it had started to expand its campaigning into rural districts. Handbills across the district had extensively publicised the meeting at Bremhill in the previous days. It was preceded by another Anti-Corn Law meeting at Goatacre shortly before.

Fig. 91: National Anti-Corn Law League membership card.

There were three reporters present at the Bremhill meeting. One from the *Wiltshire Independent*, based in Devizes, and others from the London based, *Morning Post* and *Morning Chronicle*.[167] As the proceedings began, these journalists were implored to give an accurate version of what they saw.[168] It was important because while many other accounts were made in the press, they were lifted from these three original pieces. These testimonies portrayed different perspectives on events, and it was particularly true of the critical account of the *Morning Post*. It was their report that formed the basis of the most scathing of later accounts.

According to their observer, the meeting was not a spontaneous assembly of labourers from the surrounding district. Instead, 'the gathering was promoted by persons distinct from the class of which it was composed, everything about the meeting proved this.' He pointed out that the 'prime mover' was Mr Edwards of Marlborough.[169] It caused many to argue that outside forces had manipulated local people.

However, the *Wiltshire Independent* attacked the accuracy of this version, particularly when its fellow Devizes publication, the protectionist *Devizes and Wiltshire Gazette*, rehashed and embellished the story from the *Morning Post*. The mortified *Independent* stated, 'the Gazette seeks to cast ridicule on the meeting and discredit the speakers!' [170]

The most influential account was probably that of the *Morning Chronicle*, whose journalist wrote 'the meeting originated entirely with the working men.' Their collective 'hunger brought them together.'[171] He pointed out, 'every influence was brought to bear, first to prevent [the meeting] from taking place and second to keep the labourers from attending.' This influence included the local clergyman, Rev. Henry Drury, who had taken legal advice to see if the villagers could be prevented from attending. When that failed, he managed to get 'a great number of constables in private clothes' to participate in the gathering to disperse the crowd at the first sign of trouble. In the event, the constables were not needed. Rev. Drury also told the man putting up handbills to advertise the meeting, he would be ejected not merely from his job but from 'the country' if he continued. Despite attempts by Drury and farmers to stop local people from attending, they participated in great numbers.[172]

Fig. 93: Rev. Henry Drury is buried in St Martin's churchyard, Bremhill.

Fig. 94: Charles Dickens wrote the poem *Hymn of the Wiltshire Labourer* which was published in the national *Daily News*.

O God, remind them!
In the bread

They break upon the knee,

These sacred words may
yet be read

"In Memory of Me!"

O, God! Remind them of
His sweet

Compassion for the poor,

And how He gave them
Bread to eat

And went from door to
door!

Sometime between seven and eight in the evening, the proceedings began. The chairman of the meeting was Job Gingell, a local labourer, who sat on one of the cross's stone steps. In his hands, he held a flickering candle and called the meeting to order. 'Around the cross, the people clustered, forming a dense impenetrable mass.' [173] The reporters sat to one side in a make-shift tent.

The *Chronicle* painted a picture of the unsophisticated labourers, 'who knew nothing of the rules of such assemblages,' but who instead spoke sharing their own stories, 'their own history of slow starvation'.[174] The meeting did not have an overtly political agenda, even if the Anti-Corn Law League had helped set it up. Instead, the labourers and their wives quietly shared their accounts, which exposed the harsh and challenging nature of their daily struggles.

The *Morning Chronicle* and *Wiltshire Independent* noted with pleasure how the crowd dispatched members of the radical Chartist movement, who tried to infiltrate the proceedings.[175] Towards the end, a woman in a long grey coat and old bonnet rose to speak, and by the illumination from Job Gingell's candle, she partly read partly recited her speech.[176] It was Lucy Simpkins. Her speech was long and passionate:

Don't you think we have a great need to cry to our God,

to put in the hearts of our gracious Queen and her Members

of Parliament, to grant us free trade, that a poor father and

mother may sit down with a great loaf, and give their children

a good meal of bread a long time which they have been strangers to.[177]

It ended with loud cheers from the assembly.

Accounts of the meeting were published in the press on 12 February. In London, a new liberal and Anti-Corn Law paper, the *Daily News*, had just gone into production the previous month, under the editorship of author Charles Dickens.[178] The *Daily News* published their account of the Bremhill meeting on 13 February. The article was probably neither edited nor even written by Dickens. He had stopped managing the paper a few days before.[179] However, he reacted to the report with lightning speed as his poem, inspired by events in Bremhill and particularly by Lucy Simpkin's speech, was published in the *Daily News* the following day.[180]

The poem, *Hymn of the Wiltshire Labourers*, was designed to 'elicit sympathy for the people and the repeal of the Corn Laws'. He portrayed 'a landscape fraught with exploitation and social inequalities, embedded with myth and corrupted by religious, political and economic greed and ambition' which ignored the well-being of ordinary citizens.[181] In a few lines, he criticised protectionists for supporting a system that kept bread beyond the reach of the poor:

What of the aftermath and the influence of these events? Farmer Stephen Stiles Jeffreys of Spirthill sacked five of his workers who had attended the meeting.[182] It is unclear whether this was a common experience. References to the meeting at Bremhill would find their way into the parliamentary debate on the topic of the Corn Laws.[183] Allusions in the press also continued for much of the rest of the month. However, the direct influence of Dickens's poem or Lucy Simpkin's speech on Westminster or the political classes more broadly is not clear. Suffice to say, nationally a crisis-point had been achieved in favour of abolishing the Corn Laws.

Fig. 95: Prime Minister Robert Peel was an advocate of abolishing the Corn Laws.

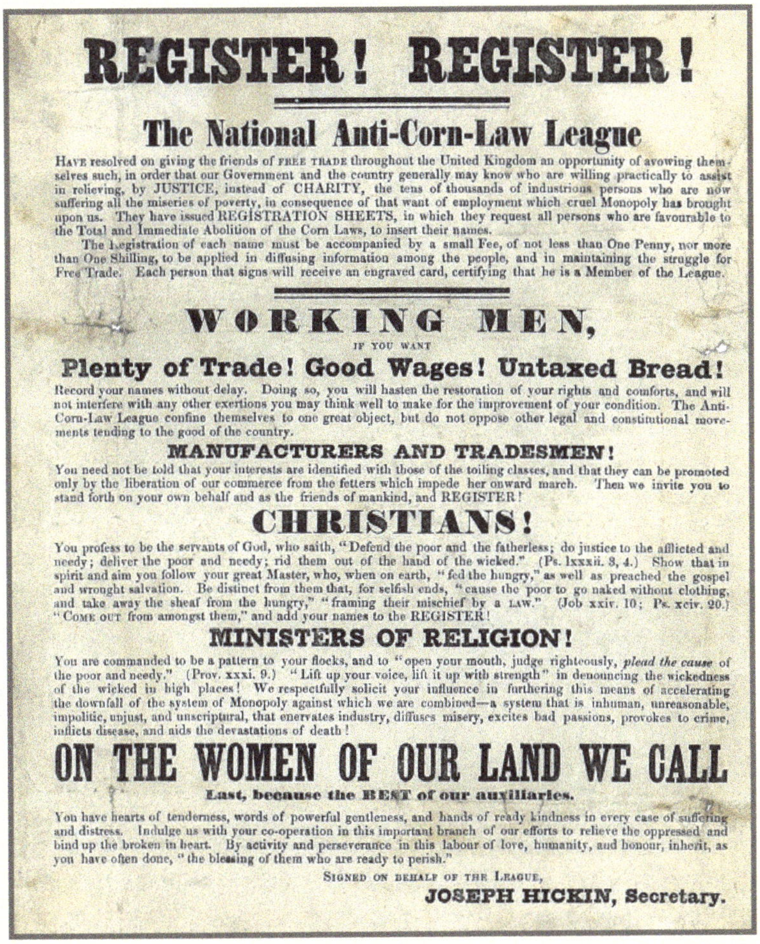

REGISTER! REGISTER!

The National Anti-Corn-Law League

HAVE resolved on giving the friends of FREE TRADE throughout the United Kingdom an opportunity of avowing themselves such, in order that our Government and the country generally may know who are willing practically to assist in relieving, by JUSTICE, instead of CHARITY, the tens of thousands of industrious persons who are now suffering all the miseries of poverty, in consequence of that want of employment which cruel Monopoly has brought upon us. They have issued REGISTRATION SHEETS, in which they request all persons who are favourable to the Total and Immediate Abolition of the Corn Laws, to insert their names.

The Registration of each name must be accompanied by a small Fee, of not less than One Penny, nor more than One Shilling, to be applied in diffusing information among the people, and in maintaining the struggle for Free Trade. Each person that signs will receive an engraved card, certifying that he is a Member of the League.

WORKING MEN,
IF YOU WANT

Plenty of Trade! Good Wages! Untaxed Bread!

Record your names without delay. Doing so, you will hasten the restoration of your rights and comforts, and will not interfere with any other exertions you may think well to make for the improvement of your condition. The Anti-Corn-Law League confine themselves to one great object, but do not oppose other legal and constitutional movements tending to the good of the country.

MANUFACTURERS AND TRADESMEN!

You need not be told that your interests are identified with those of the toiling classes, and that they can be promoted only by the liberation of our commerce from the fetters which impede her onward march. Then we invite you to stand forth on your own behalf and as the friends of mankind, and REGISTER!

CHRISTIANS!

You profess to be the servants of God, who saith, "Defend the poor and the fatherless; do justice to the afflicted and needy; deliver the poor and needy; rid them out of the hand of the wicked." (Ps. lxxxii. 3, 4.) Show that in spirit and aim you follow your great Master, who, when on earth, "fed the hungry," as well as preached the gospel and wrought salvation. Be distinct from them that, for selfish ends, "cause the poor to go naked without clothing, and take away the sheaf from the hungry," "framing their mischief by a LAW." (Job xxiv. 10; Ps. xciv. 20.) "COME OUT from amongst them," and add your names to the REGISTER!

MINISTERS OF RELIGION!

You are commanded to be a pattern to your flocks, and to "open your mouth, judge righteously, plead the cause of the poor and needy." (Prov. xxxi. 9.) "Lift up your voice, lift it up with strength" in denouncing the wickedness of the wicked in high places! We respectfully solicit your influence in furthering this means of accelerating the downfall of the system of Monopoly against which we are combined—a system that is inhuman, unreasonable, impolitic, unjust, and unscriptural, that enervates industry, diffuses misery, excites bad passions, provokes to crime, inflicts disease, and aids the devastations of death!

ON THE WOMEN OF OUR LAND WE CALL

Last, because the BEST of our auxiliaries.

You have hearts of tenderness, words of powerful gentleness, and hands of ready kindness in every case of suffering and distress. Indulge us with your co-operation in this important branch of our efforts to relieve the oppressed and bind up the broken in heart. By activity and perseverance in this labour of love, humanity, and honour, inherit, as you have often done, "the blessing of them who are ready to perish."

SIGNED ON BEHALF OF THE LEAGUE,

JOSEPH HICKIN, Secretary.

Fig. 96: Anti-Corn Law League publicity material was issued nationally.

Prime Minister Robert Peel was in support of it by the beginning of 1846. The issue was deeply contentious, and Peel was only able to get it through parliament, later in the year, with the help of the opposition. It would split the Conservative party. As for Lucy Simpkin herself, after the meeting she quietly resumed the hard life of a labourer's wife. In his sixties, her husband, William, became a gardener, and hopefully, this provided more security. Lucy died, aged seventy-five in 1878. Her death was unmarked in the press. However, the events of the fated night in 1846 were to be long remembered, and Dickens' poem would ensure she was not to be forgotten.

3.2 Textile Manufacture

Fig. 97: Woman spinning from *Labours of the Fields* by J. F. Millet (1814-1875).

Fig. 98: A cottage weaving loom c1890.

Fig. 99: Fulling stocks.

Although sheep were not a popular livestock choice for local yeomen, for centuries woollen cloth manufacture took place across Bremhill. This production was organised by local clothiers who used out workers to spin the wool into yarn and to weave the yarn into cloth. Spinning was mainly the preserve of women and the more lucrative weaving was undertaken by men. It could occur within the same household, but the wives of local agricultural labourers also spun yarn. Weaving took place within the home in the 'shop'. It was a work of skill and looms were valuable. Bremhill weaver Robert Davis left his loom to his son, also Robert, in his will. However, by the time his probate inventory was taken four days after his death, it had been judiciously removed.[184]

Zachariah Bradbury, a Quaker of Charlcutt, was a local weaver producing serge from worsted yarn. The type of heavy cloth he made was probably used for tailored items such as greatcoats or suits. The presence of two looms and a bed in his shop chamber suggests he may have had an apprentice. His 1729 inventory at over £200 was a reasonable estate. He had done well.[185]

After production, the woven cloth was taken to a local fulling mill to finish; before the clothier arranged for its sale, usually in the markets of London.[186] This industry had taken place in Bremhill, from at least the twelfth century when a cloth mill was listed at Stanley Abbey. [187]

Fulling was the only aspect of the manufacture which was mechanised, and it took place at several neighbourhood mills, including Hazeland. These mills were water powered. They took advantage of the River Marden and their presence helped to encourage the development of local transport links.

When cloth arrived at the mill, it was scoured and cleaned to remove oils. Fulling was the process by which fabric was shrunk and thickened. Mighty hammers, called fulling stocks, driven by the water lashed the sodden fibres. Outside the mill, there was generally ground on which stood a rack where the shrunken textile was stretched on big frames known as tenters (a link to the origin of the phrase 'on tenterhooks'). Inventories of local fullers contain references to fuller's earth, used in the cleansing process.

Bremhill fuller, William Hewes, had so much of it on his death, in 1711, that it had the same value as his most expensive household items; his two bedsteads with their mattresses, blankets, bolsters, pillows and sheets included.[188] It may have been expensive, but it was preferable to the local alternative of human urine and pig dung.[189]

Bremhill fullers were supremely adaptive to changing economic circumstances. Michael Feats, described as a 'fuller' in his 1679 will, was according to the manor rent roll of the same year, in possession of Stanley Abbey a 'grist mill', and therefore grinding grain not finishing cloth.[190] The inventory of 'fuller' William Hort suggests that he too was probably not working cloth but rather working grain on his death.[191] This flexibility allowed fullers to weather any short-term trade disruptions or slumps.

By the early eighteenth century, government returns list four mills used locally in cloth production. The most productive by far was Hazeland Mill which finished cloth on behalf of five local clothiers, Goldney, Farr, Turnford, Nayes and Figgins. Mr Goldney was undoubtedly part of the influential Goldney family of clothiers of Chippenham. The three lesser mills were Scotts, Stanley and Avon. The clothiers who used Hazeland did not frequent the other mills who instead used Scotts and Stanley, or Ray Mill at Lacock. The small mill at Avon produced only 6 per cent of the cloth they did at Hazeland. Miller, William Fry's only customer, was Robert Fry, a clothier, probably a relative. The miller, at Hazeland, was the fuller, Peter Lane.[192] At the time, the Wiltshire cloth trade was doing well. On his death in 1748, Lane left a good-sized estate that included bonds, securities, capital and several cottages in Calne. The property went to his daughters, and money, perhaps suspicious of his sons-in-law, was entrusted to his friends John Warne of Calne and John Jones, a weaver, from Derry Hill. They were charged with using it to provide an income for his daughters and grandchildren.

Fig. 100: The encased grinding stones at Hazeland Mill.

Fig. 101: William Henry Fox Talbot's photograph of Hazeland Mill.

—HAZELAND MILL,—
Calne, Wilts, Aug 30 1900
Mr C. Bridges
Bought of CHAS. T. PAVY,
Pure Barley-Meal, Offals, Corn, &c.

Received for C. T. PAVY
the sum of £
Signature
With thanks.

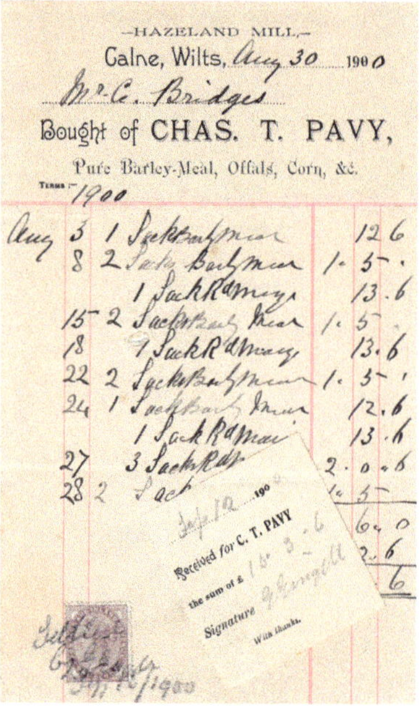

Fig. 102: Receipted invoice for sacks of cereal etc. dated 30 August 1900.

Fullers, weavers and serge makers were less in evidence in local probate records as the eighteenth century progressed, suggesting a contraction in the local trade. One reason for the demise of the Wiltshire woollen trade overall was the local persistence in the use of water power. In Yorkshire, production far more quickly used new steam technology. Whereas in Wiltshire, the introduction of mechanisation precipitated riots in Chippenham in 1801-3.

However, the tide of industrialisation was unstoppable and spelt the demise of Bremhill cloth production.[193] By 1826, the trade in Chippenham had already ceased when a prospective MP bought a mill and promised to keep it continually working.[194] It is hardly surprising that Hazeland Mill stopped production sometime shortly after 1838 when in a 'daring burglary', ninety yards of cloth was stolen. Perhaps it was the last straw with trade struggling.[195] However, indicative of the flexibility in the local trade, the mill adapted and reverted to milling grain and continued to do so into the twentieth century.[196]

3.3 Other Trades

By the mid-eighteenth century, there was a small but burgeoning service sector, particularly in establishments selling alcohol. Ann Ruddle and Simeon Oatridge were victuallers, licenced to sell alcohol during the 1750s and 1760s.[197] Shopkeepers too were making an appearance, including Abraham Brookes, who in 1781 left all the stock from his shop not to his family but to business friends, one a grocer from Calne and the other, fuller Thomas Welles of Stanley. One of the more unusual local trades was practised by William Ruming of Spirthill, a soap boiler (maker). He left his son, John, his furnace and the utensils of his trade.[198]

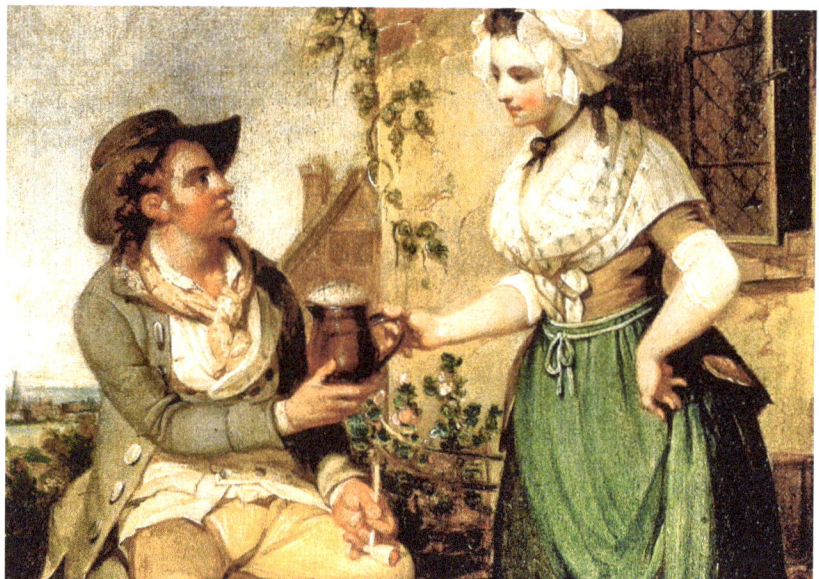

Fig. 103: *The Ale House Door* by Henry Singleton, 1790.

3.4 Side-lines

It was common for those in trade, such as fullers and clothiers, to grow produce and keep a few pigs and a cow or two for household consumption. Some individuals also kept bees or brewed beer.[199] Even among the poor, in the early nineteenth century, it was reported, 'there is not a single labourer without a pig and a plot of ground for a garden.'[200] However, for some, farming was a significant side-line. In the late seventeenth century, parish clerk John Wootten of Tytherton Lucas was also an arable farmer.[201] In the early eighteenth century, Edward Wilcox, a successful local maltster, was a dairy farmer and produced his own cheese.[202]

In the nineteenth century, Rev. Bowles did a little farming too. However, it appears from a household inventory that the vicar or his staff was producing beer in large quantities.[203] These secondary businesses are in evidence later in the nineteenth century also, although not just in farming. In *Kelly's Directory of Wiltshire* during the 1850s, John Palmer was listed as both a carpenter and wheelwright. Later in the 1860s, he was a carpenter, wheelwright and had become responsible for the post office.[204] However, in the 1851 census, a John Palmer is listed as a carpenter and labourer.

Fig. 104: Coloured drawing by George Morland.

Fig. 105: 19th century carpenters tools.

Trades

63

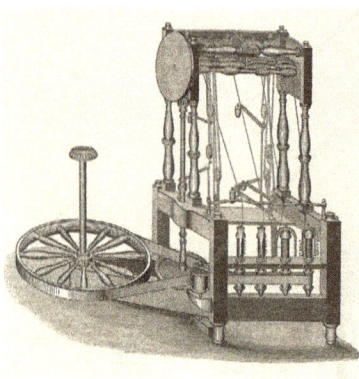

Fig. 106: Water powered spinning frame.

Fig. 107: Woman holding a distaff and spindle, with cows.

Further down the social strata, auxiliary forms of income could be critical. Many local women during the seventeenth and eighteenth century contributed to their household income by spinning wool into yarn.[205] However, as the nineteenth century dawned, one local observer wrote, 'this compensation seems likely soon to be at an end, by the general introduction of machines to supply the place of manual labour.'

He continued, 'the dearness of provisions, the scarcity of fuel, and above all the failure of spinning-work for the women and children, have put it almost out of the power of the village poor to live by their industry, and have unfortunately broken that independent spirit.'[206]

3.5 Women's Work

A number of women are mentioned on manor rent rolls and surveys during the seventeenth centuries as being landholders.[207] In 1830, out of sixty-one local farmers, eight were women. They farmed 750 acres and, between them, employed up to twenty-six labourers.[208] At the time, the farms included West End Farm in Foxham, a 153-acre mixed dairy and arable holding, which was run successfully by Sarah Hancock for decades until her retirement in 1853.[209] The smallest was one of just sixteen acres run by 'Mrs Pegler'.[210] At the 1841 census, along with Sarah Hancock, were farmers Rebecca Turk at Godsell Farm; Ann Smalcomb at Bremhill Field; Ann Riches at Stockham Marsh Farm and Hester Butler at Hazeland. While these women wielded economic power, they are likely to have enjoyed it by virtue of being widows.[211]

Although the death of a spouse provided an opportunity to run a business, it was not a forgone conclusion. In 1797, Charlcutt baker William Reeves directed that his wife, Sarah, continue his bakery business after his death. However, he left two trustees. One of these, Joseph Perkins, was also a baker in Calne. These trustees had the job of checking in on her and giving any 'directions' they thought she needed. If they noticed any 'sinking or deficiency' in the business, they were empowered to close the bakery down.[212] As Sarah's father, Paul, had been a baker in Bremhill, she presumably had the business experience, so direction was probably unjustified.[213] William was, however, by no means the only husband to leave such stipulations in his will.[214]

Fig. 108: 19th century baker engraving.

His attitude reflected the expectations of women, which ensured, their business and employment opportunities were limited. Local women could undertake caring roles or domestic service and duties in support of their husband's or father's occupation, but other employment outside the home was a different matter.

One employed in a more domestic and thus socially acceptable role was Mrs Garlic, who in the 1770s and 1780s was paid by the parish to deliver babies of poor families.[215] Other women were employed in the same period to tend the sick, although there were odd occasions where a 'man nurse' was used. More numerous than women employed by the parish were those engaged by wealthier families as domestic servants.

Elizabeth Richman, for example, was employed as a servant by the Pinnell family at Naish House Farm during the late seventeenth century. The Pinnells had owned the house for several generations. Elizabeth lived through one of the most tumultuous periods of English history, the Civil War, Interregnum and the restoration of the monarchy. She was devoted to young Master Pinnell, leaving him £5 in her will.[216] Young Henry grew up to become an MP and owner of Bradenstoke Abbey.[217]

Fig. 109: *Scullery Maid* by Anne Claude de Caylus, 1737.

Given their limited opportunities, it is not surprising that in 1828, Rev. Bowles observed five out of six local single women under thirty were unemployed over the winter.[218] This is also reflected in a government report by the testimony of the Marquess of Lansdowne's land agent, in 1843, who stated women made up only a small proportion of the number employed in agriculture in Bremhill. However, under the right circumstances, attitudes softened. Consequently, when demand for labour was high during harvest, women were required in the fields and accounted for up to half the workforce. Revealing opinions towards women at the time, the agent was able to report this agricultural employment was 'healthy' for them and had not led to a lapse in their morals.[219]

Fig. 110: Blacksmith's anvil *c.* 1890.

However, while occupations were restricted for women, there are some local surprises. In 1790, a girl named Selina Barton was apprenticed into the usually male-dominated trade of making serge cloth. All the more surprising, she was also apprenticed to a woman, Bremhill resident, Sarah Newman.[220] Sixty years later, a Bremhill woman named Ann Collar had a commercial listing in the 1855 edition of *Kelly's Directory of Wiltshire*, in another male-dominated profession, as a blacksmith.[221]

3.6 Learning a Trade and Raising Money

Fig. 111: Apprenticeships for shoemaking were a long arduous process until mechanisation.

Until the early nineteenth century, apprenticeships were an essential mechanism to learn a trade, especially if one was to avoid the ubiquitous employment of an agricultural labourer. Parents arranged most placements. The children of the more affluent were likely to be sent long distances to learn valued skills and make lucrative contacts. The victualler, John Mansell, left provision in his will in 1811 to ensure all five of his children, including daughters Eliza and Elizabeth, were apprenticed.[222]

The national register reveals some of the local trades children were apprenticed into; these include carpentry, tailoring, masonry, serge weaving, wool combing and shoemaking. The parish also recognised the importance of learning a trade, so sometimes paid the fees for local poor children to become apprentices or even purchase clothes for girls going into service.[223]

It had the benefit of removing the necessity of providing for their support because they became the responsibility of their 'master'. Hopefully, it also ensured that as adults, they would become economically productive so as not to require welfare in the future. These arrangements made on behalf of the less affluent were likely to be into less valuable trades.

By the early nineteenth century, the benefits of apprenticeships were already being questioned in the face of mechanisation. Local clothier, Abraham Eldridge told a select committee on woollen cloth manufacture that 'apprentices are not better workmen than the ordinary workmen.' He stated all his cloth workers and many weavers were 'unapprenticed'.[224] It had been very different 200 years before when Bremhill weaver Robert Davys had been in trouble with the law for 'using the craft of weaver not having served as an apprentice'.[225] In 1851, there were just two apprentices in the parish, William Lewis, an apprentice basketmaker in Spirthill, and Edward Hillier, an apprentice carpenter in Bremhill. William later moved back to his family in Lacock, where ten years later, symptomatic of the decline in local handicrafts, he was an unemployed basket maker.

Greasing the wheels of commerce in Bremhill were the lines of credit that were allowed by local traders. On his death in 1635, Hazeland clothier, John Tayler, was owed more money than the value of his business assets and possessions combined.[226] In the centuries before banking services were generally available, this was an important mechanism. This credit may have included money-lending, such as undertaken by 'servant' Mary Crook, who lent money to the local gentry in the early seventeenth century.[227]

However, it was more often in the form of deferred payment terms for goods or services rendered. During the seventeenth and eighteenth centuries, this credit was mostly locally generated and received. More substantial loans, mortgages or commercialised debt sometimes provided the exception. Some obligations were formalised in written agreements called bonds which were enforceable under law, but most were not. Many contracts, therefore, rested on trust and goodwill. It appears from local probate inventories that some traders allowed very high levels of credit. In 1711, the household possessions of fuller William Hewes accounted for only £14 compared to debts both good and bad owed to him of £125 with a further £20 upon bond. He also had £40 in cash in his possession.[228] Due to the provision of unformalised credit, less cautious or astute judges of character could be burdened with bad or 'desperate' debts. In 1721, for example, almost 20 per cent of the money owed to maltster Edward Wilcox was in the form of such liability.[229] On the other hand, Stanley fuller, William Hort, ensured all the credit services he provided, which extended to mortgages, were made formal.[230] Being in debt to others could have consequences. For example, Bremhill butcher John Aycliffe languished in Devizes Gaol in 1769 imprisoned for debt.[231]

Fig. 112: Typical 17th century bond of credit.

Fig. 113: A new gaol at Devizes was opened in 1817 next to the bridge which spanned the Kennet & Avon Canal.

3.7 Emigration

Fig. 114: Moving from your home parish could require legal documentation if you were poor so that you were not sent back again.

Although most residents lived and worked within the parish for their whole lives, a few individuals moved away. Until the mid-nineteenth century, the state tried to regulate the movement of people from their home parish through the Settlement Acts. The surviving documentary evidence arising from this legislation suggests that on leaving Bremhill, most people moved just a few miles away. For example, to Lyneham or Christian Malford or towns like Calne and Chippenham. However, a very few moved further. It did not always work out. In 1776, Joseph Slater, his wife and two children were resident in the parish of Great Glen in Leicestershire. Unfortunately, the family had fallen on hard times. The Justices of the Peace in Leicestershire informed Bremhill parish officers that as the family had a legal 'settlement' in Bremhill, they were required to pay to support the family.[232]

Although the documentation is slim, what is available suggests that people moved for economic reasons, to take up apprenticeships or new jobs, or find job opportunities elsewhere. People also moved into Bremhill for economic reasons. Again, this was usually within the county, and often not very far, but as with those people moving away from Bremhill before the mid-nineteenth century, it sometimes involved getting legal permission. William Ruming and his wife moved just two miles from Hilmarton into Spirthill sometime around 1708 but were still obliged to adhere to this legal process; otherwise they may have been sent back again.[233] It is likely the same William Ruming who was a soap boiler and died in 1755.[234]

In the nineteenth century, the parish even helped to finance some moves. Joseph Hatherill was given £10 to help him emigrate to America. For reasons not properly explained, the cost was born under the 'incidental expenses' in the highways account, which should have been used to repair parish roads.[235]

Fig. 115: Emigrating to America in the 19th century could mean a voyage of between 6 weeks and 3 months depending on the weather.

Bremhill Boys at Sea[236]

One of the most surprising job opportunities pursued by men of Bremhill parish was to join the Royal Marines, the Navy's ship-borne infantry arm. Most enlisted at Chippenham. Recruitment parties were sent from the naval barracks at Portsmouth into Wiltshire.[237] Posters would announce the arrival of the party, and men from the locality would apply, in-person to a recruitment officer.[238] A contemporary newspaper correspondent described the process as 'not only disreputable but actually disgraceful'. He depicted officers 'decoying and entrapping their victims' having stationed themselves at a public-house or beer shop or at fairs and marketplaces, where they related fancy tales which 'fascinate and enchain those not accustomed to think for themselves'. The hapless recruit was likely to be under the influence of alcohol.[239]

Nonetheless, this life choice may have been an easy decision. Most Bremhill recruits had previously worked as agricultural labourers. They came from poor families and had limited prospects. On joining the Navy, they received a lump sum or 'bounty'. In 1841, the bounty paid was the sizeable sum of £3 17s 6d.[240] The Marines offered accommodation, regular meals, a wage and the prospect of 'prize' money awarded for the capture of an enemy ship or city. There was, also, the excitement of adventure. Additionally, no sea-faring knowledge was required, helpful for recruits from a landlocked county.

Although the Navy was looking for men of a particular age and general fitness, it seems they were flexible. Samuel Alexander was only sixteen when he joined in 1810. He was small, only 5' 1"; fair-faced with hazel eyes and brown hair, he passed a physical, likely a very superficial exam. Samuel was later discharged on medical grounds aged about twenty. He was suffering from rheumatism. He returned home and died at the age of twenty-three.

For some, the reality of life in the Navy came as a shock. Jacob Fry was twenty-one when he joined up on 17 December 1855. He lasted less than a week running away two days before Christmas. He returned to Woolwich Barracks on 29 December to complete his training. He was discharged from his military service five years later, described as an 'invalid'

Fig. 116: *The King's Shilling*, painting by James Campbell, 1871.

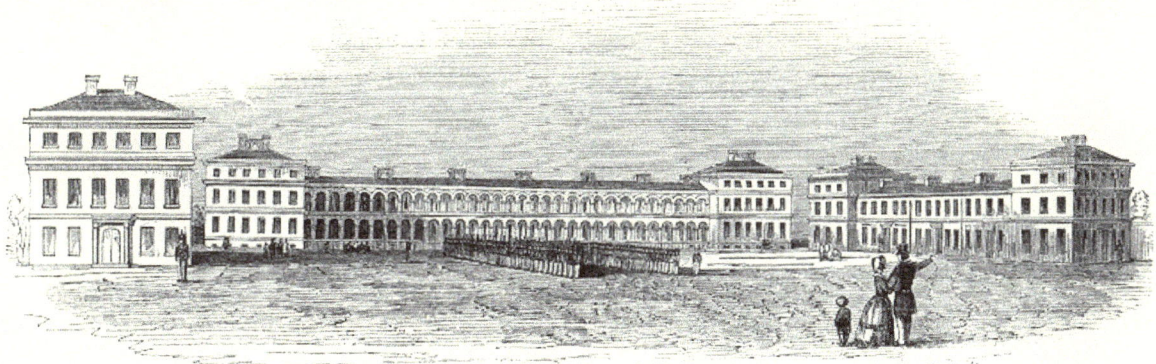

Fig. 117: The Royal Marines Barracks in Woolwich, London.

Fig. 118: HMS *Franchise* was a French Navy frigate captured by the British in 1803 and was taken into the Royal Navy under her own name.

Fig. 119: Sailor's hammock slung from the deck beams mostly in cramped conditions.

Once training was done, the ultimate fulfilment of a marine was to become part of a detachment on board a naval vessel. Meshach Alexander, a sixteen-year-old labourer, joined up just after Christmas 1809. In 1810, he was transferred from Portsmouth to HMS *Franchise*, a former French frigate. The vessel had a crew of over 200 and likely a detachment of around thirty marines. In May, Meshach sailed to Newfoundland, Canada.[241] Conditions on-board *Franchise* were uncomfortable. A marine officer described his berth on a ship during the period as 'a place between two guns, about seven foot long and four foot wide, and divided from some hundred hammocks by a little canvas, or an old sail, where there is no light but for a candle, nor no air but what is unavoidably very foul and as unwholesome as it is unpleasant.'[242]

Apart from taking watches and providing guard duty, marines, like Meshach, were usually given labour-intensive tasks such as pumping water. Tragically, by October, Meshach had died, aged just seventeen. There are no details provided and no reference to the ship being engaged in enemy action. It is likely Meshach died of natural causes. In the close quarters of naval vessels, disease spread quickly. Indeed, at this time, marines were more likely to die of disease than enemy action.

One of the worst crimes for a marine to commit was desertion. It was, however, commonplace. William Provis was a twenty-three-year-old labourer when he joined the Marines. He was serving with 8th Company at the Marines' Woolwich Barracks, when in July 1836, he fled. He made his way back to Wiltshire. In December, he was committed for trial on the oath of John Groom of Devizes who had reported him to the authorities.[243] But he was then handed back to the Navy. In March 1837, he was dismissed from the Marines after he had been punished. William had received the extraordinary punishment of being 'branded' with the letter 'D', possibly under his armpit on his left side.

Fig. 120: HMS *Inconstant*, built in 1868.

Fig. 121: HMS *Boadicea*, a Bacchante class corvette built in 1875.

A few Bremhill parish recruits were in the service for the long-haul and did well. Born in 1854, Henry Woodward joined the Navy aged just fourteen. By the time he was sixteen, he was on board the huge iron-hulled steam frigate, HMS *Inconstant*, one of 600 crew. Firstly, sailing to Gibraltar and then to various Scandinavian ports. In 1872, *Inconstant* was temporarily moved into the reserve fleet, and Henry now an ordinary seaman, was assigned to the Naval flagship, HMS *Duke of York* at Portsmouth. In 1876, he was aboard HMS *Unicorn* in Dundee, and between 1877 and 1879, he was on HMS *Raleigh*, sometimes at Cyprus. Henry acquitted himself well and became a Petty Officer 2nd class. In 1880, he was stationed on the new gun vessel, HMS *Rambler* and became Petty Officer 1st class or bosun, a foreman for the ship's deck crew. He was then assigned to HMS *Boadicea* and then HMS *Thalia*. In 1882, still in his twenties, Henry signed up for another ten years. In his first thirteen years of service, the only wound he had sustained was to his left forefinger. His next ship was HMS *Northampton*, in North America and the West Indies, on whom he served for the next four years.[244] Back on dry land, he married Kate Hill in Salisbury in 1886. His last years of service were on the Royal Yacht *Osborne*, taking the royal family on foreign trips or to Osborne House on the Isle of Wight. Henry retired to Portsmouth.

Fig. 122: HMS *Northampton*, launched in 1876, a Nelson class armoured cruiser.

3.8 Continuity and Change: 1881-1911

Despite the economic and social changes in Britain, on the surface, the economy of Bremhill parish changed little between 1881 and 1911. Most people who earned a living still did so in agriculture.[245] But the community was not immune from what was happening elsewhere. Between 1881 and 1891 the number of farms increased, as farming recovered from an agricultural depression that affected the country from the late 1870s. However, after 1891 there was no significant reduction in the number of farms, suggesting the consolidation of local farm holdings had not yet taken place as it had elsewhere. The allied trades which farming had traditionally required, such as carpenters, wheelwrights, blacksmiths and carters, were still very much in evidence, although their numbers were now slowly diminishing. By 1911, there was no longer a harness maker or thatcher in the parish, after harness maker Frederick Freegard had emigrated to America and thatcher, William Norton, died in the 1880s.

The community remained largely self-sustaining. For most farmers and the general population, their needs were quickly supplied by someone in the community, be it a horseshoe, dress or loaf of bread. There was a baker, grocer and post office in Bremhill and East Tytherton where a total of ten people were employed in retail according to the 1911 census. There was also a grocer at Charlcutt and Foxham.[246] Most worshipped on a Sunday, either in church or a chapel, and church or chapel also provided much of the social focus of the parish.

There were some small differences between the settlements. At the beginning of the twentieth century, all the farms within East Tytherton were dairy. It contrasted with other settlements that either had no or only a small proportion. East Tytherton had a higher percentage of households with servants and those living on their 'own account' or by private means.

It was not coincidental that the settlement also had some people employed with horses, as coachman, groom, horseman or farrier. As the location for several schools, there were more significant numbers of people who worked in education. Most of those employed in the retail and service sector lived in the largest settlement, at Bremhill, where the police constable and vicar also lived.

Fig. 123: Horse drawn farm waggons gradually gave way to the combustion engine from the early 1900s.

Fig. 124: Fry's Bakery in Bremhill, established in 1875.

Fig. 125: East Tytherton in the 1930s.

Some socio-economic changes revealed by the census affected the parish fairly equitably. By 1911, some who would have previously had to work until they were physically unable to do so were instead able to retire. However, by no means all either chose to or were able to do so. The state pension was still discretionary. The Bremhill gamekeeper, John Summers, was still working at seventy-five. At Spirthill, another John Summers was still working as a labourer at seventy-seven. But earlier, some residents were employed into their eighties.

An increasing number of parishioners were now born outside the county suggesting higher geographical mobility than previous generations. However, very few people were born out of the country, and those were often staff or boarders at the Moravian school. No one born outside the country lived in Foxham with West End or Stanley over the period. The few born elsewhere, aside from those associated with the Moravian school at East Tytherton, included James Davy from Ireland. He lived on a private income and boarded in Spirthill with the Ing family in 1891 and 1911. The Ings seem to have welcomed a few lodgers from overseas.

Many Bremhill families supplemented their income by taking in one or more boarders. Charles Hales was a carter, living with his wife Emily and young family in a cottage in Charlcutt in 1911. Their family income was supplemented by the rent of William Smith, also a carter. At Ivy House, Spirthill, Dulcie Blanche, the elementary teacher lodged with the Hilliers.

Several of those listed at Charlcutt and Spirthill that year were very young children, such as three-year-old George King, who lived with Henry Whale, an agricultural labourer, his wife Elizabeth, and their children. Evaline Knight had been a 'boarder' with the Haddrells since she was a baby, her mother, Emily, had been unmarried. It appears the Haddrells were paid to look after Evaline, and her mother returned to work.

In 1911, a question on the census asked couples how many children they had and how many had died. Tragically, some parishioners had lost children. The blacksmith, William Matthews and his wife, Mary, of the Forge in Foxham had sixteen children of whom six had died; at Avon Farm, Joseph and Eliza Amor had lost six of their eleven children, and at Bremhill vicarage, Rev. George Long and his wife had buried two of their four children.

Fig. 126. Engraving of the Moravian settlement by Alexander Anderson.

Fig. 127. The death of a child required 3 months of 'deep mourning' in the early 1900s to demonstrate the brevity of life.

CHAPTER FOUR

Society,
Support & Education

4.1 Welfare

Fig. 128: Locally raised taxes named as 'poor rates' supported the needy.

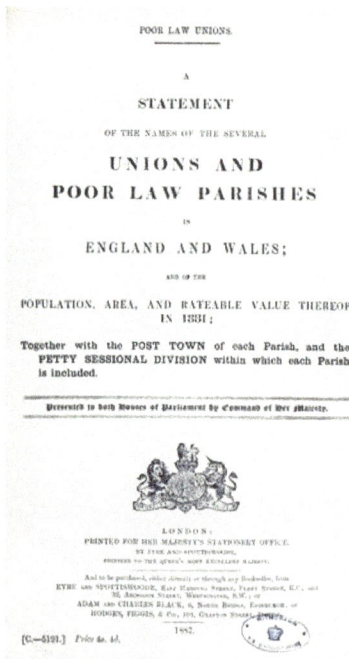

Fig. 129: The Poor Law system was revised by the Poor Law Amendment Act of 1834.

Fig. 130: (previous page) Edward Jenner vaccinating his own child, pioneering work which helped develop the smallpox vaccine.

The English welfare system before 1834 was based on legislation passed in the reign of Queen Elizabeth I. Under this system, every parish was responsible for supporting its own poor, paid for by a locally raised tax, called the poor rates. Despite being enshrined in legislation, take-up was slow. It is possible some parishes took exception to the new tax or felt it was unnecessary.[247] By 1660 only around one-third of parishes were using the system, however, among these was Bremhill.[248]

One of the earliest recorded welfare interventions made by the parish arose from the problem of who belonged to what parish. It was important because residents inevitably only wanted to support their 'own'. Over time legislation was passed which regulated who was legally settled (and therefore could apply for parish relief) and who was not. And, indeed, how such status could be acquired. Before that in 1649-50, Roger Harding his wife and five children fell foul of the system. The family needed relief. They were resident in Calne, but Calne parish opposed supporting them as they believed they were the responsibility of Bremhill. There then started a spat between the two parishes which involved the courts, and the hapless family were passed between the two places as the issue played out in the Quarter Sessions. Finally, a compromise was reached whereby Roger, his wife and three children remained in Bremhill. At the same time, his two older daughters were apprenticed by overseers in Calne.[249]

From the eighteenth century, there are several examination and removal orders which suggest that Bremhill was trying to police who was living in the settlement. For example, in 1762, Jane Watts and her six children moved into the parish. However, Jane and her family were ordered to be removed to Avebury after an examination by local Justices decided that is where she had a legal settlement.

The system was unpleasant for those examined and removed. It is likely that proceedings were only started when families were in danger of becoming destitute. Women were particularly vulnerable. In 1777, Ann Painter was a widow. Although she was local, on her marriage under the law, she had taken the settlement status of her husband, Joseph Painter. Unfortunately, despite working in Bremhill when they met, Joseph had been born and had settled status in Berkshire. On his death, it was ordered that Ann and her children be removed there.[250]

One way to avoid intrusive examinations and threats of removal without cause was to obtain a certificate from your home parish that promised to cover the cost of your removal should you need relief. It would generally stop any parish you moved into from moving you on without just cause. It meant a person could move to Calne or Chippenham from Bremhill for a new job without being sent straight back again. A few individuals moving into Bremhill obtained these certificates. Interestingly, Bremhill parish did sometimes assist those who wanted to move away. In 1783, for example, the parish paid 6s to Robert Barrington and his son who were going to London.[251]

In 1692 the parish relieved twenty-two people in the community at the cost of £21.[252] By 1776 the cost of supporting the poor had rocketed to £738.[253] According to a list of paupers taken in March that year, there were over 100 receiving welfare from the parish. This included five people who had 'settlement' outside the village (i.e. who had legal residency elsewhere).[254] The support the parish provided in the year was wide-ranging. It included house or room rents ('pays'), medical expenses (covering the services of a surgeon, nurse and midwife), coal, clothing, linen and shoes. One-off costs underwritten by the parish were broad. In July 1775, it paid one unnamed individual 3s for 'cleaning Widow Banger'. Thomas Killings was paid 14s in 1783 for glazing the home of William Fisher.[255] Sometimes these expenses appear particularly altruistic. In 1774, James Pegler had been receiving parish welfare for some time. When his son died in January, the parish paid for his funeral, but this does not appear to have been the usual pauper burial. Instead, the boy was provided with a 'bel and grave'. The ringing of the church bell gave the occasion some dignity and solemnity. Unusually the parish also paid for refreshments afterwards.[256]

In 1781, the vestry felt that despite the 'great burden' of providing for the local 'numerous poor' they remained in a 'deplorable condition'.[257] The solution they identified may come as a surprise. It was to create a workhouse to look after all the parish poor. Legislation in 1723 had amended the Elizabethan welfare system by allowing parishes to set up a workhouse to provide accommodation and work for the poor. Consequently, workhouses became increasingly popular throughout the eighteenth century. These early institutions were different from those set up after 1834.

Fig. 131: Legislation passed in 1662 and later amended required legal settlement status otherwise justices could remove a family from the parish.

Fig. 132: One of the reasons why workhouses evolved was due to the burden of providing for the numerous poor.

Fig. 133: A typical workhouse diet plan from post 1834.

		Breakfast		Dinner				Supper	
		Bread. oz.	Gruel. pints.	Cooked Meat with Vegetables. oz.	Soup. pints.	Bread. oz.	Cheese. oz.	Bread. oz.	Cheese. oz.
Sunday	Men	7	2	5	..	..	..	7	2
	Women	5	2	5	..	..	..	5	1½
Monday	Men	7	2	..	2	7	..	7	2
	Women	5	2	..	2	5	..	5	1½
Tuesday	Men	7	2	Bacon. 4	..	..	..	7	2
	Women	5	2	4	..	..	..	5	1½
Wednesday	Men	7	2	..	2	7	..	7	2
	Women	5	2	..	2	5	..	5	1½
Thursday	Men	7	2	..	..	7	2	7	2
	Women	5	2	..	..	5	1½	5	1½
Friday	Men	7	2	4	..	..	..	7	2
	Women	5	2	4	..	..	..	5	1½
Saturday	Men	7	2	..	2	7	..	7	2
	Women	5	2	..	2	5	..	5	1½

In this system, living conditions were intentionally made less pleasant than that of the lowest-paid labourers living independently; whereas earlier, some workhouse regimes were very altruistic.

The workhouse at Bremhill is likely to have been somewhere between the two, particularly as the cost of relief had not increased dramatically in the preceding few years. Its stated objective was that 'the aged and other impotent maybe with all humanity protected: the able kept to reasonable labour and employment: the industrious encouraged: the idle coerced: the profligate, as far as practicable, reclaimed: and the contumacious and incorrigible given up to the Justice of the Law.'[258] In other words, by creating a workhouse relief would be improved for those unable to support themselves. While employment would be found and labour encouraged for the able-bodied. It is also likely that they hoped relief costs would fall.

The site identified for Bremhill's new workhouse was the 'Church House'. A church house was an early version of a church hall and therefore under the care of the churchwardens. However, this one was by 1781 the property of William Chivers.[259] We do not know much about William; he was not among the village's larger landowners.[260] His own home was next to the church house, so a wall was built between the two to separate the premises properly.

The conversion of the church house was a community effort. Local landowners were to cover the expense. While their tenants were to 'supply and perform all manner of carriage' in proportion to the poor rates they paid. A mason and carpenter were employed to carry out the work with due haste.

There are indications that the workhouse was not planned to be disagreeable, but it was not necessarily pleasant either. One requirement was that no doors or windows were to face the street. Inmates were to attend church twice on Sunday, to say grace before and after meals and to recite the Lord's Prayer twice a day. The minister and parish officers were entreated to visit the workhouse from time to time to ensure the condition of 'the House and Family' was adequate. Once opened, the numbers of those accommodated were usually between twenty-two and thirty-two. As the figure rose and fell, it is likely that for many, it was merely a short-term solution. A lack of evidence makes it difficult to deduce what life was like at the workhouse. (But, given the large quantities of malt and hops recorded, the house was at least brewing and serving beer.)[261]

Fig. 134: The workhouse regime for women and girls could involve sewing, spinning and weaving.

The first master and matron of Bremhill workhouse were Paul and Sarah Newman.[262] Paul was born in 1721. He married twice, firstly to Mary Gale in 1747, and after her death in 1777 to Sarah Reeves. Sarah was a good deal younger than her husband. Indeed, she had been born the year Paul had married his first wife. Unusually, she may have been a serge maker during the time she was employed at the workhouse.[263] As Paul had initially been in the cloth trade, the work done in the institution probably revolved around woollen cloth manufacture.[264]

Despite the grand objectives Bremhill workhouse had at the beginning; it had only ever looked after a proportion of the local poor. As the number of local people who required support increased, the people who could be accommodated stayed the same, the proportion who were looked after in the workhouse (as compared to out in the community) fell. By 1803, the number of people who received parish help had reached an incredible 449 of which only twenty-six were in the workhouse.[265]

By 1834 the cost of welfare nationally had soared, and the government was forced to act. A new national system was introduced. Parishes across England and Wales were joined together into poor law unions. In March 1835, Bremhill joined the new Calne Poor Law Union, made up of the parishes of Calne, Bremhill, Blackland, Bowood, Cherhill, Calstone Wellington, Compton Bassett, Heddington, Highway, Hilmarton and Yatesbury. After that, the ability of the Bremhill community to look after its own was progressively undermined. A relieving officer, Mr Maundrell, arrived from Calne at Bremhill by 8 a.m. every Tuesday. He sat in a room, let to the union by William Powney at £2 a year, to grant relief to the local poor. In the winter, the Calne board ordered that coal and a fire was to be made up for Mr Maundrell's visit.[266] Usually accommodating twenty people, the union had considered extending Bremhill workhouse but instead side-lined it.[267] In its place, Bremhill paupers were increasingly ordered into Calne workhouse. It included the unaccompanied (probably orphaned) children looked after within the village's own institution.

Fig. 135: 'Visiting the poor', an engraving by Karl Girardet.

The children were thus removed from the family and friends they may still have had nearby. This left a handful of old residents in the Bremhill workhouse. There were more subtle hints that the Calne board were taking control and not intending to continue the more humane regime previously adopted at Bremhill. First the contract to bathe the residents was quietly dropped then the union ordered 'the allowance of soap to the inmates of Bremhill workhouse be discontinued'.[268] These were little details, but they made life more bearable and provided a little dignity to the predominately elderly residents.

4.2 Charity and Friendly Societies

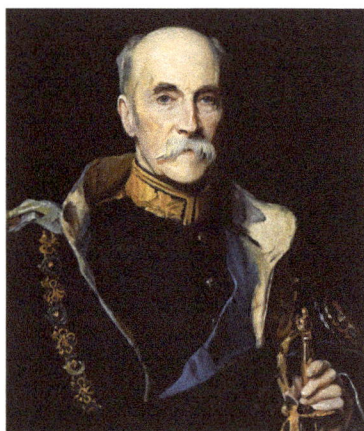

Fig. 136: Henry Petty-Fitzmaurice, 5th Marquess of Lansdowne (1845-1927).

Local people benefited from the generosity of estate owners. Pre-eminent among these families were the Lansdownes of Bowood House, who owned much of the area from the late eighteenth century until the twentieth century. Their generosity included substantial support for the renovation and rebuilding of Foxham chapel, a school, and the provision of local allotments. They also provided occasional assistance to individual residents. However, possibly the most significant contributions of the family were the three reading rooms established in the parish at Bremhill, Charlcutt and Foxham, by Lord Fitzmaurice with his brother the Marquess of Lansdowne.[269] The Bremhill library and reading room were opened in 1882, the Charlcutt reading room in 1883 and one at Foxham the following year. In 1915, the Bremhill reading room librarian was John Palmer. It was later run by his wife. Its membership was in decline by the 1920s but was still in use during the 1930s.[270] Up until 1918, it was still financially supported by the Lansdowne family as well as by subscriptions from members.[271] The declining membership during the early twentieth century was partly blamed on 'disorder which frequently prevails'.[272]

The Hungerfords, owners of Cadenham Manor until the early eighteenth century were also local benefactors, particularly in their support of Foxham chapel. According to a local tradition, the Hungerfords also provided three cottages for the local poor. However, by 1834 two of the three cottages were being lived in by Shadrach Smith, a local carpenter and Henry Silvester, the basket maker who both claimed to own them.[273] By the early twentieth century, the charity was deemed 'lost'.[274]

There was one charity which could have had a direct benefit to the local poor. In the early 1680s, the Bremhill vicar Rev. John Tounson established eight small alms-houses in Calne for poor widows (over the age of fifty) and the children of clergymen. Each tiny home was arranged on two floors, with access to the upper level bedroom by ladder. Tounson endowed the charity with lands to provide it with a perpetual income.

Fig. 137: Sir George Hungerford of Cadenham.

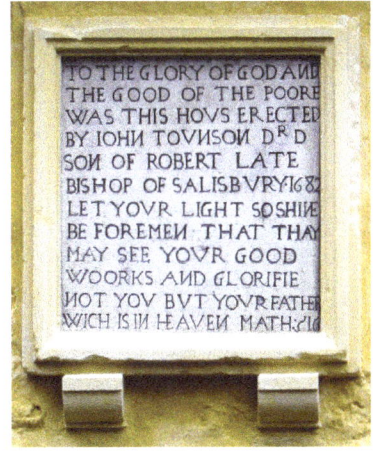

Fig. 138: Calne Alms-houses established in the 1680s by Bremhill vicar Rev. John Tounson.

In his will every fourth and fifth vacancy was to be filled by a Bremhill resident.[275] However, later reports by charity commissioners suggested that possibly no parish resident had ever taken advantage of this largesse. An unnamed Bremhill woman was provided with one in the 1890s but immediately gave it up.[276] The alms-houses are still in use, albeit as three flats and one studio, managed by the Calne Welfare Charities.[277]

To guard against the necessity for charity or welfare, local people could join a friendly society. For regular subscriptions members would receive payments in the event of illness or infirmity. By the early nineteenth century, there were two local friendly societies with a combined membership of 105; this rose to 130 during the Napoleonic Wars and 186 in 1863 when funds were valued at £359.[278]

The Dumb Post Friendly Society was established as early as 1770. Despite its funds being stolen in 1837 it survived and provided much needed support to local people for almost 100 years. Its festival day was cause for a celebratory drink, lunch and procession. However, not all was rosy. In 1863, a case was brought in the Calne Petty Sessions against John Palmer, secretary of the society by a local member, John Ferris. Ferris had been a part of the friendly society for thirty-six years but had become infirm, so he sought and received a medical certificate from 'the medical officer' which proved his incapacity. However, rather than paying him relief he was due, the society excluded him from their membership as he had 'assisted his son-in-law to fill a cart with dung'. The court reinstated his membership and, hopefully, he was thereafter paid.[279] Yet, the incident may have hastened the demise of the club, just two years later and despite a large membership and healthy funds, the society was dissolved.[280] In 1979 the Friends of St Martin's was established reviving the spirit of the Dumb Post Friendly Society. Today, it raises money in support of the church and projects and groups in the community.

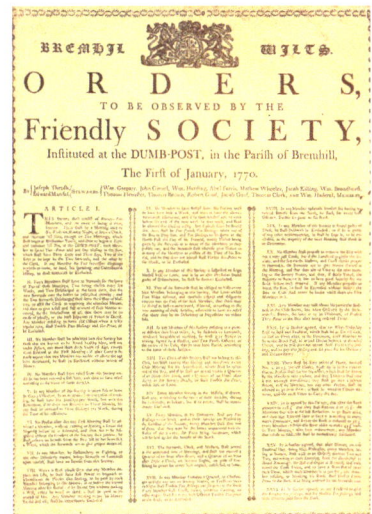

Fig. 139: The original charter of The Dumb Post Friendly Society 1770.

Fig. 140: Illustration from the Post Office first day cover for the quincentenary of Maud Heath's Causeway.

Fig. 141: Apothecary bottles containing herbal remedies.

Fig. 142: Engraving of surgeon bleeding a patient.

The most significant local charity or society was, and continues to be, Maud Heath's Trust created to maintain a causeway from Bremhill through East Tytherton and Langley Burrell to Chippenham.[281] The trust was formed by a fifteenth-century legacy of land and premises left by Maud Heath who lived at Tytherton Kellaways. According to Rev. William Lisle Bowles, a trustee of the charity in 1828, 'The tradition is that Maud Heath had acquired her property by carrying her farm produce, between Bremhill . . . and Chippenham; and having thus acquired the property, left in perpetuity a sum to be applied to the sole purpose of keeping in repair the accommodation of a more clean and convenient foot-way.'[282] As enchanting as the legend is, Maud Heath was a substantial property-owner and there is little possibility she was able to acquire the five houses and several closes of land in Chippenham by selling butter and eggs at market.[283] To learn more about the route of Maud Heath's causeway, sites of interest along its route and more about its history, see chapter 2.

4.3 Medical Care

Unlike welfare, medical provision to the poor was not mandatory under Elizabethan law. However, by the early nineteenth century, most English parishes were beginning to provide it. It could be interpreted as a kind move on behalf of many communities. Still, at a time when parishes paid for the relief of those unable to work, it also made practicable sense to help people get better sooner. When a community was faced with an epidemical infection, a community-centred approach was also recognised as being most effective.

Medical care to the poor began early in Bremhill, from at least 1763. The earliest surgeon's bill indicates the service consisted of visits and prescriptions for powders, syrups, tinctures, pills or draughts often for 'purging'. Treatments also included the application of blisters, bleedings and vomiting. The remedies prescribed, in some instances, sound barbaric. Although it should be conceded that the cases which demanded the attention of the parish surgeon are likely to have been serious. There was also little alternative.

On 31 May 1763, the wife of Nicolas Bailey received a visit from the surgeon, Mr Wheeler. At the consultation, the unfortunate woman was given a 'bleeding and a vomit', 'a purging mixture', 'three bolus [large pills]' and four enemas. The following day, Mr Wheeler visited again, and Mrs Bailey had 'three doses of purging pills' and three 'purging' enemas. She was also given a pot of ointment. On the third day, she had 'three doses of opening pills' and on the final day 'an opening mixture'.[284] Despite the best efforts of the medical practitioner, the prognosis was not good. A lady by the name of Mary Bailey, wife of Nicolas Bailey, was buried at Christian Malford two days later. Unfortunately, there is no indication of what Mrs Bailey had been suffering from at the time of her treatment.

Ten years later, the surgeon's methods were less invasive. There were no bleedings or vomiting but a range of 'juleps', linctus and even honey and lemon prescribed. However, the value of the care remained limited with the medical knowledge of the time. In a rare instance of a medical diagnosis being recorded, the daughter of Robert Wicks was identified as suffering from smallpox. The surgeon was called in. The girl in question was either Mary or Susannah Wickes, daughters of Robert and Eleanor. They had been baptised at Bremhill in 1759 and 1763, so the patient is likely to have been in her teens.

Smallpox was possibly the most feared disease of the age. It was infectious and affected both rich and poor alike. The risk of death was one in three. Those who survived could be made blind or at the very least extensively scarred. The Wickes family was already afflicted with problems as Robert was on the list of those receiving parochial relief. He was also called 'a crippel'. Whichever daughter was infected, the medical care she received over the subsequent weeks consisted of possibly everything within the attending surgeon Mr Allsup's power to provide. It was also somewhat cutting edge within the context of the period. Treatments included juleps for fever, mixtures for opening her bowels, linctus for a cough, 'anodyne draughts' for pain, a 'pomatum [pomander] box' to perfume the air and guard against infection, ointment for the sores and even 'alterative bolus' probably designed to cure her of the affliction. The surgeon visited on several occasions. The girl had an attendant nurse. Surprisingly, one of those who cared for her was listed as a 'man nurse'. There was even an indication, given several purges prescribed to one of the attendants, that the surgeon was at least considering taking the unusual step of inoculating the nurse against smallpox (purging was the first step in the process).

It was decades before Edward Jenner's discovery of the smallpox vaccination which eradicated the disease during the twentieth century. At the time, Allsup would have had to infect the nurse with a mild version of the disease. The process which was beset with risk would provide her with immunity. It seems credible that Allsup may have been trying to contain the outbreak. As a different physician was attending to the girl's family, she was likely in some kind of quarantine. There are also allusions made to visits to her and other patients which are to 'Marshfield' and not to the patient's home.[285]

In Christopher Allsup the Bremhill poor had access to an 'eminent physician' and influential man. It seems likely given the nature of cases he attended that he was used when circumstances were particularly difficult. Allsup was physician to the Lansdowne family at Bowood. Within local society, Allsup was important too. He was credited in collaboration with the Marquess for improvements made to the centre of Calne. His legacy remains visible on the Wiltshire landscape as the Cherhill White Horse was cut under his direction.[286]

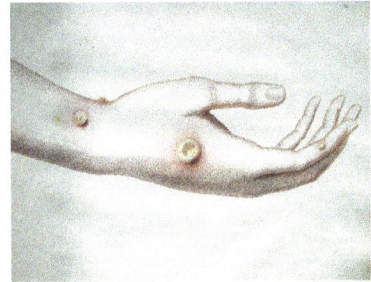

Fig. 143: Pustules on the hand of a small-pox victim.

Fig. 144: Edward Jenner infected a young patient with cowpox to help him prove it provided protection against smallpox.

Fig. 145. Edward Jenner using cowpox to find the world's first vaccine, one against smallpox.

Allsup was not the only one who was tending to residents with smallpox according to amounts paid by local overseers. Mr Bruck's 'small pox bill' of £3 5s was settled in May; in July Robert Holly was paid 'for tending smallpox' 13s and Peter Ruming £1 6s 'his bill smallpox'. Robert Holly may have been the 'man nurse' mentioned in Allsup's itemized bill. The last smallpox related bill was in September 1773.[287] Unfortunately, smallpox was to return in 1782. We do not have any itemised bills to assess the care given on that occasion. Still, intriguingly for several months, there were payments made 'for beer for the smallpox'.[288] What the beer was used for is open to conjecture.

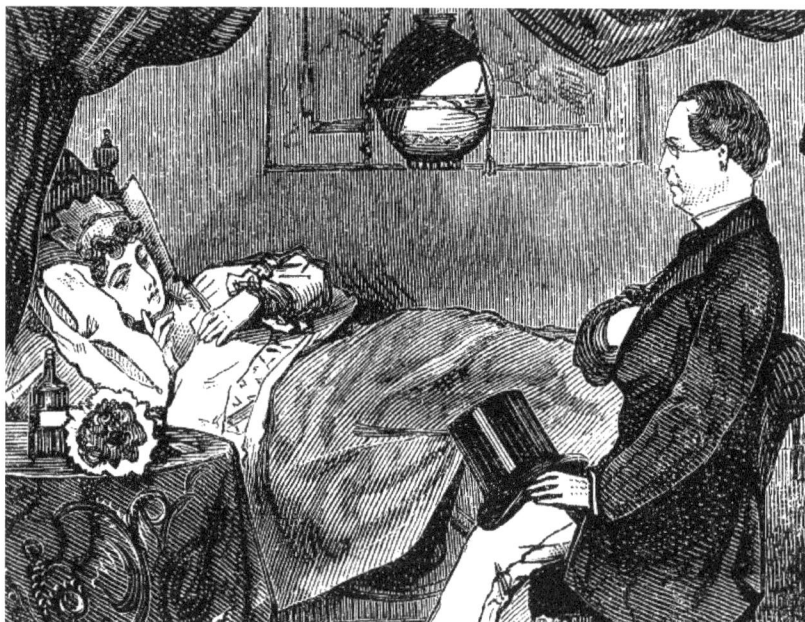

Fig. 146: 19th century print of doctor and patient.

Sickness and infirmity accounted for the reason why some Bremhill residents turned to the parish for support. In 1776 when overseers noted all the names of the residents of the village receiving poor relief, they also noted a few of the medical ailments they were suffering from. In March, this included Betty Harding, who was blind and 'Widow Banger' who was bedridden. The extraordinary expenses listed also indicate other people received one-off medical care. In the same month, John Smallcomb had his broken leg set and 'Hollys Wife' was delivered of her baby and received some post-natal domiciliary care. The following month Mrs Garlic was paid 'for delivering several women' and for 'tending Ceens wife 3 shillings Jery Packers wife 2 shillings'. Unfortunately, not all ailments are elaborated, so the number of those receiving medical care or financial assistance for reasons of sickness or infirmity are likely to have been higher.[289]

Medical care continued to be given under the Calne Poor Law Union. It was needed. In 1865, it was noted in the Bremhill School journal that five children had died of scarlet fever.[290]

Home-made Remedies:

The Gardiner Family

The alternative to medical intervention paid for privately or by the parish was to self-medicate. From the seventeenth to the nineteenth century there is evidence that parish residents resorted to what we might now consider bizarre practice.

In Tytherton Lucas during the late seventeenth and early eighteenth century, three generations of the Gardiner family made notes in a book of what they considered essential information. It included accounts, lists of tithingman, dates of bad weather and a record of remedies which had been transcribed from a volume entitled *The Queen's Closet Opened: Incomparable in Physick, Chirurgery, Preserving, Candying and Cookery, as they were presented to the Queen.*

The book had been supposedly written by one of Queen Henrietta Maria's own servants and had been first published in 1655, at a time when the queen herself was in exile. It was a bestseller. A copy found its way from London to Wiltshire and into the hands of Thomas Gardiner, a local farmer, who copied what he considered the most useful remedies. He did not reproduce cures for the worst illness or afflictions, such as the plague or cancer, but for more common-or-garden ailments like the common cold.

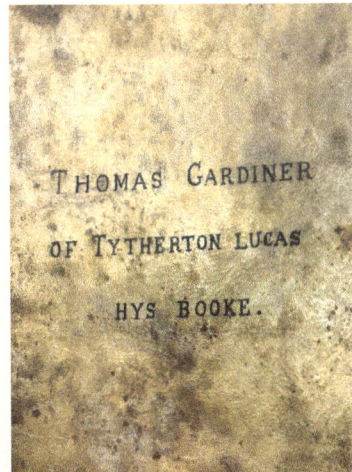

Fig.147: Images of Thomas Gardiner's most useful remedies from a book entitled *The Queen's Closet Opened.*

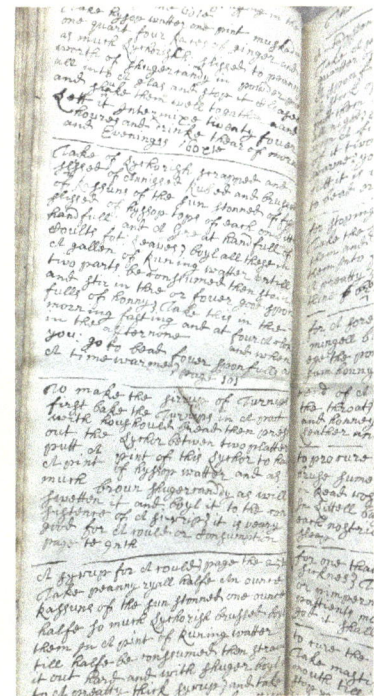

There were also several for toothache and a sore throat, for which the remedy appears the most peculiar. It reads: 'mingell burnt Allom (alum) the yolk of an ege (egg) the powder of a white dog turd, and sum honey togather tye A clout one the end of A stick and thear with rube the throat Or mix white dog turd and honney and spread one sheeps (sheep) Leather and apply it to the throat.' We have no way of knowing if Thomas actually tried any of the cures he wrote down, but can assume, given the trouble he went to write them into his 'commonplace book', they were ones he wanted to remember.[291]

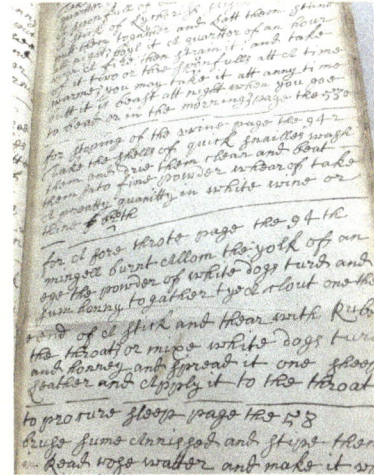

4.4 Education

There was a school at Bremhill as early as the late sixteenth century run by Mr Collier, who later became vicar at Bremhill around 1596.[292] In the early 1780s, parish accounts include regular monthly payments for 'Thomas Pointings Scholling'. Unfortunately, they do not elaborate why the parish was paying for the education of one child; and indeed, whether he was going to school locally.[293] In 1803, a government report stated the village had a 'school of industry'.[294] The school was short-lived.

However, by 1818, educational provision had burgeoned. There was a school which had been established by the Marchioness of Lansdowne at Foxham. It had seventy-two children. Another was being run by the wife of the local parish clerk which had twenty pupils; and two or three dame schools each contained eight or nine. On top of this, Rev. Bowles ran a Sunday school for forty boys and Mrs Bowles another for fifty girls.[295] In 1835, three Sunday schools were also identified. One each run by the Church of England, Wesleyans and Moravians.[296]

Fig. 148: The space above the porch at St Martin's Church was used as a small school room.

In 1846, a new Bremhill National school was planned which included accommodation for a schoolmaster. It was paid for by a parliamentary grant of £150 and £173 raised by local promoters.[297] The design was simple. One school room of 30 x 15 feet with an area adjoining of 15 x 12 feet was planned to provide for 100 children. The pupils also had use of a small schoolyard with toilets at one end. The master's accommodation was connected to both the schoolroom and the schoolyard.[298] Ten years after its construction a school inspector noted 'the schoolroom is a very fair one, with boarded floor and parallel desks.'[299]

The school provided elementary education to boys and girls of local poor families. The ethos was Christian. Like many such schools created throughout the country, the building was planned next to the church. This was likely on the site of the old parish workhouse. During the first decades, the curriculum was narrow. It primarily comprised reading, writing and arithmetic. Pupils regularly attended church services, and scripture lessons were given at school several times a week. The children also had regular singing practice.[300] From the 1860s, the children were taught by a schoolmistress who was assisted by a 'pupil-teacher'.[301]

Fig. 149: Bremhill School opposite the village cross.

Bremhill School was visited regularly by school inspectors sent from London. The church diocese sent others. In 1850, the school was scrutinised by Mr Warburton. His report was brief: 'Sixty-five boys and girls taught by a mistress. The children are very young and very ignorant. The school is, however, improving.'[302] Another noted the scholars were 'taught by an untrained mistress of fair abilities and anxious to learn'.[303]

Generally, the inspectors seem to have had a low opinion of village children. In 1864, pupils were described as 'not very intelligent'.[304] The following year they were 'not very bright or forward'.[305] Aspiration was likely to be low. The diocesan inspectors were concerned mainly with whether children knew their catechism, scripture and prayers. However, as time went on, complaints were made about the standard of attainment.[306] These seem to have finally precipitated a reduction to the grant provided by the central government in 1869.[307]

Fig. 150: A school inspector was regularly sent from London to assess the elementary education of Bremhill pupils.

Although low standards were unfortunate, it is to be remembered that at the time there was no compulsory education and any provision was better than none. Indeed, attainment was probably made worse by the fact that attendance for many children was sporadic. It rose and fell with the seasons, as children were needed for haymaking or planting; although low attendance was also attributed to wet weather and snow.

On 4 March 1867, there were 'very few children at school owing to a wild beast show in Calne'.[308] On 17 July 1871, a list was made of the children who were being kept off, and why. It shows six boys were absent for hay-making, and two for 'bird keeping' and one for 'nursing'. Only one boy was sick. Of the girls, five were nursing, one was pea picking, and one was at home while her mother was in the fields.

In 1871, according to government returns, there were four schools in the parish. Of these, three were either national schools or affiliated to the Church of England. It would have comprised Bremhill National School, Foxham School and one other, probably at Charlcutt.[309] On the day enquiries were made a total of 160 local children were attending. The capacity of the schools combined was 195.[310]

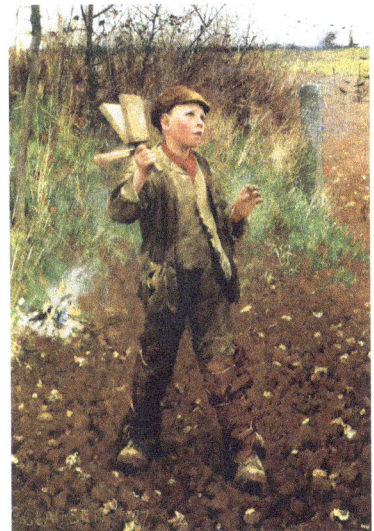

By 1875, the state was supporting three schools at Bremhill, Foxham and Charlcutt. Charlcutt had twenty-one pupils, but the largest in pupil numbers was the school at Foxham which had 39.[311] Twenty years later, state support was also provided to the Moravian school at East Tytherton. Although local capacity had risen to 345, attendance was static at 160.[312] By the end of the 1890s attendance at Charlcutt was down to just seven pupils, and shortly after the school closed.[313] The Foxham School was closed in 1930, and in 1969 Bremhill School was also shut.[314]

Fig. 151: Boys seasonally missed some schooldays due to farm tasks in the fields such as bird scaring.

Schooldays: Bremhill 1913-19

Fig. 152: Bremhill School with adjoining teacher's accommodation.

On a June morning in 1913, Frederick Herbert Freegard, known as Herbert, not yet four years of age and accompanied by his older brother John, set out for the first time on his walk from Bencroft Farm to Bremhill School.[315] By coincidence, the previous day had also been the first for twenty-four-year-old Lucy Singleton as headteacher of the school. For her it was not an auspicious start. As she wrote in her log: 'The school is somewhat out of systematic working order. There are no schemes for the current year. This is due to the fact that there has been no permanent mistress for some time.'[316]

Herbert, however, quickly began to enjoy life in the 'Little Room' with the other infants. As he later wrote: 'Some of the little things we used to do then were greatly to my liking, we had strips of wood with notches in, of varying lengths with which to make models, paper strips of varying colours to thread through, mat shape patterns, on a square sheet of paper cut across many times parallel, but not quite to the edges. Then we also sewed fancy wools around patterns of Birds, Animals etc, which were thereupon hung up around the walls.'[317] Not all activities were viewed in the same positive light, however: 'Several of the other odd occupations with which I had less patience were sewing and knitting, especially the latter. I have know(n) myself have a piece of knitting (we didn't have a special piece to ourselves) at the start of the lesson & at the close of which there was less knitting done than before I had started, I never could get on with that job.'

Fig. 153: Typical school desks of the period.

Herbert was able to give a very detailed description of his schoolroom: 'The little room was very pleasant & well I remember how it was furnished, a stove stood in the front with a door in the corner behind - adjacent in the next wall the other door led into the big room, it had glass panels at the top - directly opposite was the window, overlooking the playground. The cupboard stood, with the blackboard, to the window side of the stove - all around the walls were mottoes, a print of the crucified Lord, two photos of fire engines - the which I remember most plainly. One of the mottoes I tried to write down one evening after school on the whiteness of the back kitchen window in the courtyard at Bencroft. There the legend said "Thest the tucker" which being interpreted reads "Speak the truth" - my spelling was too primitive then but I remembered in later years what the symbols stood for.'

Meanwhile, Lucy Singleton's first autumn at the school did not run smoothly. In October 1913 she recorded in her log that Miss Potter, her recently appointed assistant teacher, 'behaved in a very insubordinate manner to me this afternoon'. Angry that her salary had not been paid as the General Education Council had not sanctioned her appointment, Miss Potter accused Lucy Singleton of untruths in relation to her dismissal. After her departure the Education Committee appointed a Miss Ruth Singleton, Lucy's eighteen-year-old sister, as her replacement.

In November 1913 there was an outbreak of measles and both Freegard brothers were absent from school. In December the fire in the school could not be lit as the coke which had been ordered had not arrived. The temperature in the big room was recorded as thirteen degrees Celsius and in the little room as fourteen degrees Celsius. Practical problems continued into January 1914 when Lucy Singleton wrote in her log: 'The stove in the class room is out of repair, the pipe having almost worn through, it is very unsafe and not at all advisable for the little ones to be in the room. As all the children are in the big room it is not quite possible to follow the timetable.' An inspector's report in the same year demanded that the condition of the offices (toilets) be improved without delay and that a plan for rearranging the cloakroom be submitted.

Fig. 154: An icon of early school life- the satchel.

Miss Singleton was the earliest teacher of whom Herbert had any recollection. This was not Lucy Singleton, however, nor was it Ruth Singleton, but the third sister Una who had been enrolled as a pupil at the school in September 1913 at the age of twelve. During her eight months at the school before departing the following May for secondary school, Una clearly made a great impression on the young Herbert. He wrote of her: 'I shall always be gratefull to her for numerous stories of giants & a certain warning which there & then entered into my head to abide therein my thoughts, to harrass my sleepless nights - The road at the bottom of Bremhill, if you go below a certain place, will open & swallow you up. That thought haunted me in after years, the fear of the dark was upon me thereafter.'

Herbert's walk home from school with his brother would have caused him some anxiety, particularly on afternoons when it was growing dark. The boys are likely to have cut across the fields and through the woods to Bencroft, rather than following the road. Occasionally Edward Long, the adult son of the curate, accompanied them home and stayed for tea. Generally it was the Gingells who lived at the top of Bencroft Hill who escorted them, and one incident stood out in Frederick's memory: 'I probably owe my life to one of them - in this wise, me prowling about, as seems to have been & always will be my habit I fell into the slimy muddy waters of the pond in Six Acres from whence one of the above girls did fish me out not hurt but terribly frightened.'

Fig. 155: Bremhill School pageant c.1917.

In time, Herbert was duly promoted at school to the 'big room'. A little overawed at first, he soon came to enjoy himself there: 'Plasticine modelling was one of our occupations & thoroughly enjoyable, we made it up into all shapes and conditions of forms & when 'Gif Fry' made a model of a coach & pair with two human figures seated on the box we thought it very good, as did also the teacher when told that the two on the box were supposed to represent her fiancée & herself.' In June 1919 Herbert left Bremhill School to go to secondary school. By 1916 Lucy Singleton had married her fiancé and left the school expecting her first child and Ruth Singleton had entered Bath Hospital as a probationary nurse. Una, who in Herbert's eyes had showed such aptitude for teaching, in fact went on to nurse seafarers at the Dreadnought Seamen's Hospital in Greenwich.

4.5 The Schools of East Tytherton

Fig. 156: Thomas Collett was the only boy in the Moravian Girls School in 1915.

A Moravian girl's boarding and day school was opened at East Tytherton in 1794, under headmistress Ann Grigg, with six boarders and seven day-pupils. The school admitted children from Moravian and non-Moravian families alike.[318] Later in 1818, Rev. Bowles reported the day school accommodated four boys and girls, although boys may have attended only to the age of nine.[319] In 1859, a government report stated, 'At the hamlet of East Tytherton there is a Moravian Settlement, and about 20 to 30 children are taught in a nice little thatched room with a wooden floor, by a mistress of the Moravian persuasion.'[320] The description suggests that while the boarding school continued to accommodate day-pupils a separate establishment was also founded.

Fig. 157: The new Maud Heath School was built in 1870 on the site of the Moravian School.

Given the importance of education within the Moravian church and the low aspiration for pupils in schools in the wider area, a Moravian-run day-school is likely to have been an attractive option for many local families. This commitment by the local Moravians to providing education to local families was further reinforced by the building of a new school in 1870-1 on the site of the old school room.[321] Ten years later Her Majesty's inspector of schools for Wiltshire, Dorset, Hampshire and Somerset, Rev. S. Fraser was able to declare the school one of the few he had assessed which were deemed efficient. While the school had been scrutinised by an inspector, the parish still declined government funding.[322] However, by the end of the 1880s the school had begun to accept a small parliamentary grant.[323] A decade later this amount had increased six times over and the number of children in regular attendance had more than doubled. The school buildings could accommodate 102, and at the turn of the twentieth century, it was the most popular school in the parish with an average attendance of fifty-two, which rose to sixty-nine in 1906.[324] That same year, the local education authority took over the running of the school.[325] The twenty-first century was difficult, the school roll dwindled and in 2005, the school was finally closed.[326]

Fig. 158: Maud Heath School staff in 1976.

4.6 Leisure

A crucial part of the social life of the village was bound up with drinking alcohol. In the 1780s the vestry complained that their attempts to protect and reform the poor were met with 'the never-failing obstruction from the swarm of ale-houses, too many of which are the standing nurseries of idleness, beggary and vice'.[327] The situation did not improve (in the minds of some) in 1830 when a change in the law meant that 'beerhouses' could be set up without seeking a licence from magistrates. Local beerhouses were implicated in disturbances.

In 1835, two brothers fought a 'pitched battle' in Spirthill which lasted over an hour and drew a crowd of onlookers. 'At the close, the parties adjourned to a beerhouse where several other battles were fought.'[328] Drinking to excess was considered an evil in the minds of Rev. Bowles and his wife. Indeed, Mrs Bowles was inspired to pen a pamphlet, published the year following the battle of Spirthill. It was titled *Summer Visits to Cottages in a Country Village with Observations on the Morals and Habits of the Inhabitants, and particularly Exemplifying the Pernicious Effects of Beerhouses*. In it, she emphasised the positive outcomes of temperance. The following account, taken from her publication, should be viewed considering Mrs Bowles's undoubted prejudices. Still, it undoubtedly had a basis in truth. Mrs Bowles does not give many names. Yet, from her account and assumptions regarding the ages of the protagonists and proximity of a drinking establishment, she may have been referring to Ann Hadrell. Ann's story is outlined in the next case study.

Christmas in the nineteenth century was cause for great festivity. During the time of Rev. Bowles, the village often engaged in communal celebrations sponsored by the vicar. In 1819, fifty-five girls attending Mrs Bowles school had a Christmas lunch of beef and pudding at the rectory. At two local pubs, 'the parochial choir and 50 poor men and women had a substantial dinner of beef and beer; and on the same day bread and soup was distributed to upwards of 200.'[329] Also on Christmas Day, those who had subscribed to the local 'penny a week club' received their share of a distribution of blankets, stockings, cloaks, shirts, shifts, petticoats, handkerchiefs, shoes and frocks. 'At this meeting, the clergyman (the Rev. W. L. Bowles) addressed some of his assembled parishioners, in a speech replete with the most affectionate admonition.'[330] Hopefully, this did not distract from the merriment of the day. The polite revels were, at times, extensive. In 1824, a dinner 'of old English fare' was provided to 400.[331] These celebrations continued into the 1830s.[332]

Fig. 159: From 1830 beerhouses did not need a licence from a magistrate to ply their trade.

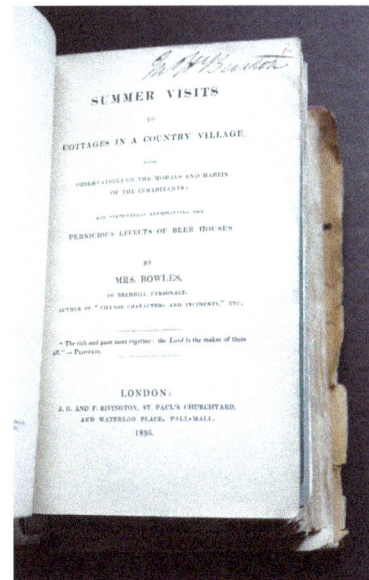

Fig. 160: Mrs. Bowles considered drinking alcohol to excess was an evil and penned several articles about the need for temperance.

Beer Shops:

Fig. 161: Engraving demonstrating the evils of intoxication.

Ann Wheeler was married as a teen to a local labourer, John Hadrell. She may have been pregnant when they married.[333] John was about fifteen years older than his wife. Babies followed their marriage: Henry in 1820, Simon in 1821, Emma in 1824, Mary in 1826, Jane in 1827, Anne in 1830 (who died the year after the incident outlined below), Sarah in 1831 and William in 1837. Probably sometime in the summer of 1835, Mrs Bowles was conducting cottage visits around the village of Bremhill and witnessed an incident: 'Proceeding homewards, I was roused from a train of thought by hearing loud screams, and seeing a woman running out from her cottage followed by her husband, who had returned home, in a state of intoxication, from a neighbouring beerhouse. The poor wife had not offended him; but it was his constant custom, when in this degraded state, to put her in bodily fear, sometimes by threats, other times by breaking and demolishing everything that was in his way: if any endeavours were used by herself and children to restrain him, he was furious; and the poor woman fled . . . '

Later talking to Mrs Bowles, Ann said of her husband, 'John is so sorrowful, when he is sober, for what he has done, that if I could but keep him steady to his work, and no idle companions and beerhouses were in his way home, no family in the parish would be happier than ourselves. The worst is, when he gets a little drink, he is never at rest till he has had enough to make him quarrelsome; then he comes home, and a word or a look will bring his fury upon his wife. As to the poor children, they run and hide themselves the moment they see their father staggering. He did a deal of mischief before he assaulted me. The little crockery I had is now almost all broken; and, in trying to save some of the things, he was so provoked, that I verily thought, if I staid any longer, he would have killed me; but I would not be hard upon him, for he is a kind-hearted man when he is sober.'

Mrs Bowles account continued: 'After giving her some relief, and all the consolation in my power, I rose and left the cottage, telling her I would call upon her the next day. In my way to the parsonage, I saw her husband reeling towards a stile in my homeward road, followed by some idle boys, who kept laughing at his zigzag walk . . . The next morning, I visited the poor woman, according to my promise. She was surrounded by her infant family, like little steps one above another. The table was newly propped up, having been thrown down and broken when this madman, in his blind fury, demolished everything that was near. He was now sober, silent, and apparently penitent; and seeing me coming towards the house, he turned out of sight.

The cottage stands in a beautiful part of the village: the sun was shining upon its white walls, and it looked as if it ought to be the abode of peace and love; and so it would have been, had not this terrible vice opened the door to want and its long train of grievances. The poor woman had ventured home when she found her husband had become calmer. The children nestled round her; and she divided the last bit of bread that remained in the cottage amongst them. Her quiet habits and patient enduring of all the ill-treatment she received, had made her much beloved and pitied by her neighbours; and often food was given to the little ones by those who could ill spare to part with any. Once already had she, by the persuasion of her friends, been to a neighbouring magistrate to swear the peace against the man who had so harshly used her; but it was one of her hardest trials and was of little avail. . . her neighbours expect that she will at last fall a victim to his ill-usage.'

Fig. 162: Illustration of a mother and children anticipating the homecoming of a drunken father.

4.7 Morality and Gossip

Standards of morality have shifted significantly over the centuries. Rev. and Mrs Bowles were worried about the licentiousness of local labouring families, particularly resulting from over-generous welfare payments and excessive drinking. Both tried to mitigate the effects locally through sponsoring moral education and the encouragement of self-help and temperance.

Pre-marital sex, adultery and children born out of wedlock were other 'problems' of public morality which no doubt also concerned them. In 1631, George Cooke of Bremhill ended up in the church courts as he wished to sleep with his betrothed before the wedding, but her uncle, with whom she lived, objected in the strongest manner.[334]

However, despite attempts to improve public morality through persuasion, education, vilification, or other sanctions, relationships that did not adhere to societal or religious expectations occurred. To circumvent possible consequences, individuals inevitably took measures to reduce the possibility of detection. In his attempt to be honest about the relationship he wished to conduct with his intended, George Cooke was likely to have been in the minority. Repercussions could be particularly acute for women, the possibility of pregnancy, the different moral expectations of their sex and their reduced status within society compared to men. It is little wonder, therefore, that some women took drastic measures.

Fig. 163: Morality was a hot topic among the village gossips.

Forbidden Love: The Secret Marriage of Susanna Scott

This is the story of Susanna Scott, alias Newman of Bremhill, and of an alleged secret marriage and a will disputed in court.

Susanna was most likely to have been the daughter of Robert Scott of Bremhill. She was baptised on 6 August 1645 in Bremhill and buried there on 27 June 1672. She died a young woman from what seems to have been a short illness, leaving no written will. There existed, however, two nuncupative wills, which were allegedly spoken by her before witnesses and later written down. The first was made on or around the 9 June preceding her death. It instructed, 'all my goods I now stand possessed of, of what kind or sort soever' should be left to 'my welbeloved friend Adam Newman of Titherton in the Parish of Bremhill'. She appointed the same Adam Newman to be sole executor of her will, which was witnessed by William Newman, Joane Newman and Frances Sollman.

The second nuncupative will was said to have been made a couple of weeks later, on or around 25 June. This will left £5 to Adam Newman and small gifts to Joane Newman, to Thomas Jones, with whom she lived in Bremhill Grove and all his children. To Rebecca Davies and Ann Chivers, she left 12d apiece. Furthermore, she said that her sister Edith Scott would give them 'full satisfaction for their attendance in wayting upon her during the tyme of her sycknes'. To her sister Edith, she left her annuity, bonds, monies, and other possessions. This will was witnessed by the aforementioned Thomas Jones and Rebecca Davies.

Susanna died soon after this second will was made. An inventory of her possessions was taken on 10 July with William Newman Senior as one of the appraisers. Described as a spinster, there is no evidence that Susanna had her own home or household possessions. Apart from her chest, her bible and her wearing apparel, her assets consisted of the annuity and bonds, which were together valued at £56.

The scene then moved to the Court of the Archdeaconry of Wiltshire in Sarum. Documents including allegations, depositions and examinations show a dispute between Adam Newman and Edith Scott over which of Susanna's wills was the genuine one. Adam's claim rested on the fact that he and Susanna had lawfully wed three years previously. Even if she had not made a will naming him as her executor, he would nevertheless, as her husband, have had all rights in law to her goods and chattels.

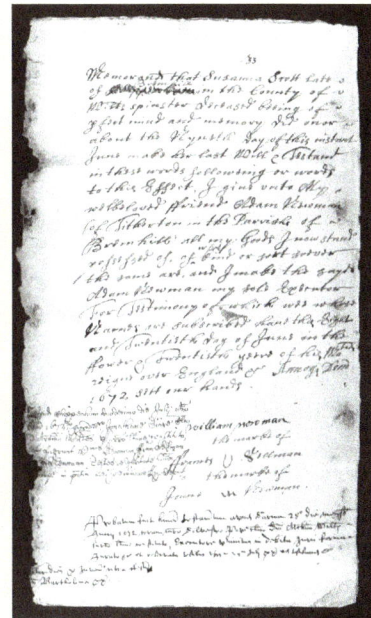

Fig. 164: Written down evidence of the nuncupative wills and court proceedings.

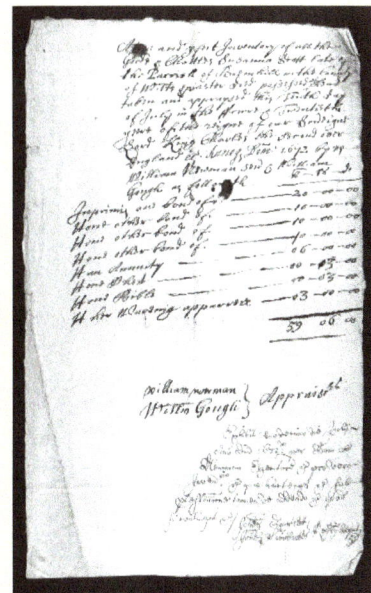

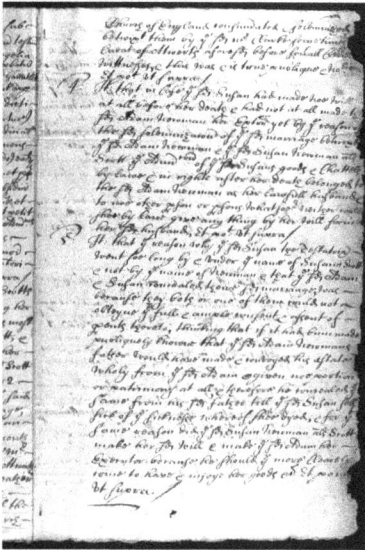

Fig. 165: Depositions made at the Court of Archdeaconry of Wiltshire.

The circumstances of this alleged marriage were examined by the court, and witness statements were produced. It was said to have taken place in or around May 1669. The ceremony was performed by Mr John Clarke, then curate of Atworth, 'according to the liturgie and the ceremonies of the Church of England'. There were two others present at the marriage who provided testimonies on Adam's behalf. The first was Thomas Wilshire, a yeoman of Atworth, who stated that he had known Adam for seven years. On the day of the marriage, he happened to be in Atworth when Adam Newman asked him to accompany him to Mr Clarke's house 'for he intended to be that morning married to Susan Scott'. This Thomas Wilshire did, and he confirmed that he gave Susanna in marriage to Adam. The other witness present at the wedding was Ann Clarke, the wife of curate John Clarke. She confirmed that following the lawful ceremony conducted by her husband, she knew Susanna by the name of Susanna Newman. Both she and Thomas Wilshire stated that they had heard that after the solemnisation of the marriage, Susanna and Adam 'did lye in bed togeither'.

The marriage was not made public, it seemed the couple did not live together, and Susanna continued to go by the name of Scott. It was said on Adam's behalf that the reason for this was because one or both could not obtain the full consent of parents to the marriage. More specifically, had Adam Newman's father known of the wedding, he would have 'conveyed his astate wholy from Adam and given noe portion or patrimony at all'. This, it was claimed, also explained why Susanna would have made a will naming Adam as her executor, 'because he should the more clearly come to have and injoye her goods'.

Adam, therefore, concealed the marriage from his father until Susanna fell sick. Adam was likely to be the son of William Newman, who was baptised in Bremhill on 8 January 1640. It was probably his father who witnessed Susanna's will in favour of his son and who was one of the appraisers of her inventory. Records show a Newman family of yeomen resident in Tytherton Kellaways at the time, but this is conjecture only.

A certain amount of character defamation formed part of the dispute over the will. It was claimed on Adam's behalf that no faith was to be given to the sayings and depositions of Thomas Jones, Ann Chivers and Rebecca Davies, described as 'poore indigent and needy people of noe credit or riputation in the parishes where they dwell'. It was allegedly no coincidence that they were beneficiaries of the will they had witnessed. They were known to be people who could be easily persuaded to make a deposition for gain and reward and indeed had received promises of rewards from Edith Scott. Furthermore, they had known of Susanna's marriage to Adam Newman but had nevertheless persuaded her over some weeks to make the unlawful will in favour of Edith.

So what of Edith Scott's version of events? Records only show the questions regarding the details of Adam's story, which were put on her behalf to his witnesses. These were asked to declare in the first instance any pressure put upon them in wording their depositions by Mr Henry Butler, Adam Newman's proctor. Very detailed information was required about the will made verbally in Adam's favour, 'in what howse, in what parish, in what room of such howse' and even, regarding Susanna, 'was shee in bed, upon the bed, walking, standing or sitting, or in what other postion was shee then in'. They were asked about her sickness, why she had decided to make a will at that time and whether she had called to mind mortality and the frailty of mankind.

Questions about the claimed marriage ceremony were just as probing and included 'what were the very prayers then used and in what words did he joyn them together'. Information was even sought on whether the marriage had been consummated 'by lying in naked bed together' and where precisely this had taken place, which may not have been so easy to verify.

This story ends with many questions unanswered. Though some documents submitted to the Archdeaconry Court in Sarum were dated as late as the January following Susanna's death, there is no record of any judgement made. The dispute seems to have moved on to the Prerogative Court of Canterbury, where it was the will favouring Edith Scott that was copied sometime later into the register. So, was Susanna Scott a spinster being exploited by the Newman family for financial gain? Or possibly a woman who married for love a man to whose family she would not have been socially acceptable? Either way, her life was cut sadly short.

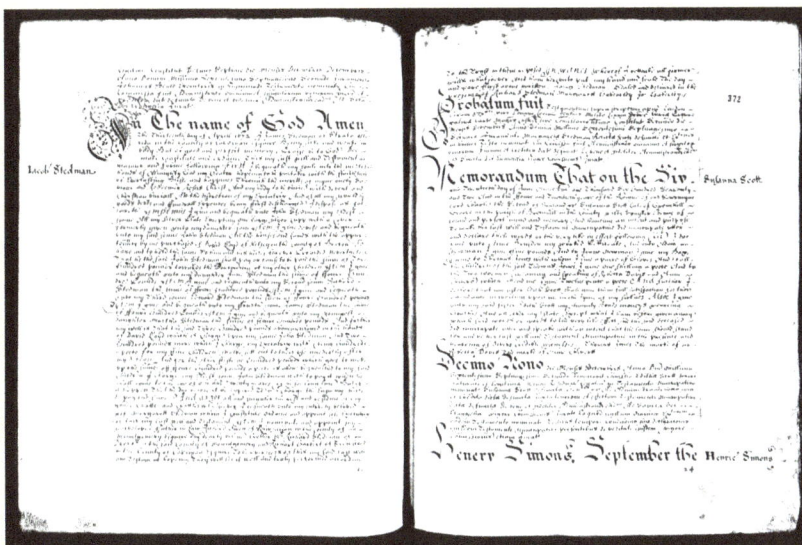

Fig. 166: Susanna Scott's will copied into the register of Prerogative Court of Canterbury and held at the National Archives.

Fig. 167: An unmarried mother with a baseborn child was frowned upon by society.

Despite the efforts of the parish, clergy and families to police personal relationships, instances of pre-marital sex took place and consequently babies were born out of wedlock. In Bremhill, like many villages, it was particularly frowned upon if the parish had to pick up the bill for looking after them. These children were routinely labelled 'bastard' or 'baseborn'. A derogatory term. However, parish records reveal that baptisms of illegitimate children were a regular occurrence.

It was not only unmarried mothers and their children who caused concern in previous centuries. Society could be unforgiving of many situations outside of what was deemed acceptable behaviour. The results were sometimes tragic. Isaac Woodfield was a Bremhill mason. In April 1835, at the age of twenty-four, he had a wife and three children. For reasons not described, Isaac deserted his family. Left destitute, Mrs Woodfield turned to the authorities for help. For centuries past, when left in this predicament, a wife so abandoned would have approached one of the up to eight parish overseers to ask for help. They may even have come to her to offer support. These overseers were annually appointed to both collect in the poor rates and distribute relief. Each Bremhill overseer had responsibility for a different part of the parish. If Isaac's wife had been in this situation the previous year, she would likely have known the overseer. He may have known the history of the family. However, in 1835 circumstances had changed and she now had to approach the new Calne Poor Law Union for help.

By December 1835, the union noted Isaac now had only two children living. The circumstances around the death of one of them are not described. The authorities looked for Isaac. They took a dim view of a husband's abandonment of his family for moral, legal (and probably financial) reasons. Isaac was eventually located and prosecuted for abandoning his family. He received a custodial sentence over Christmas. His wife received relief but only until his release. On his discharge, he was returned to the family.

Fig. 168. Abandonment of a family by the husband could mean a custodial sentence.

Fig. 169: 19th century engraving, Reading of the verdict in a magistrate's court.

Whatever the problems were within the household, they were not resolved, as the following February he fled again. He was pursued, located and taken back before the magistrates in March. However, he 'promised' he would support his wife and family in the future.[335] His protestations worked, and he was set free, but in July, Isaac ran away once again. Mrs Woodfield was forced to turn to the union for help.[336] By August, he was still missing. At this point, the decision seems to have been made that he was not coming back. His wife and remaining children were taken to the Calne workhouse.[337] Once there, the family were probably separated. Had Isaac absconded a year or two before they would have remained in Bremhill and the outcome would have been very different.

Fig. 170: The new Union Workhouse was built in 1847-8 at a site on the north side of Curzon Street, Calne.

Fig. 171: OS Map showing the site.

The historic community of Bremhill looked after its own, and in many respects functioned well. As described earlier, the parish was early to provide welfare and medical care to the poor. In the seventeenth century, the manorial court records would suggest life was bound up with the rhythms of rural life. When community disputes arose, such as those over scouring ditches, making boundaries or overgrazing cattle, they were quickly resolved.[338]

However, this did not mean that points of friction ran just below the surface. As with most village communities, village gossip was a constant through the centuries. Several times in the early seventeenth century, however, this became vicious and the objects of the scandal, became objects of ridicule and possible defamation; upon which they turned to the courts.

A Village Scandal: The Pregnancy of Sibil Ledges

In late 1600, one morning after prayers, the Bremhill vicar was walking in the nave of St Martin's Church.[339] He overheard two men arguing; one was John Bull and the other Robert Herne. The topic was John's pregnant step-daughter, Sibil, or more particularly, the likely father of her child. Robert was adamant; it was not his son, Matthew, as John alleged. Instead, he argued the culprit was Edmund Trimnell who often 'used the company of her.' He made much reference to late-night trysts in John's ox house.

The Trimnells and the Hernes were respectable yeoman families. Neither wished to be associated with Sibil's baby. Allegedly the Hernes tried to arrange for the Bayntuns (owners of Bremhill Manor) to 'find another father for Sibil's child'. At the same time, the Trimnells tried to pay Sibil off. Ultimately the families brought defamation cases against each other to the church court.

The truth is impossible to deduce. Despite owning oxen, Sibil's stepfather, John, was evidently a poor man. He lived in a rented cottage owned by the Trimnells. It probably suited him better if someone outside the Trimnell family had fathered Sibil's child. Moreover, according to testimony, he bore a grudge against the Hernes. However, Robert Herne was portrayed as a desperate man prepared to defame the reputation of the Trimnells to exonerate the Hernes.

Much came down to witness testimony, and there was no witness more controversial than the Trimnell's star witness, farmer, William Scott. The Hernes tried to paint William Scott as an unreliable source. Testimonies bore witness to the fact William 'walke with a visard before his face & is a man of stout & stubborn disposicion'.

One story alleged he had once taken a pet deer which belonged to Margaret Norborne. The Oliffes, another yeoman family, claimed he had broken into their house. Tanner, John Scott, alleged William had threatened him with a dagger. And local tailor Edmund King declared that one night in the early hours of the morning, William Scott had galloped his horse through the village while carrying an eight-foot staff.

Fig. 172: Feelings ran high in the 17th century when a woman was found to be pregnant outside wedlock.

In December the parish register notes the christening of 'Matthew, the base child of Matthew Hearne and Sible'. However, the antagonism between the Hernes and the Trimnells continued in court proceedings for some months. The outcome of the defamation cases is, unfortunately, unclear. Matthew Herne moved away from Bremhill and got married, but not to Sibil. What became of her or their son is not recorded.

The narrative reveals something of the time that Sibil herself was not called to give evidence. She was, after all, a woman and poor. Worse still, she had sinned by being pregnant out of wedlock. Of more importance, than any slight to Sibil or the truth about the parentage of her child, was the reputation of the local farming families of Trimnell and Herne.

Fig. 173: Interior of St Martin's Church, Bremhill.

CHAPTER FIVE

Folklore, Superstition & Witchcraft

Chapter 5: Folklore, Superstition and Witchcraft

Fig. 174: The hand-carved crown post in the roof space of Bremhill Court suggests it was the site of a very much older building.

One way in which Bremhill parish life has changed are the superstitions and customs that local people previously observed. By the 1980s, it was reported no such traditions were locally practised, it was assumed none had ever been, and 'Bremhill must have been a most conservative or unimaginative village.' However, this was very much not the case. Nor has the village been immune from tales of supernatural occurrences.

In one of the most recent paranormal events, the inhabitant of one old house in Bremhill was bothered by the apparition of a man in Victorian labouring clothes moving through the upstairs rooms of their home. She turned to the Rev. Jim Scott of Bremhill, who called in the diocesan expert and an exorcism was performed.[340]

Another example within living memory was in 1986 when renovations took place of Bremhill Court (formerly the Old Vicarage); the roof over the earliest part of the building was taken off to reveal remains of a timber-framed hall. This older core was dated by a historic buildings surveyor, at the time, as possibly fifteenth century but no later than sixteenth century. Concealed among the timbers were items associated with warding off evil spirits. A dried cat's head loosely enclosed by sewn leather, a well-worn child's shoe and some simple wooden toys. The position of them demonstrated that these had been carefully placed and not simply discarded. The common belief was that the personalised items acted as a defiant, and permanent, reminder to the spiritual world of the primacy of human beings. Some of these items were removed and are to be found in a display case commissioned by The Friends of St Martin in the adjacent building of St Martin's Church in Bremhill.

Fig. 175: Some of the items discovered in the rafters of Bremhill Court during renovations in 1986.

Fig. 176: (previous page) Woodcut from *The History of Witchcraft*.

In centuries gone by, in agricultural communities like Bremhill, people's lives depended on their own good health and local agriculture for their livelihoods – they needed bountiful harvests and healthy livestock. People were vigilant for signs of looming disaster, of portents and signs. In Foxham, black dogs were believed by local people to be a warning of death, sickness or calamity.[341] When things went wrong, inhabitants sometimes drew not what we may consider logical conclusions but instead placed blame at the door of the evil eye, fairies or witchcraft and devilry. In seeking solutions when things went sour, local people also did things that, even accounting for a lack of modern scientific knowledge, seem to a twenty-first-century eye bizarre or ridiculous. Thus, for hundreds of years, the settlements of Bremhill parish were rich with superstitious practices.

Fig. 177: 17th century woodcut of a black dog.

Chapter 4 looked at how local people tried to cure ailments with homemade remedies, but alongside this were the local rites to effect cures that may have origins in pre-Christian times. One such rite utilised the healing power of the maiden ash tree (an ash tree that had not been pruned); in particular the tree's ability to cure babies and infants of 'ruptures', a term used for hernias. To be cured, the trunk of the maiden ash tree had to be split in two. At sunrise, the patient was passed through the opening of the trunk with their face turned towards the rising sun. The rite needed to be carried out on 1 May, a date associated with the pagan festival of Beltane (although how far back in Bremhill's history this tradition went is impossible to ascertain). After the rite took place, the tree was bound back together again to grow to maturity. The fate of the child and the tree were tied. The cure would not work if the tree did not thrive.[342]

The initiation of Summer

*She turned to the
sunlight*

*And shook her
yellow head*

*And whispered
to her neighbour*

Winter is dead

A A Milne

One local child to undergo this treatment, was likely Henry Head, who was born in 1875. It is difficult to be sure but given the evidence it is likely that Henry suffered from an inguinal hernia. The physical manifestation of the condition, which is now easily treated by surgery, is a bulge in the groin area. His parents tried their best to help him. He was trussed, made to wear a leather strap or belt, which would have stopped the hernia protruding and may have relieved his discomfort. They set store by local customs and, hoping to cure Henry, carried him naked on a blanket into local woods and passed him through the split trunk of an ash, on 1 May, as the sun rose.

The tree had been prepared by his father the night before. Unfortunately for Henry, after the rite, the woodland was thinned, and the tree cut down. His cure failed. Regrettably, Victorian times could be unforgiving to those with a physical or mental ailment or abnormality. Untreated, Henry's hernia may have grown, and his pain could have increased significantly.

Fig. 178: Young ash tree saplings.

Fig. 179: The Wiltshire County Lunatic Asylum.

Fig. 180: The lodge to the Asylum.

This may have contributed to the mental health problems he developed as a young man, and which caused him to be committed to the Wiltshire County Lunatic Asylum, where he died still in his twenties.

Several parish traditions associated with remedies seem to have been a hybrid of Christian beliefs and country folklore. One of these was the conviction that a half-crown given in a collection at holy communion at St Martin's and fashioned into a ring could cure epileptic fits.[343] An old woman of Charlcutt could cure ulcers by reciting the words:

> Our blessed Saviour Christ was of the Virgin Mary born, And on His head was crowned with a crown of thorn, Which never did canker, fester, or swell, And God Almighty grant this may do as well.

As she spoke the first two lines, her finger passed around the ulcer; during the third, her finger went in the opposite direction, and at the last, the sign of the cross was made over the afflicted area. The lady charged 1s a time. There were also local people, who through the centuries, believed they were imbued with healing powers.

For at least two generations, a family in Spirthill cured jaundice or rather 'yaller jarndice' by burning the patient's urine and performing a rite that involved the ashes of a maiden ash tree. However, the exact process was a secret, as, on its telling, the practitioner's power would be lost.[344] During the sixteenth century, superstitious beliefs were to have tragic consequences.

The Stanley Witch:

Agnes Mylles and the Death of William Bayntun

In 1564 the Bayntuns were regarded as one of the most eminent Wiltshire families. In February 1564, the head of the family, Sir Andrew Bayntun, died.[345] In 1560, Andrew entailed the Bayntun fortune, in the event of his death, to his younger brother, Edward.[346] However, on his death, Edward Bayntun did not enjoy this inheritance. But, rather due to his brother's financial mismanagement (possibly due to Andrew Bayntun's naivety or the fact he was easily manipulated), Edward Bayntun was embroiled in a court battle to gain full possession of his legacy. The details of Andrew's poor financial decisions have led one historian to conclude he was 'simple minded'.[347] In the later genealogical telling of the family history, Andrew is sometimes expunged, a dynastic link to be forgotten.[348] In life, there was likely no love lost between brothers Andrew and Edward. However, the drama within the Bayntun family in 1564 did not abate.

Much of the ensuing tragedy was related to other troubled relationships within the family.[349] Edward and Andrew had a younger brother, Henry, who was married to Dorothy.[350] In the preceding years, Dorothy's family had become 'ruined' firstly by the execution of her elder brother for murder and later by the execution of a nephew and another brother for treason.[351] It is likely given this and Henry Bayntun's status as a younger brother, together with the events that followed, that Henry and Dorothy's financial circumstances were difficult and their relations with Edward strained.

Fig. 181: Early 16th century execution scene.

Fig. 182: The coat of arms for Sir William Stourton.

Edward Bayntun had married late in life. While by 1564, his brother Henry already had sons and daughters, Edward had only one child, an infant son, William, by his marriage to Agnes, whom he had wed over ten years previously. Agnes Bayntun's grandfather was the 2nd Duke of Norfolk, who was also grandfather to Anne Boleyn and Catherine Howard. Her father had been executed on possibly false charges of treason. Scandalously, Agnes then had an affair with a married Wiltshire gentleman, Sir William Stourton, who, on his death, had left her a fortune.[352] She married Edward Bayntun, who helped her to fight through the courts to retrieve this inheritance.[353] Suffice to say, William Bayntun's family was embroiled in scandal and intrigue. Through his mother, he was also distantly related to Elizabeth I. If William died and Edward and Agnes Bayntun had no more children, then Henry and Dorothy Bayntuns' children would inherit. Before Easter 1564, disaster struck, and William Bayntun, the infant heir to the Bayntun wealth, died.

Edward and Agnes Bayntun were to have thirteen children, ten of which were to predecease their father. It was, therefore, likely that William was not their only child to die in infancy.[354] However, it appears William was their first. Like Henry VIII a few decades before, Edward Bayntun was under intense pressure to produce a male heir. In 1564, this was particularly acute. He was fighting for much of his inheritance. The birth of a longed-for son and then his, possibly, sudden death with no apparent cause was too much. The timing was heady. Elizabeth I had recently ascended the throne. There had been several catholic plots against her in which witchcraft had been implicated. John Jewel, bishop of Salisbury, had preached a sermon for the queen in which he had called for action. Some historians have suggested that this and his writings resulted in a Witchcraft Act in 1563.[355] Its first provision made death 'caused' by witchcraft a crime, one punishable by death.[356] Coincidentally the legislation passed through parliament in the same year that William's father, Edward Bayntun, first entered the Commons as an MP. Perhaps it is unsurprising that he or indeed others would consider William's death was not natural and may have had a supernatural cause.

Fig. 183: Woodcut of a witch trial in 1598.

There were around 1,000 witchcraft trials in England over the centuries, and fewer than half resulted in execution.[357] Wiltshire witchcraft cases are rare. Despite popular perceptions of the hearings, prosecutions were problematic because of the difficulty of gathering necessary evidence.

It is not known who made the first accusation. However, soon after the death of baby William Bayntun, witchcraft was being suggested as the probable cause. Allegations centred on a widow from the village of Stanley, Agnes Mylles. Edward and Agnes Bayntun later described how Agnes Mylles 'not having God before her eyes but being seduced with a devilish instigation by using of Sorcerer's charms and witchcraft' had murdered their son.

Fig. 184: Thumb Screws, a torturer's device to force a confession.

Given at this time 'secular justice followed accusatory principles where the onus lay with ordinary accusers', it is probable that the indictment and considerable momentum of the case stemmed from William's parents.[358] Agnes Mylles was taken to the county gaol at Fisherton Anger. It is unlikely, although not impossible, that she was tortured (it was not allowed under English law in this context). Nonetheless, likely scared, Agnes Mylles confessed her guilt of the charge of murder by witchcraft to several justices and Bishop John Jewel, a man who believed in sorcery.[359] One would assume, guilt in Jewel's eyes would have been clear, as there was also witness testimony. However, this was not the case.

A connection between Agnes Mylles and the Bayntuns is difficult to deduce. Andrew Bayntun based himself at both Stanley in Bremhill from where Agnes came and at nearby Bromham. Andrew had endowed the chapelry at Foxham in Bremhill.[360] His ties with the parish are likely to have been close.[361] It is conceivable, given Agnes Mylles knowledge of the family, the allusion to witness testimony and mention of charms, presumably requiring access to the child, that Agnes Mylles was known to the family before William's death. She may have been a servant in one of the Bayntun properties at Bremhill or Stanley, or she may have been a local 'cunning' person who dispensed remedies, as did another alleged Wiltshire witch, Anne Bodenham, who almost a century later was to share her fate.[362] Unfortunately, there are no parish registers at Bremhill for the period. Consequently, we know little of who Agnes was with any certainty. Those who faced trial were generally older impoverished women.[363] Certainly, as a widow, Agnes Mylles may well have been elderly, and she may have had no family to protect her.

Fig. 185: Late 16th century woodcut from *The History of Witches*.

Whoever she was, Edward and Agnes Bayntun were confident Agnes Mylles had killed their son. However, Bishop John Jewel was not so persuaded by her confession.[364] In this, the bishop may have been influenced. Bishop Jewel's friend and patron was Henry Sharington, who in the last years of Andrew Bayntun's life had 'clearly schemed' to acquire property from him.

Fig. 186; Engraving of the notorious Matthew Hopkins, professional witchfinder.

Sharington was Andrew Bayntun's executor and beneficiary of a possibly forged will. He and Edward Bayntun were engaged in a court battle. Edward Bayntun was also considered lukewarm in his Protestant faith. It may have rankled the bishop, who had been obliged to flee the country under Mary.[365] But there was also the complicating factor that not only did Agnes Mylles confess to murdering William Bayntun, she also stated that she had done so at the instigation of none other than Dorothy Bayntun, the child's aunt, whose husband and children would inherit should Edward Bayntun fail to produce a male heir. An assertion the alleged witch also made in front of witnesses 'unto the said Dorothy's face'.[366]

The bishop sought further evidence by calling on the services of one Jane Marshe, a Somerset woman, who had a skill in detecting those who used witchcraft, a witchfinder. This is unusual in the sixteenth-century context but a concept which has found its way into popular culture through the activities of the self-proclaimed witchfinder general, Matthew Hopkins, a century later.

If the bishop hoped that Jane Marshe's testimony would call into doubt the witch's guilt or even put the blame elsewhere, he was to be disappointed. Even before she visited the site of William Bayntun's alleged murder, she declared Agnes Mylles and Dorothy Bayntun guilty. The bishop ordered the witchfinder to be imprisoned, where she languished for six months. Meanwhile, Agnes Mylles, her guilt confirmed by the witchfinder, was tried and hanged at the command of the judges of the Assizes.

Fig 187: Witch hanging was a crude affair, with the victim carried up a ladder on the shoulder of the hangman and thrown off to choke to death.

Fig. 188: Fisherton, a suburb of Salisbury, hosted a county gaol from about 1485 until 1870 on several different sites. The building where Agnes was incarcerated is lost, but fragments of its replacement, built in 1568 a few years later, survive as the base of Salisbury's Victorian clock tower.

It does not appear Dorothy Bayntun was punished for the procuring of a witch to murder her nephew. When a county tour of inspection was undertaken in 1565 by King of Arms, William Harvey, to document the pedigree of the Wiltshire nobility, Henry Bayntun's name was recorded, but his marriage and children were not, unlike his siblings.[367] Later, heraldic histories did not record Henry's existence, like his uncle Andrew, it may have been a name that the family wished to forget.

It is possible no more information will be uncovered about the Stanley witch, Agnes Mylles. The circumstances surrounding the death of William Bayntun are thus likely to remain unknown. Despite being mentioned in local histories the case has been overlooked by historians working on witchcraft.[368] There are reasons for this omission. The documentary evidence for the case of Agnes Mylles comes from an unusual source for this type of research, the Court of Chancery. The records of the original witchcraft trial at the assizes are lost. If this Wiltshire case had not involved an 'elite' family, knowledge of it and its context would probably be lost. Crucially it also predates the first 'witchcraft pamphlet' in 1566, *The Examination and Confession of Certaine Wytches*, which includes the case of Agnes Waterhouse, often called the first person to be executed in England for witchcraft.[369]

Indeed the first case in current academic historiography is that of Elizabeth Lowys who was executed in Essex in March 1565.[370] So the case of a convicted witch from Stanley in 1564 is significant and not just in Wiltshire. Agnes Mylles was one of the first, if not the first person, to be executed for witchcraft in England.

Fig. 189: The confession of Agnes Waterhouse who was executed as a witch in 1566.

CHAPTER SIX

Government, Crime & Punishment

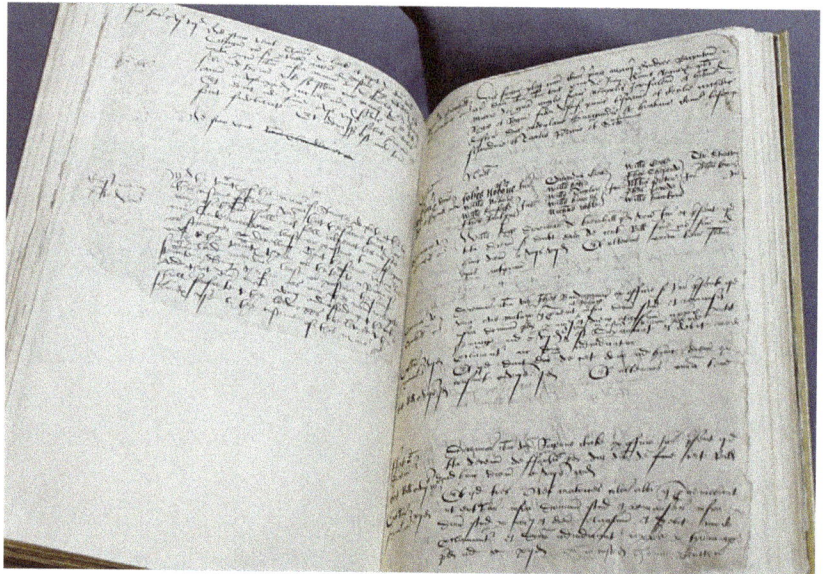

Fig. 190: The court book for the Manor of Bremhill 1545-1557.

For 500 years Bremhill parish was mostly self-governing, responsible for much of its law and order, welfare, roads and bridges and much more.

6.1 The Manor

After the dissolution of the monasteries in the reign of Henry VIII, much local law and order and matters of government were administered under the local manorial court system. Much of what is now Bremhill parish was divided into the manors of Stanley and Bremhill. The lord of these manors was the same, Sir Edward Bayntun.[371] For administrative purposes, Bremhill was subdivided into the separate 'tithings' of Bremhill, Foxham and Spirthill with Charlcutt.

A court generally met twice a year although sometimes it met more frequently, as the centuries passed it was increasingly sporadic. There was also a court for Tytherton Lucas between 1677 and 1749 but there is much less documentary evidence for it. Although Cadenham was also a manor, it did not appear to have held a court. Manor courts had limited jurisdiction, and a lot of its business had to do with organising land tenure (for example, to pass a tenanted farm from father to son).[372]

However, its range of activities was wide. Under the local organisation of the manorial system, a 'tithingman' was selected for Stanley, Bremhill, Foxham and Spirthill with Charlcutt, and separately for Tytherton Lucas. The tithingman was a petty constable or law enforcement officer. The position was unpaid but probably not arduous.

Fig. 191: (Previous page) Engraving, *The Bottle* after George Cruikshank.

Most infractions local tithingmen had to deal with were minor. They involved little more than presenting small misdemeanours at the manor court, such as tenants who had failed to pay the molecatcher. There were a few occasions, however, which demanded a tithingman acted decisively.[373] In 1600, 'Old John Oliff' called in his local tithingman during the night 'as a suspicious man was about the house'. The local tithingman was summoned and searched the property but found nothing.[374]

Surprisingly, a local tithingman was not necessarily the most law-abiding person. In Bremhill it appeared he was sometimes elected on other criteria. In October 1651, on the day Thomas Hayward was elected as tithingman for Foxham he was fined by the court for not doing his share to repair local roads and warned that unless he 'scoured' (cleared) his ditches by November, he would face another fine. Despite his new role, Thomas was unperturbed and had not scoured them six months later. If the post was given to encourage his good behaviour, it failed, as it was by no means his last offence for not clearing trenches. He was also later charged with not controlling his grazing livestock and not digging ditches.[375]

Not everyone welcomed their election as tithingman either. William Sheppard, a gentleman of Hazeland, refused to take the post. He also failed to find a replacement when directed to do so and was finally told to find one within a day of the court sitting or face a £5 fine. Like Thomas Hayward, William had fallen foul of the court previously. He had failed to maintain his bridges at Hazeland Mill for years. However, at the last minute, the post was given to someone else, a previous occupier of the mill. Despite the reprieve, William showed contempt to the court by failing to repair the bridges, despite a hefty £8 fine. Six months later, at the next court, William's penalty for the lack of bridge repair was raised to £16. He was given another for £5 for failing to take the oath of tithingman and warned unless he did so within ten days, he would get more. Unfortunately, there are no available court records for the following year to know if he eventually complied.[376]

As well as a tithingman, local manor courts also elected 'haywards'. It was a hayward's role to maintain hedges and fences, mainly to ensure cattle did not breakthrough from local commons, like Stockham Marsh into enclosed fields.[377] Locally they also served notice when livestock should be taken on and off the commons and collected fines for infringements. There were often more haywards than tithingmen, up to four for Stockham alone, probably because the role demanded more effort than that of tithingman. There are occasional references to tenants paying haywards' fees, and again it is likely for the same reason. Sometimes, 'overseers' of commons were also appointed with a specific right to impound cattle, probably as a backup to haywards and likely because such imposition would be controversial.[378]

Fig. 192: The tithing man, a satirical image from 1770.

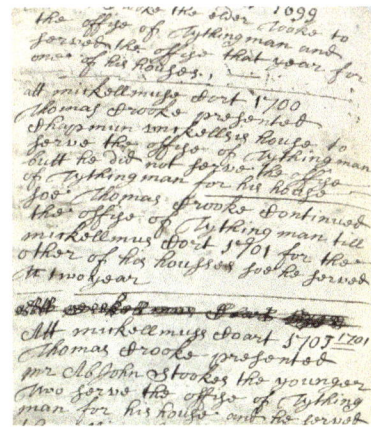

Fig. 193: Comments about the tithingman were a frequent entry in the commonplace book.

Fig. 194: A hayward looking after free-roaming stock would have been an everyday sight in Foxham.

Misdemeanours recorded by the court generally concerned those who neglected to repair boundaries, fences, highways and bridges, or to scour ditches and those who had encroached on land which was not their own. Occasionally, there were public disorder offences. Later manor courts were quieter, although the misdemeanours which were recorded were very similar.

In 1752, Stanley Manor court dealt with only one case, that of a neighbourhood dispute. From the little recorded in the court book, it appeared to have started when William Watts made 'a new hole in his garden for the reception of water from his house'. Unfortunately, the hole caused his neighbours garden to 'overflow' with wastewater. His neighbour, Thomas Hood, was understandably, not pleased. Hood then decided to cut his hedge. The hedge cuttings were dropped, likely in a fit of anger, onto his neighbours' house 'whereby' according to the court recording 'his house is damaged.'

For some years the court had made an annual plea to the lord of the manor, to provide village stocks. If they had been installed by 1752, Watts, Hood or both might have suffered public humiliation by being placed into the stocks and having refuse thrown at them. But instead, both men were ordered to put right the damage or face 5s fine. How Hood and Watts fared after their altercation is not recorded; although given the fact they do not appear again in the court recording, it is likely that they were reconciled.[379]

Fig. 195: Watercolour of The Assize Court, Devizes, built in the 1830s.

Not all public order or crime was dealt with locally by the manor courts. Many of the successive generations of the Bayntun and Hungerford families who lived locally were also magistrates who presided at the Quarter Sessions. These courts were held every three months at different locations across the county. The most serious crimes were tried by the judges of the assizes who visited Wiltshire twice a year. In matters of religion and morality, there were also the Bishop of Salisbury's ecclesiastical courts.

Fig. 196: Engraving of a church court.

These took cases of drunkenness, wife-beating, Sunday trading or more commonly those involving sex (such as adultery and prostitution). If these outlets were unsatisfactory, then recourse could be made to higher courts in London. In 1672, several Bremhill residents and Sir George Hungerford took legal action against the Bremhill vicar, Rev. John Tounson, in the bishop's consistory court for not providing a curate at Foxham chapel. The court ruled against the vicar who then appealed to the Court of Arches in London where the case was still unresolved ten years later.[380]

In the first instance, the community could decide not to resort to a tithingman, Justice or court, but instead police misdemeanours itself. In the following case, the actions of a particular family offended the wider community, and they received a public humiliation. The move proved a misfire, however, as the family then raised a libel lawsuit against a large number of defendants from the parish.

Fig. 197: Sir George Hungerford.

'Infamous, Scurrilous and Scandalous'

A Seventeenth-Century Sex Scandal in East Tytherton

Fig. 198: 17th century painting, A country scene by unknown artist.

In 1619, a libel case was brought to the Star Chamber Court based at the Palace of Westminster by John Harrys, of the Elms at East Tytherton, his daughter and son-in-law.[381] The case alleged many Bremhill residents had conspired against them to produce a scandalous libel which was spread around the village and far beyond. The subject matter focused on Harrys who, among other things it alleged, committed adultery with several women, coerced others into prostitution and shockingly committed incest with his daughter, by whom he may have had a baby. According to the accusation, the plot to libel Harrys was hatched in December 1618. In January, it gained traction when the accused started to 'scatter, disperse publishe and divulge the saied several writings' across Bremhill and 'other adioyninge townes and parishes within the saied Countye'.

The libel was in the form of two rhymes made by a real or imaginary author, William Isbelis. Isbelis had signed the work but was never seen. The accusations contained in the poems chiefly concerned the behaviour of John Harrys, who was given the nickname 'Blanchute', something by which he was also known around the village. Apparently, a literary play on the colour white, maybe a reference to his supposed purity, but the full meaning may now be lost.

Fig. 199: The cuckhold departs for the hunt, 18th century print.

Both rhymes alleged John or Blanchute had 'cuckolded' Michael Robbins with his wife Elizabeth. A cuckold is the husband of an adulterous wife, a label associated with shame and humiliation which implied the husband, in this case Michael, could not control his spouse, or that he was impotent. A child of a cuckolded husband was a cuckoo in the family nest. As John was Michael's father-in-law, it is more shocking. It was not only adultery but incest.

The poem further alleged John had engaged a wet-nurse for Elizabeth's baby so they could continue their assignations ('he fetcheth the nurse to give the Childe sucke, that he may have fytt tyme thy wyffe for to fucke'). It called Michael a 'silly asse' for not realising his wife's behaviour which included romping in the hay or under hedges with John depending on the strength of the wind. It was common for accusations of this kind to be elaborated by references to beastliness, filth and disease, and this was no different. A second rhyme asserted that John had kept Michael busy working so he could spend time with Elizabeth, who was described as a 'wattle chapped whore', a reference to Elizabeth having venereal disease.

This liaison aside the poems also talked about several other women. One given the derogatory label of 'whore' lived near Underdowns. She was described as a 'sillye owlde woman' who did not see any harm in a sexual relationship with John 'because shee have stronge beare for Colde ffleshe to warme'. Sexual misconduct was also alleged with unspecified corrupt women for whom, it said, John 'drawes out his weapon by daye or by night'. The poem went on to accuse him of encouraging sexual immorality by enticing women into prostitution. One ruse was to offer a woman a house rent-free along with a white cow if she agreed 'to deale with him by the yeare'. He was sometimes shunned by the women he tried to tempt or coerce into having sex. One, a tenant of his, was virtuous and honest and rejected his advances. Consequently, they were soon 'att strife'. The poem ended 'this woman was forced from thence soone to goe, or else shee Coulde not live honeste the truthe was soe.'

On 13 January, to spread their libel more widely, one of the plotters, Edyth Sommerell 'found' a wax-sealed copy of a poem at the bottom of Barton Hill. She took it to Hazeland Mill. There, Walter Webb (the younger) opened it and in the presence of several individuals read the contents with much scoffing. Later that same day, a larger crowd gathered at Hazeland, and the libel was again communicated by Walter 'by waye of a ieste and merriment'.

Thereafter, the libellous poetry came to be read, published and divulged around the village. The following day, Walter's father, Robert, on the instigation of other conspirators took the now 'infamous' libel to Devizes for market day. There Robert met another plotter, and the two in the 'open marketplace' read, published and communicated it to several others.

Fig. 200: *Lovers in a hay field*, by A.Aldorfer.

Fig. 201: Devizes open market place.

Fig. 202: Tower and belfry of St Martin's Church, Bremhill.

In Bremhill, meanwhile, Edyth's role in disseminating the libel continued. The following day she took it to a local clothier, intending to encourage him to circulate it further. After her visit, he 'unlawfullye and maliciously reade, publishe and divulge the saied infamous and scurrilous libels and copies thereof both in his owne dwelling howse, and in diverse other Townes, parishes and places'. On the next Sunday, the poem was sung and otherwise disseminated from the belfry of St Martin's Church by young Walter Webb, 'to the greate profaninge of the sabbothe daye, and to the exceeding great slaunderinge, defaming and disgracinge of your [majesty's] said subiectes'.

Later in the accusatory testimony, these Sunday revels became more elaborate. Firstly, one conspirator journeyed to and from morning prayers reading and singing the rhyme 'with much laughter and reioycinge' as he went. Later the poetry was performed within the church at evening prayers, while John Harrys was in the congregation. The vicar was encouraged to join in but refused. Later the vicar received the poems in a letter which he declined to read.

The testimony of the defendants sought to distance themselves from any conspiracy or wrongdoing. The statements include Walter's father who said he had taken the rhymes off his son when Edyth had brought them to the Hazeland Mill. He had realised their defamatory nature and tucked them into his pocket for safe keeping. They had not been broadcast. He had gone to Devizes where he had shown them to one other, to get his opinion. Unfortunately, the libel had been read out loud (to work out who had written it), and in doing so, its contents may inadvertently have been broadcast. In his testimony, another defendant confessed that as he left morning prayers at St Martin's Church and later from its belfry 'in the hearing of somme fewe of the parishioners of Bremhill he spake some fewe words of the saide libel, But What those Wordes were he then spake he this defendant rembereth not.'

The creation of the doggerel and its transmission in public was designed to humiliate the Harrys family. Its performance entertained many within the community. It articulated communal displeasure of their behaviour, while the plot, in part, protected the conspirators' anonymity. The vicar and the church-wardens were also invited to condemn them. It is possible conspirators hoped this would bring the issue to the attention of the bishop's court. In both respects, they failed. A typical response by those in receipt of this type of condemnation by neighbours and peers was fear. However, in this case, the family went on the offensive and created a lawsuit. Their case warned the court 'yt woulde be a greate incourageemente to other like evill disposed persons to sommytt the like offences, yf theise soe fowle and notorious offendours shoulde escape vunpunished.' Unfortunately, its outcome is not recorded.

The manorial system was in steep decline by the eighteenth century, and other agencies took much of its jurisdiction and that of manorial lords. However, it persisted in Bremhill, albeit in a diluted form, up until the late nineteenth century. Locally, the last of the parish's manorial courts was held for Stanley Manor in the name of its lord, Sir Gabriel Goldney, in 1879.[382] Goldney had purchased the estate in the previous decade from John Bayntun-Starky, a descendant of its original Bayntun owner. After this, although a 'lord of the manor' was noted in trade directories until well into the twentieth century, it was largely honorific. With the assembling of the last Stanley court, centuries of traditional government ended.[383]

6.2 The Parish

The manorial court system did not exist in isolation. From the seventeenth century, if not before, other branches of local government also existed and filled in gaps which the manorial system did not address. These were organised by the parish vestry, a parish committee of local ratepayers, and so named as such committees traditionally met in the vestry of a local church. The vestry appointed unsalaried officers to undertake particular tasks. Later as new services were added, or as the tasks became more arduous, salaries were paid. Parish officers included overseers, who were responsible for collecting poor rates and distributing relief to the poor, and churchwardens who raised church rates and looked after church property.

The vestry tried to provide public services, while encouraging public morality and delivering value-for-money. A concern in many communities were children born to unmarried parents. Fathers were expected to support their offspring and 'bastardy' enquiries were routinely made into the parentage of any child born 'out of wedlock'. In some years, community officers noted the number of children born to unmarried mothers the parish supported. Between 1786 and 1800, for example, it was usually between fifteen and eighteen.

Fig. 203: Caricature of Sir Gabriel Goldney by Delfico, 1872.

Fig. 204: Illustration by Emma Brownlow, image depicts the Foundling Hospital.

Fig. 205: *The Outcast*, 1851. Painting by Richard Redgrave.

Charity Peirce and The Cadenham Kitchen Affair

A bastardy case aimed to identify the father of an illegitimate child to ensure that responsibility for its maintenance was placed on him and was not a financial burden on the parish. Bastardy examinations took place before the Justices of the Peace, and women were questioned about the circumstances in which the child was conceived.

The following information is part of the deposition of Charity Peirce, a single woman who likely worked in the kitchens at Cadenham Manor in Foxham. It was recorded on 6 February 1692.[384]

Fig. 206: *Kitchen maid*, (detail) by Anthony Oberman.

> On her oath, [Charity Peirce] says that Francis Hicks is the only natural father of the bastard child of which she was lately delivered. And that the said Francis Hicks begot her, this examinant, with child in the kitchen at Cadnam in the evening when the election was last at Calne, it being done in the settle [a wooden bench] in the said kitchen while neat's [cow or ox] tongues were boiling over the fire. And further, she says that she was delivered of her said bastard child about three weeks and some odd days after Midsummer last past. And she further says that the said Francis Hicks had carnal knowledge of her body twice, it being about a week between the first time being in the kitchen at Cadnam aforesaid and further she says not.

The election at Calne would have been a source of much interest in the household at Cadenham. In 1690, Sir George Hungerford, owner of Cadenham Manor, had considered standing as MP for Calne in the general election, in part because his local rival, Henry Bayntun (owner of the manor of Bremhill), was running. In 1691, Bayntun died and George Hungerford took the opportunity to stand at the by-election. He was unsuccessful.

Fig. 207: *Peasants in a tavern*, by A. V. Oustade.

However, at this time, Charity became pregnant. Possibly, the drunken revels that often characterised elections resulted in the bawdy episode in the manor kitchen, with labourer Francis Hicks, that left her pregnant. The only other tryst Charity admitted to having with Francis was in a local punch house, a type of tavern of low repute. One of Charity's depositions was sworn in front of Sir George himself, possibly by then her ex-employer, who was a magistrate. Unfortunately, what became of Charity or her baby is not recorded. However, it is likely Francis, the father of her baby, was ordered to provide for his child as a result of the bastardy action.

As the manorial system waned, parish government also stepped in, for example, to maintain Bremhill's bridges. Like parish overseers, locally selected 'surveyors of the highway' were responsible for separate tithings and raised funds for the work by locally collected rates and sometimes by selling the 'scrapings' off local roads.[385] They were often local farmers who had little or no experience in the construction and maintenance of local highways and bridges. Highly unusually, locally they could also be women. For example, Ann Vines was selected for Spirthill in 1842 and Ann Pegler for Foxham in 1857.[386] In some years the duties of the post were undoubtedly arduous. In the year 1839-40, John Morris collected over £60 of rates, sold £2 of road scrapings that was added to his cash in hand. He then spent this money on 200 yards of stone from a quarry at Hazeland, for which he organised and paid for the labour to dig it out and also to pay for its transportation by boat to Foxham Wharf. Subsequently, John arranged carriage to where it was needed on the roads of Foxham. The roads were then repaired under his direction, with the help of local labourers, a carpenter and mason. He also had time to pay for a large number of sparrows heads from the local poor, slaughtered for fear the birds were eating crops.

Until the late eighteenth century, local tithingmen were selected and provided rudimentary law-enforcement under the local manor court, and occasionally supported county magistrates. In 1842, the government passed the Parish Constables Act which formally removed the rights of manorial courts for policing. Wiltshire County Constabulary had been formed some years before, but the legislation also allowed magistrates to plug gaps in policing provision not yet addressed by the constabulary, and crucially more cheaply. Bremhill was quick to respond following encouragement by local magistrates who had probably drawn up a list of suitable appointees. A constable was selected (or possibly conscripted) for each of the four parish tithings of Bremhill, Foxham, Spirthill and Tytherton with Studley.[387] These posts were more arduous than the previous role of tithingman. The position was, however, part-time. A constable was only required to work in his parish, and only should the need arise. The effectiveness of these officers relied heavily on their public spirit and physical ability. Provisions of the Act suggested appointees should be fit and healthy ratepayers between twenty-five and fifty-five. It is difficult to believe that they would have been willing to peril themselves to arrest offenders.

However, it seems they may well have done. In 1846, one of the Bremhill constables, George Bournes was assaulted and beaten in the line of duty, and his assailant was imprisoned.[388] Nonetheless, these constables were probably viewed as secondary to those employed directly by the Wiltshire County Constabulary. For a large Anti-Corn Law meeting held in Bremhill, in February 1846, the local vicar Henry Drury asked for and received several officers from the constabulary to police the event.[389] He did not ask the parish's own law enforcement.

Fig. 208: *Sparrows,* an engraving by A. Brehms in 1797.

Fig. 209: A well-fed parish constable illustrated by satirist and artist Paul Sandby.

Fig. 210: Reaping corn using a scythe.

One of the men to be appointed as a parish constable, was the constable for Bremhill, James Smallcomb.[390] Along with the other appointees, James was from a local farming family. He most likely had little or no experience in law enforcement. In his thirties, James undertook the role for several years. After serving the community in this way, he stepped back. How effective James was as a constable is difficult to ascertain.

However, after his service, James's personal history took a sad turn. He had a small farm, but it was just fourteen acres, comprising the local fields of Elder Wells and Bremhill Field.[391] The ability to support a family on such a small plot is likely to have been difficult. Although he employed a labourer in 1851, he also had four children under ten. More children are likely to have followed. This put immense pressure on the household finances, and it appears that after he stopped receiving the remuneration of a constable, the family may have got into financial difficulties. By 1853, he seems to have been employed as a labourer by Charles Vines who ran one of the largest farms in the parish. James was one of a workforce of seven labourers.[392] However, in that year, he was charged with stealing a pair of stockings that belonged to Vines while they were hanging on a washing line. James was acquitted, but it likely made his employment untenable.[393] He died at the age of only forty-nine in the following year.[394]

6.3 Local Crime & Punishment

Fig. 211: The Dumb Post Inn, Bremhill.

One of the most notorious crimes to take place in Bremhill parish, during the eighteenth or nineteenth century, occurred on the night of 27 January 1837. After dark, 'three villains with crape over their faces' burgled the Dumb Post Inn. The felons were well organised, gaining entry through an upper storey window, after first fastening the front door. While inside they also secured an internal door, a bedroom containing two young men, who presumably may have jeopardised their success. They were, however, confronted by the landlord's daughter who they knocked over. The miscreants stole two chests belonging to local friendly societies and containing £50, and a box with an undisclosed sum belonging to the landlord, Mr Frayling. The assailants were not caught.[395]

Most crimes involved petty theft or minor assault. A fine or short internment at the House of Correction at Devizes often sufficed. However, in the late eighteenth and early nineteenth century, sentences could be exceedingly harsh, even for offences which today appear minor. In 1826, a sentence of seven years transportation to Australia was given to Bremhill labourers, Haddrell and Long for stealing poultry. Rev. William Lisle Bowles, the parish vicar and a magistrate, petitioned the king through the home secretary, Robert Peel, and their sentences were commuted to one-year imprisonment.[396]

A perennial problem reported to local magistrates was poaching, the suspicion of poaching or even having a dog (such as a lurcher or greyhound) which could be used for poaching. Such was the 'crime' of William Pinniger of Foxham who was reported several times in the 1770s to the neighbourhood magistrate, Robert Ashe.[397]

Convictions for the most heinous of personal crimes, such as serious assault or murder were practically unheard of in Bremhill. For centuries, all unexplained deaths were subject to a coroner's inquiry. These provide us with some early glimpses of these offences or potential offences in the parish. In the 1240s a stranger was found dead in Bremble Field; the parish, for whatever reason, did not follow due process and arrange for an inquest and they were fined for the breach. Unfortunately, no further details were recorded. Later, when Adam, son of Maud, was found dead after being run over by a waggon, due process was followed. Enquiries revealed Walter son of Seywe had driven the waggon and fled the scene, leaving Adam to be found by his mother. The incident was judged an accident and Walter acquitted.[398]

Like the stranger found dead in the thirteenth century, there are instances through the centuries where the reporting of the judicial process leaves many questions. In 1824, an inquiry took place when the Bremhill labourer, Robert Slade, was found in a field impaled on a pitchfork. The accompanying investigation concluded, he had been on top of a straw rick and had decided to assist himself down by using his pitchfork, spikes facing uppermost. In undertaking the manoeuvre, he slipped, and the fork penetrated his heart 'and killed him on the spot'.[399]

Some decades later, Beata Brewer, wife of a Bremhill labourer, alleged Frank Gale had thrown her to the ground and indecently assaulted her, while she was on the way to work. The case was dismissed due to insufficient evidence.[400] In both instances, the deliberations appear to have been cursory.

In recognition of a perceived increase in local crime, the number of parish constables increased to eight by the end of the 1860s.[401] By this time, it was apparent that unprofessional law enforcement was no longer working (if indeed it ever had). By 1874 the parish stopped appointing its constables. In 1888 and 1894, the system of English local government was reformed. By then the system of parish autonomy in local government had been undermined. It was no longer working but local society was also no longer the same. It was not possible to base local service provision on annually selected, largely unpaid officers with no experience or skill other than their public spirit.

Fig. 212: Poacher setting a snare.

Fig. 213: Haystack in the process of being built using a pitchfork.

Fig. 214: Wiltshire County Police in the mid - 19th century.

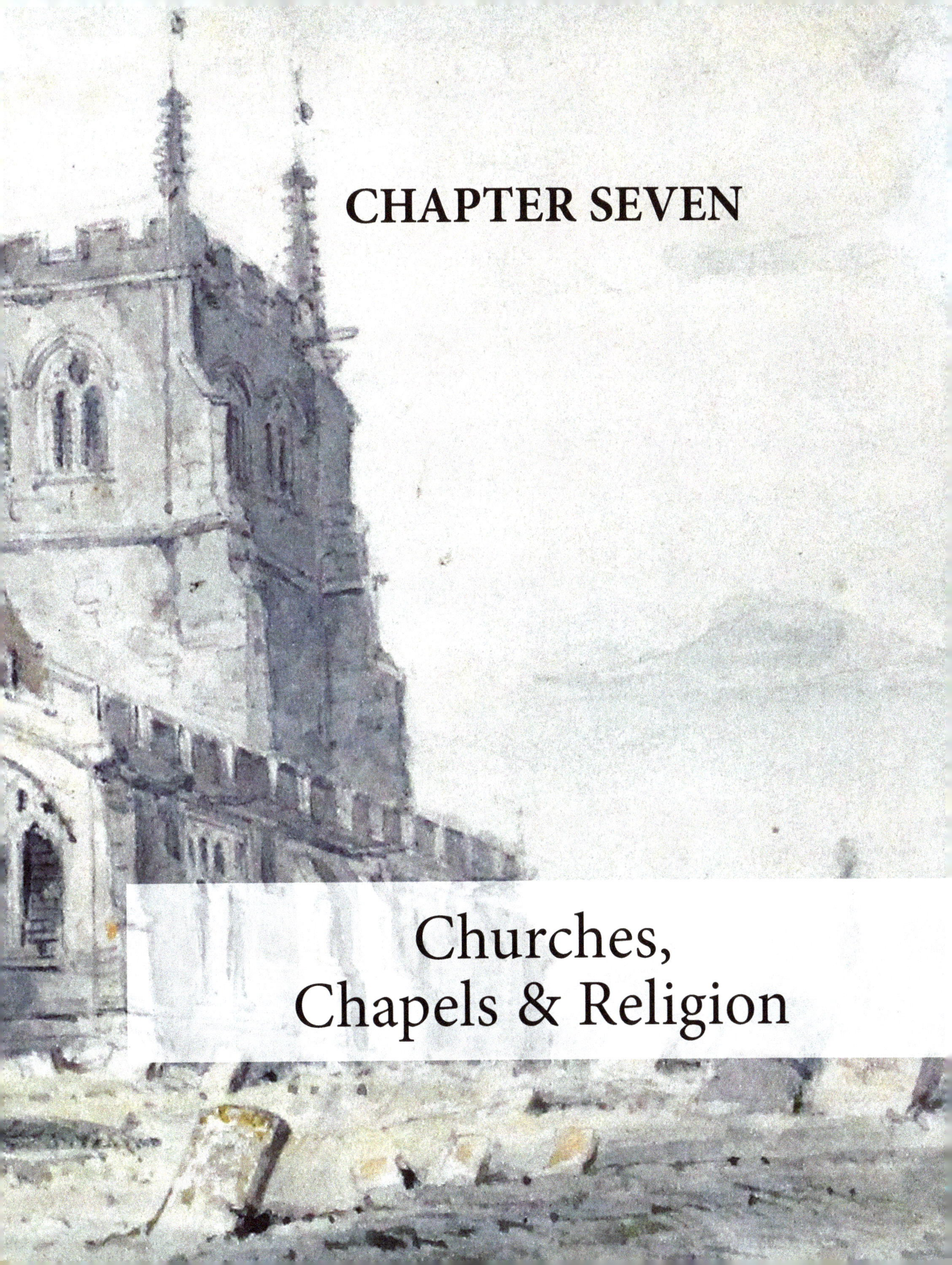

CHAPTER SEVEN

Churches, Chapels & Religion

Chapter 7.1: St Martin's, Bremhill and St John the Baptist, Foxham

Fig. 215: Bremhill churchyard from an engraving in 1809.

Fig. 216: The former chapel at Foxham rebuilt in 1778-81.

Fig. 217: St Peter's Church at Highway.

Fig. 218: (previous page) Watercolour of St Martin's Church, Bremhill by William Bartlett in 1824.

The Church of St Martin's Bremhill was the focus of village life for many centuries. It was a place to worship and to pray. But also, to celebrate weddings and baptisms, to meet and decide parish matters such as who should receive poor relief or whether local ditches needed clearing. Sometimes it was a place where children were educated and where neighbourly arguments came to blows or to be resolved.

St Martin's Church has ancient origins. Although there was no mention of it in the Domesday Book, the presence of Saxon masonry and an enclosure around the building suggests it may have been a tenth-century church foundation by Malmesbury Abbey, who owned Bremhill Manor, or an earlier Anglo-Saxon minster church.[402] According to Dr Simon Draper, it is likely that Malmesbury Abbey acquired Bremhill Manor, not from the king but from a thegn, a Saxon aristocrat. The thegn built a manor house and church within an enclosure which he gave to the abbey prior to 1066.[403] Under the care of Malmesbury Abbey, a weekly or monthly officiant was provided.

Malmesbury Abbey was in the unusual position of being under the direct control of the pope in Rome rather than the local bishop. As the centuries progressed, this became a source of irritation to the bishop of Salisbury, as he felt it undermined his local authority. Finally, in 1218, the pope ordered an examination of the issue. A compromise was agreed. Malmesbury retained its special status, but the bishop was compensated by receiving the manor of Highway and the patronage of churches at Bremhill and Highway and a chapel at Foxham.[404] This dates the original structure at Foxham to the early thirteenth century at the latest.

From this point on, the bishop of Salisbury could choose who became vicar of Bremhill. The vicar had responsibility for St Martin's at Bremhill, St John the Baptist Chapel at Foxham and St Peter's Church at Highway. The first recorded incumbent was Johannes Hackeneye in 1299.[405] We know very little about Hackeneye, but we do know what weekly provisions were provided for him in 1308. These included twenty-one loaves of bread, forty-two gallons of ale, six cartloads of hay, seven bushels of oats (for his horse) and two quarters of wheat. Rev. William Lisle Bowles thought the grant somewhat excessive. He quipped 'such a vicar might be considered the prototype of [Alexander] Pope's parson, "much bemus'd by beer"'.[406] The postholder, whether befuddled by beer or otherwise was a hugely influential figure in village life.

However, not all Bremhill vicars had a good reputation among their parishioners. One such was John Tounson or Townson.[407] Tounson was the son of a bishop of Salisbury, Robert Townson.[408] At his father's death in 1621, his uncle, John Davenant became the bishop.[409] John Tounson benefited from the family connection and was given the rich living of Bremhill in 1639. As his father appears to have been without a fortune and Tounson had fourteen siblings, the gift was a great personal boon. Unfortunately, during the English Civil War and interregnum (1642–60) 'by reason of his loyalties' the benefice of Bremhill was confiscated by parliament.[410] The loss of income and possible political exile seems to have had a permanent effect on Tounson when the living was eventually returned to him in 1660. He became irascible; prepared to defend his income and his rights as he saw them to the hilt. Perhaps it was unsurprising, the median income for Wiltshire clergymen in the late seventeenth century was a little over £80 whereas he earned £300 at Bremhill.[411] He had a parsonage, which he may have extended, land, barns, stabling at Bremhill and further property in Highway.[412]

Fig. 219: Bremhill Parsonage contains a 15th century core (or earlier) but is mainly 17th century with later additions.

However, Tounson pushed things too far. The churchwardens at Bremhill saw fit to mention to the bishop that their vicar grazed his cattle in the churchyard, likely it had caused some irritation.[413] But, Tounson became more than a source of annoyance to his parishioners, he became 'one of the most litigious clerics in Wiltshire', bringing lawsuits against nineteen Bremhill defendants for the non-payment of tithes, alone, in the period 1664–83.[414] Tithes were the local levy for the support of the clergy and an essential aspect of their income, perhaps excusable, but his lawsuits included ones against local elites including Sir George Hungerford, owner of Cadenham Manor. Tounson's persecution of the leader of local Quakers, Joane Hale, bordered on the obsessive.

Religious Persecution: The Suffering of Joane Hale

On Boxing Day 1649, the year in which King Charles I was executed following the upheaval of the Civil Wars, a marriage was recorded between a Joane Hayward and a David Hale.[415] Little is known before this time of the woman thereafter known as Joane Hale, who was to become not only a strong support to her Quaker husband during his years of persecution but also herself an actively committed and leading member of the Quaker community in Charlcutt.

In the decade following Joane's marriage, the couple became members of the growing Quaker movement. For Joane this time was characterised in part by domestic happiness with the growth of her own family. She was blessed with the birth of a daughter Edith in 1650, another daughter Margaret in 1652 and a son William in 1656. In 1660 twins David and Joane were born. Although the births of Edith and Margaret were recorded in parish registers, the births of William and subsequent children appear in Quaker records.[416]

Fig. 220: Engraving entitled *A Short Examination of the Spirit of Quakerism* designed to ridicule Quaker beliefs.

These early years of Joane's marriage, however, were also marked by the increasingly frequent persecution of the couple for their Quaker beliefs. In 1657 David was prosecuted by the then vicar of Bremhill, James Crump, for non-payment of tithes. Appearing before the Barons of the Exchequer, he refused to remove his hat and was sent to the Fleet Prison in London where he remained for two years. While he was there, the son of James Crump, a lawyer, broke a locked gate at Joane's house, took away a load of hay and, hammering on her door, swore that he would send her to prison too. He also threatened their neighbours to such an extent that they were afraid to help Joane cut or bring in the hay. Had it not been for the support of David's brother, the crop which 'was for the relieving of the Prisoner and his wife and children' would have been completely spoiled.[417]

Fig. 221: Print of a Quaker meeting.

In the 1660s things took a much darker turn for the Hale family, as they did for the whole Quaker movement. In 1662 David was again arrested and imprisoned. At the time of his arrest Joane must have been pregnant with Jane, their sixth child, born in 1663. David remained in prison and 'after three Years Confinement he finished his Testimony by Death.'[418] There is some mystery about how he died, with one reference to his death as being in the county jail 'under the hands of violence'.[419] David was buried in 1665 in the Quaker burial ground at East Tytherton. He died intestate and an inventory valued his possessions at £203 12s 8d, a not inconsiderable sum. A further blow struck Joane the following year with the death at the age of ten of her older son William, who was buried alongside his father.

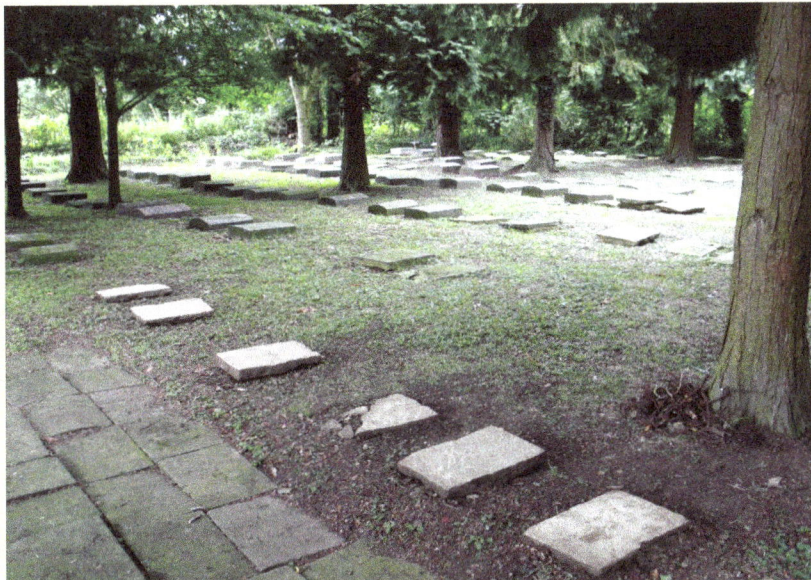

Fig. 222: Old Quaker burial ground in East Tytherton, restored in 2009.

Despite being a grieving widow with small children, Joane appeared to take on the role of her husband in fighting openly for her Quaker beliefs. In 1668 she had property seized for failure to swear an oath.

In 1669 she was fined for hosting a Quaker meeting and it seems that her house had now become the meeting house in Charlcutt.[420] In 1670 her life seems to have reached its lowest ebb when, at the instigation of the then priest, John Tounson, her possessions were confiscated for non-payment of tithes in a very punitive manner:

Anno 1670 Joane Hale, of Charlcutt, was profecuted at the Suit of John Townfon, Prieft of Brimhill, for Tithes of lefs than 6l. Value, and had taken from her on an Execution, four Cows, two Heifers, a Bull, and all her Houfhold Goods, not leaving a Bed for her Children to lie on, nor Bed-clothes to cover them. The Prieft, her Profecutor, a little before this Seizure, came to vifit her and her Fatherlefs Children, profefing much Love to them, and a great Care that they might not be wronged: But his Actions towards them did not correfpond with thofe Pretences. The poor Woman was fick of an Ague and Fever at the Time when they took away her Goods, which were but few, viz. two Beds, five Coverlets, three Bolfters, one Pillow, three Bolfter-Cafes, one Pillow-Cafe, a Bedfted, a Table-Cloth, a Pair of Curtains and Rods, three Blankets, one Pair of Fire-Irons, one Settle, fix Forms, two Table-Boards and Frames, one Brewing-Kettle, a Sack, a Pair of Fire-Dogs, two Joint-Stools, and a Pewter-Difh: They alfo took away fifteen Cheefes, and two Flitches of Bacon, provided for the Food of her Houfhold, and alfo a Gown and Petticoat, being Part of her wearing Apparel.

But Joane no doubt retained the support of her family and fellow Quakers and was not so easily defeated. Her name, together with those of other members of her family, continued to appear regularly in lists of participants at meetings. The persecutions did not stop and neither did Joane's suffering. In 1674 an official complaint was made against her for church absence and in 1681 her daughter Edith died, only three years after her marriage. In 1684 Joane was again fined for holding a meeting at her house, this time '20l for which eight Cows were taken from her'.[422] Two years later her son David died.

It was to be hoped that the Toleration Act of 1689, granting the Quakers religious freedom, would allow Joane a more peaceful life in her twilight years. Sadly, this was not to be. In 1694 she had ten cows and two heifers confiscated, to the value of £46, this time by the priest, John Wilson. Evidencing the frequency of these occurrences, she said the 'Priests demand was 35th for 7 Years Tythes'.[423] In 1696 Joane died intestate but comfortably off and was buried with her husband, son and daughter in the Quaker Burial Ground in East Tytherton. Her legacy is one of a strong woman, characterised by determination, self-sacrifice and complete loyalty to her faith.

Fig. 223: The modern section of the burial ground (post 1927).

In 1674, Rev. Tounson, complained to the bishop about his parishioners. His congregation had chosen a woman to be churchwarden. Worse still, Matthew Clarke had laughed at him and cocked his hat during service, and when he was ordered to be removed 'he shewed himself ye more irreverent; and aftersaid threatened, let any come to take off his hat be dared.'[424] These incidents reveal his congregation sometimes enjoyed baiting their minister. However, Tounson's reporting of those who did not attend communion to the church authorities did convince some to resume proper worship.[425]

Fig. 224: Modern image of St John the Baptist church at Foxham.

Tounson's most protracted legal action was over Foxham chapel.[426] St John the Baptist at Foxham presented a problem to local vicars; how to provide services at three places: Bremhill, Foxham and Highway. However, Highway had its own curate. Foxham residents wished for the same, but Tounson refused to pay for one, despite his sizeable income. The situation is somewhat confused, various gifts by the Bayntun family (who owned Bremhill Manor) and the Hungerfords at Cadenham had endowed the chapel. Tounson, therefore, argued that Foxham residents should arrange a minister themselves.[427] However, George Hungerford and local people believed otherwise. Neither would compromise. The legal action which began in 1666 was still ongoing at Tounson's death in the 1680s. On his death, Tounson pointedly left £5 to the church-going poor of Bremhill, provided they did not live in Foxham.[428] By then his reputation had been irrevocably damaged.

The livelihood of the vicar at Bremhill remained one of the richest in the county. In the early nineteenth century, the poet, Robert Southey remarked 'there are not many better livings, there are few more pleasantly situated.'[429] This made the position highly sought after.

Fig. 225: The worn memorial stone of Rev. Tounson in front of the altar in St Martin's, Bremhill.

One hundred years after Tounson's death, the minor poet and cleric Rev. Bowles was promised the post by John Moore, the archbishop of Canterbury. The agreement was apparently made with Bowles's mother because Moore had 'contracted obligations' with Bowles's grandfather. Unfortunately for Bowles, the incumbent vicar, Nathaniel Hume, lived on many years. Bowles was informed of his death in 1804 by the bishop of Salisbury. Bowles raced to Lambeth Palace to see the archbishop, but Moore's mental facilities were fading, and Bowles was obliged to repeat his mother's name, over and over, until the archbishop remembered his promise and made the arrangements.[430]

Fig. 226: Bremhill Parsonage from the *Beauties of Wiltshire* Vol.III.

Once in place at the parsonage, Bowles set about adding gothic embellishments to the house and garden, 'I am making quite a priory here' he wrote excitedly to another poet, Thomas Moore. He continued 'Gothic arches, turrets, pinnacles, &c. salute your arrival at Bremhill Parsonage.'[431] While the house and garden gained many plaudits over Bowles's tenure, Moore believed that, in the garden at least, Bowles 'had a good deal frittered away its beauty with grottos, hermitages and Shenstonian inscriptions'.[432] Much of Bowles's garden ornamentation has been removed. The Wiltshire commentator John Britton, another friend of Bowles, remarked, 'I wish it were in my power to compliment either the Parson or the Builder for the manifestation of either taste or judgement.'[433]

In 1836, Southey described to his daughter the eccentricities of the poet. These included a pet hawk, Peter, and two tamed swans, Lily and Snowdrop who tapped on the breakfast room window if their breakfast was served late. He continued:

Much as I had heard of Bowles's peculiarities, I should very imperfectly have understood his character if I had not passed some little time under his roof. He has indulged his natural timidity to a degree little short of insanity, yet he sees how ridiculous it makes him, and laughs himself at follies which nevertheless he is continually repeating. He is literally afraid of everything. His oddity, his untidyness, his simplicity, his benevolence, his fears, and his good nature, make him one of the most entertaining and extraordinary characters I ever met with. He is in his seventy-third year, and for that age is certainly a fine old man, in full possession of all his faculties, though so afraid of being deaf, when a slight cold affects his hearing, that he puts a watch to his ear twenty times in the course of the day. Our reception was as hospitable as possible, Mrs. Bowles was as kind as himself, and every thing was done to make us comfortable.[434]

Britton described Bowles as 'Devoid of guile, as harmless as the dimpled infant, as bland as affable as courtesy and kindness in union, he gained the love and excited the sympathy of all who knew him.'[435] Bowles was generous, and his work and that of his wife, Madeline, ensured many local children were educated. In 1836, it was reported in the press that he spent £400 a year on supporting charities.[436]

However, particularly on questions of poetry Bowles could also get very upset and express his feelings with 'pugnacity' in prose and a manner rather 'noisy, flippant and fierce'; something he did in a public spat with Lord Byron over the seemingly innocuous life and work of poet Alexander Pope.[437]

Perhaps it is no surprise that the relationship between Bowles and certain sections of the community were sometimes a little strained. Like Tounson before him, the issue of St John the Baptist at Foxham was problematic. In Bowles's mind the chapel was 'private property' and he was not obliged to officiate there.[438] He paid for the renovation of the chapel roof during the 1820s, but it was to encourage inhabitants to pay for the services of their own minister.[439] It did not work. In 1834, a news report appeared in the *Devizes and Wiltshire Gazette,* 'An additional place of worship... having been long wanted, for the benefit for a portion of the inhabitants at Bremhill, who lived at a distance from the parish church, it was anxiously wished that an ancient chapel [at Foxham] should be restored. The Rev. Canon Bowles... liberally contributed towards carrying the object into effect... The rector of Bremhill, with that Christian benevolence which distinguishes his whole life, also readily consented to provide for the duty of the chapel.'

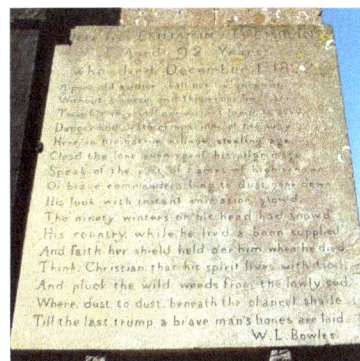

Fig. 227: Bowles wrote poems that were incised onto the markers and gravestones of deceased parishioners.

Fig. 228: The stained glass window of 1855 was formerly the east window of St Martin's, Bremhill.

The report went on to suggest that Lord Lansdowne had then been approached (the inference being by Bowles himself), and that Lansdowne 'immediately requested to be permitted to bear the whole of the remaining expenses himself, engaging to put the whole in a perfect state of repair'.[440] The report was a little odd, not least in the fact that the chapel had opened the previous summer. Its presentation of events was also skewed to shed Bowles in a favourable light. Indeed, it is likely that the report had come from Bowles himself. The people of Foxham did not stay silent. An anonymous local correspondent wrote to the paper pointing out that 'the inhabitants deserve some of the credit' and stating, 'it was they who commenced the subscription' and 'they, likewise who made the first application to the Noble Marquess'.[441] The paper, printed an almost apology admitting 'we omitted to state that the most respectable farmers, and nearly the whole of their poorer neighbours in that part of the parish, were first to subscribe.'[442]

Despite the questions over the circumstances of its renovation, the reopening of Foxham chapel was a grand affair attended by almost 1,000 people including 300 crowded into the building. The Marchioness of Lansdowne made a gift to the chapel of a bible, prayer book and cloths for the pulpit and communion table.[443] However, notwithstanding the improvements, within a few decades the building was deemed to have little architectural worth and the decision was taken to replace it. The new chapel was designed by William Butterfield, the gothic revival architect of Keble College, Oxford, and built between 1878–80 at the cost of £2,300. These were covered by subscriptions which included £850 from the Marquess of Lansdowne and £400 from the vicar of Bremhill, Edward Eddrup.[444] After the chapel was rebuilt and re-consecrated, regular services resumed.[445]

Fig. 229: St John the Baptist Church in Foxham designed by Gothic revival architect William Butterfield.

A Comfortable Benefice: Reverend Eddrup

Who might have imagined that a man like St Martin of Tours, whose shrine became an important stopping place on the road to Santiago de Compostela and considered the patron saint of France during the Third Republic, would be the patron of a church at Bremhill in rural England? He is the patron saint of beggars and wool-weavers and is known as a man full of consideration for others and who detested violence. These attributes have influenced the benefit of Bremhill as there have been many examples of long-serving rectors held in high esteem throughout the parish and diocese.

The impression is that during the nineteenth century, Bremhill Parish was held in considerable esteem by the Salisbury see and carried more importance than it does today. The congregations would have been larger than today, and entering Holy Orders was considered an acceptable route for gentlemen scholars. It may also have been because of links to the Lansdowne family at Bowood or, as it included at that time Foxham and Highway, it was a sizeable country parish, but it certainly attracted some able men.

One of these was Charles Harris, whose ministry lasted only five years, was a scholar from Oriel College, Oxford and a fellow of All Souls. He was appointed to Bremhill following time at Shaftesbury and Wilton. He became archdeacon of Wiltshire, but in 1868 was appointed bishop of Gibraltar, hence his leaving the parish. His obituary stated that 'he was singularly beloved, and his kindness of heart and his genial manner will long be remembered by the chaplains under his rule.'

This resulted in the appointment in 1868 of Edward Eddrup, who remained in the parish for thirty-seven years until his death in 1905. His family appeared in the 1881 census as one of the larger families in the village. There appears to have been nothing extraordinary about Edward Eddrup. He did not obtain high office, although he did become a canon, and didn't, as far as we know, write poetry, but he and his family did represent many typical features of Victorian life and attitudes, and it is interesting to see the development of a large family unit over time.

He was born in London, clearly into what might be described as an upper middle-class, or just upper-class, family who had wealth and society contacts. He graduated from Wadham College, Oxford and educated his sons at St Edward's School, Oxford and Keble College. In 1856 he married Helen Annette Campbell, aged twenty-one, daughter of Sir John Campbell, 2nd baronet.

Fig. 230: An interior photograph of Bremhill Parsonage at the turn of the century.

Clearly, this demonstrates he had means as it is doubtful that the Bremhill stipend would have been sufficient for such school and university fees, and his family had contacts with the gentry. This seems to mirror the idea that the sons of society families tended to choose either the army or church as a preferred profession.

The couple had nine children, six sons and three daughters, and the census returns show they could afford servants. Helen had nine children over sixteen years, with the last son born when she was thirty-eight. It is impossible to know if this child-bearing affected her health, but she died at the relatively early age of fifty-four and is buried in Bremhill.

Edward, Theodore and Ernest were seen as the more intelligent children as there are records of them at school (boarding) and university. Edward is listed in one census (1891) as 'schoolmaster', but in a later census, in London, he was listed as 'Gentleman'. Both Theodore and Ernest entered Holy Orders and then practised their ministries.

Herbert, in the 1881 census, was unmarried and aged nineteen. Later there are records of him arriving in Canada where he was resident in Montreal. It is difficult to trace his steps as the Canadian records were not easily available, but he did marry Jessie, and in 1902 and two years later, there are records of him as part of the crew on a cattle boat plying between Canada and Liverpool. He was listed as a 'cattleman'. He died in Ontario in 1943. Information on his brother Hermann has been more difficult to gather. He seems to have been an engineer or salesman of products in and around Yorkshire. He died in 1952. An interesting fact, revealed in the 1911 census, was that Hermann was listed as single but had a servant, Minnie Greig, living in his house. In 1937, they got married.

Both Lucy and Ela married and moved away from Bremhill and there is no record of their education or possible job, and one assumes they followed the pattern of their mother. The 1901 census paints a slightly sadder story, however. From a full house in 1891 with servants and nursemaid, there was now listed Rev. Charles and his eldest daughter Helen, rattling around the empty vicarage. Helen never married and spent her life, one must presume, caring for her father. Although only the two of them, they did keep, nevertheless, two maids and a cook – so perhaps she took on the role of lady of the house following her mother's death in 1889. She died in 1944 in Bournemouth, listed as living by her own means and leaving £15,000 to her brother Theodore. Charles Eddrup died in 1905 and is buried in Bremhill with his wife.

Fig. 231: The grave of Edward Eddrup in Bremhill churchyard who died in 1905.

Fig. 232: His wife Helen Eddrup died at the age of 54.

Society changed rapidly during the twentieth century. The clergy had also changed, Bremhill vicars were no longer waited on by servants. In 1952, the vicar Rev. Bradbury felt the parsonage 'far too large in size'.[446] Church attendance generally declined, but Rev. Bradbury still had a sizeable congregation at St Martin's at Christmas and Easter in 1958, when eighty-three people worshipped on Easter Sunday.[447] Both Bremhill churches had thriving Sunday schools. Circumstances at Highway, traditionally the responsibility of the Bremhill vicar, were different and St Peter's Church at Highway was converted into residential accommodation.[448]

In 1983, a new benefice was created of Bremhill with Foxham and Hilmarton.[449] From 2010, St Martin's, Bremhill and St John the Baptist, Foxham have been part of the Marden Vale benefice, along with Christ Church at Derry Hill and Holy Trinity and St Mary the Virgin at Calne and St Peter at Blackland.[450]

7.2 St Nicholas', Tytherton Lucas

The original churchyard wall is distinctly oval in shape, which indicates there might have been a Saxon settlement here before the current church building was created. The Domesday Survey of 1086 refers to land holdings in 'Terintone' or 'Tedelintone', which later became known as Tytherton Lucas.[451]

Fig. 233: An aeriel view of St Nicholas' Church highlighting the oval shape of the outer wall.

Fig. 234: The oldest church bell in Wiltshire?

Fig. 235: The 12th century tub-shaped stone font.

Fig. 236: The final resting place of Edward Stokes and his wife.

In about 1150, Empress Maud bestowed the tithes of Chippenham and Tytherton Lucas to the monastery of Monkton Farleigh (near Bradford-on-Avon). Hence St Nicholas' Church at Tytherton Lucas became annexed to St Andrew's Church at Chippenham, which continues to this day. There was a footpath across the fields and over the River Marden to and from St Andrew's Church. The vicar of St Andrew's was to provide a weekly service, 'unless prevented by the Rysing of the waters'.[452]

St Nicholas' Church is thought to have been built in the thirteenth century.[453] Some parts of the medieval chapel are still evident including: the rubble stone masonry; stone slate roof; a priest's door on the south side; a window on the east side with intersected lacery and hoodmold; the trefoil-cusped entrance and window on the north side; and an unusual squint to the left of the chancel arch. The long-waisted bell that hangs in an open cot is thought to be the oldest bell in Wiltshire. An inventory in 1553 records two bells. There may have been a smaller Sanctus bell in the small cote on the south gable.[454]

It is not uncommon for the font in a church to be the item of the greatest antiquity. The tub-shaped stone font at St Nicholas' is mid-twelfth century and decorated with characteristic Norman motifs: gabled arches and fluting. There is an anecdote that the font was removed from the church during the Civil War and used as a trough for farm animals, possibly explaining why the decoration has been chiselled away to create two bolt holes.

By 1650 the church was in a very poor state of repair, and it was eventually restored in 1802 through the generosity of Thomas Crook, a wealthy farmer who lived at Coggswell (the black and white timber-framed house built c.1600) and also farmed at Curricomb Farm.[455] He was renowned for his dairy cattle which he fed on steamed potatoes, and bred thoroughbred racehorses, including the progeny of Skyscraper who had won the 1789 Derby. The churchyard contains several listed tombstones, including members of the Crook family. The house adjacent to the churchyard dates back to 1600 and was part of the glebe (church property).[456]

Records indicate that it was only briefly used as a vicarage, as the vicar from St Andrew's, Chippenham, provided the weekly service. The house used to be called 'Stokes', presumably after the Stokes family who lived in Tytherton Lucas from about this time. Interestingly, in 1656, Edward Stokes hosted a Quaker meeting at 'his house' attended by 'several thousand'.[457] This must have caused tension with the Church of England, to which all inhabitants paid their tithes. There were a number of local Quakers from this time who are buried at East Tytherton, although Edward Stokes is buried here at St Nicholas' Church. This would indicate that, perhaps, he was just a Quaker sympathiser.

Fig. 237: St Nicholas' Church is reputed to be built in the 13th century.

7.3 Nonconformity

For several hundred years protestant dissenting, or Nonconformist sects, drew many residents away from the Church of England. By 1866, the local vicar believed three-fifths of the local population were attending local chapels.[458] This trend began in the mid-seventeenth century with the arrival of Quakerism.

Quakerism

Fig. 238: Engraving of a Quaker meeting.

Quaker teachings emphasised a direct relationship with God, rejected the sacraments, ordained ministers and set forms of worship, something which set them against the doctrine of the Church of England. They were persecuted, most often given fines for their non-attendance at church or failure to pay tithes. In Bremhill, Quakers were periodically hounded by the vicar.

Firstly, Rev. James Crump in the 1650s and then by the 'wicked' Rev. John Tounson from the 1660s to the 1680s, who according to testimony went as far as arranging for the cattle of a local Quaker to be kidnapped. Although their persecution abated on Tounson's death, a few more instances occurred until the mid-eighteenth century.[459] Their oppression was recorded at the time in the Wiltshire Friends Sufferings Book. The last to suffer for her faith, was probably 'Widow Abury of Bremhill' who was fined £10 in 1758 and forfeited several livestock and a large quantity of cheese.[460] However, there is evidence that local estate owners had some sympathy and were prepared to turn a blind eye to the activities of local Quakers, something which may have helped them ride out the harassment.[461]

In 1690, shortly after the passing of the Act of Toleration, which allowed Nonconformists freedom to worship, a Quaker meeting house was licensed at Charlcutt at the home of 'Joan Hall', probably Joane Hale who had been persecuted for decades.[462] The meeting house was administratively important within north Wiltshire. It provided a governing body to congregations in Bromham, Calne, Charlcutt, Devizes, Marlborough and Purton.[463]

However, by the first half of the eighteenth century, the position of local Quakerism had begun to be encroached. Methodist evangelists preached in the open air at Foxham during the 1740s, and a Moravian church was established in East Tytherton.[464] Quaker meetings continued but with diminishing numbers in attendance, so that by 1783, the new Bremhill vicar reported that the Quaker meeting house was disused and only three or four Quakers were left in the parish.[465]

Methodist and Baptist

John Wesley began preaching in the open-air in Bristol in 1739. Although at the time a Church of England minister and seeking to remain within the Anglican faith, Wesley and those who were inspired by him very often met with derision. Nonetheless, very quickly Wesleyan evangelists began to preach in Foxham, where a local Methodist society was soon formed.[466] Preachers such as Thomas Adams and John Cennick documented their activities, which were published and recounted their success and their struggles. Adams recorded a feast at Foxham in July 1742 where 'some who had never found our Saviour before, met with him'.[467] However, those hearing the preachers could find themselves 'very much disturbed' by local 'mobs' and 'daubed with water and dirt' or even knocked over.[468]

The first steward of the Foxham society was Richard Gotley, son of a local farmer, who had been brought up a Quaker. Gotley had seen Charles Wesley preach while on a visit to Bristol in 1739 and had met with John Cennick and his sister while they had stayed with his father in 1741. Inspired, Gotley had supported Cennick's local work while he was absent and was probably consequently chosen, despite his young age, as Foxham's local leader. He was, Cennick recorded, 'a real Christian and faithful brother'. Tragically, Gotley died in 1743 aged just twenty-one. Cennick darkly observed 'it was apparent that for some time before his sickness he had not kept up such a close communion with our Saviour as former days, and I believed the whole of his sickness and death was a chastisement.'[469]

Fig. 239: John Wesley, leader of the Methodist revival movement.

Fig. 240: John Cennick, Wesleyan evangelist.

Fig. 241: The first Methodist newspaper *The Watchman*. Copy dated 6 May, 1835, found in the rafters of Friday Street Farm.

After almost 100 years of local Methodists meeting in the open air or in homes and premises across the parish, a Wesleyan chapel was built at Spirthill in 1828.[470] The attendees did not confine themselves to religious worship; they were also politically active. Local Wesleyans petitioned parliament in 1831 for the abolition of slavery.

In the early 1840s, with acute distress among its congregation, a meeting was held by labourers 'for the purpose of stating their grievances and endeavouring to obtain information as to the cause of their distress'. Many expressed their particular suffering, but others voiced opinions against the aristocracy and established church.[471] The meeting was significant enough to be reported as far away as Scotland.[472]

Despite their differing views, by the nineteenth century relations between Nonconformists and those who followed the established Church of England were, on the surface at least, amicable. Nonconformists were no longer locally persecuted; however local religious leaders and ministers were not necessarily tolerant of each other.

Fig. 242: Wesleyan chapel built in Spirthill 1825, now a private residence.

Religious Intolerance:
The Agony of Ann Nichols

In 1816, a lady by the name of Ann Nichols became ill.[473] Ann was a Baptist but had worshipped at both Baptist meetings and at a local Anglican church (possibly due to the distance she had to walk to get to a chapel). As she became weaker, and fearing she was slipping away, her friends called on a Baptist minister to attend her. Minister Warburton did not know Ann, or if he did, not well, and on arriving at her cottage and despite her condition questioned her about the details of her worship.[474] On hearing of her attendance at church, Warburton offered no words of comfort and refused to pray with her, 'as Prayer could be of no use' or as he later told his flock because the Lord had 'stopped his mouth'.

Fig. 243: Engraving of a bedridden woman receiving visitors.

The implication was that by attending church, Ann had doomed herself. She became inconsolable. Seeing her great anguish, her friends called on Rev. Bowles to pray for her. Bowles, on hearing of her plight, and having a low opinion of 'false teachers', set about over a series of visits to both console Ann and bring about her conversion to the Church of England.[475] It is probable that he stopped Ann from receiving further visits from local Baptists, saying 'I thought it best that none of the gospel-disputers of the village should see her.' He also 'prayed for the conversion and repentance of the Baptist preacher', something which despite the clamour raised against Warburton by Bowles's publication of a pamphlet did not happen. According to this account, Ann was, through Bowles's ministration given comfort and she died back in the bosom of the Church of England.

The episode reveals the latent tension between Nonconformist sects and the Church of England. However, Ann was by no means the only one to be flexible about where she worshipped as evidence suggests local congregations often moved quite freely between the dissenting chapels and Church of England.[476] By the twentieth century, things had relaxed and in 1921 the Bremhill vicar, Rev. Arthur E.G. Peters, was even given leave to use Spirthill chapel for weeknight worship (albeit with the proviso it 'must not be used for the teaching of any doctrines or practices contrary to Methodist Standards').[477]

Fig. 244: Rev. William Lisle Bowles.

Fig. 245: Mormon Baptism involves full immersion in water.

Despite the establishment of Spirthill chapel a number of local dwellings continued to be licensed as meeting houses for those of dissenting faiths through to the 1840s. These included the cottage of Thomas Ponting for the Primitive Methodists at Bremhill and the home of Jonas Haddrell at Charlcutt. Both Thomas and Jonas were agricultural labourers. The most surprising of the establishments was the licencing of the premises of Richard Hatt, another Charlcutt labourer, as a place of worship for the Mormons, otherwise known as the Church of the Latter-Day Saints.[478] Its creation was influenced by a Wiltshire man, John Halliday, who had spent some time in America and returned an elder of the faith. Halliday's preaching was somewhat controversial. As were his assertions that he could cure disease by immersion in water or by the laying of hands.[479] Although only surviving a few decades, the Charlcutt Mormon chapel persisted until at least 1866.[480]

In 1855 Wesleyan Methodists built a second chapel at Foxham, and in 1865 another was constructed at Stanley. Both Spirthill and Foxham chapels were overseen by local boards of trustees who appointed the posts of treasurer and steward, responsible for the day-to-day organisation of the chapel and activities around it.[481] The life of these chapels was vibrant. In the late nineteenth century, they were involved in campaigns which supported abstinence from alcohol, particularly through the 'Band of Hope' movement which encouraged young people over the age of fourteen to sign pledges. These stated, 'I promise to Abstain from all Intoxicating Drinks as Beverages.' However, Foxham chapel in their support of the campaign, took things a little far by getting children as young as five to sign the pledge (or else it was signed on their behalf). Girls such as Nora Fanny Matthews and Ethel Evelyn Fry who 'signed' on 20 December 1896.[482] Ethel was to sign the pledge again ten years later at the age of fourteen. The chapels also ran Sunday schools and there was the regular celebration of anniversaries of their establishment and at harvest time. At Stanley, the chapel was linked to the Christian Endeavour youth movement which began in America during the 1880s.[483]

Fig. 246: Wesleyan chapel built in Foxham 1855, now a private residence.

Fig. 247: Members certificates were issued for the temperance organisation on signing the pledge.

However, as the twentieth century progressed, congregations started to dwindle. By the 1950s, Foxham chapel found people were coming from outside of the parish to worship.[484] In 1962, the Foxham trustees, only one of whom lived in Foxham, found that the chapel 'was in need of help'.[485] In 1977, many of the responsibilities of the chapel trustees at Spirthill were assimilated by the church council at Monkton Hill Methodist church, Chippenham, as the Spirthill brethren was deemed too small to have its own board.[486] It is likely that the Foxham board of trustees were likewise superseded, in reality, the trustees of Foxham chapel had already been meeting at Monkton Hill for many years before this date.[487]

From 1978, the Spirthill Property Committee which dealt with the maintenance of the fabric of the chapel was merged with that of Foxham.[488] In 1982, with diminishing numbers of congregants and the chapel requiring repair, the decision was taken for Spirthill chapel to close.[489] It was sold for £2,800 and converted for domestic use.[490] Chapels at Foxham and Stanley were also closed.

Fig. 248: Wesleyan Chapel built in Stanley, 1865.

Moravian Church, East Tytherton

The Moravians were born out of Eastern Europe in the sixteenth century and earlier and known as the *Unitas Fratum* (Unity of Brethren). Persecuted in Bohemia, Moravia and Saxony, they moved to England. Beginning with a visionary founder, the movement was the first major global missionary movement in the UK in the 1700s. It included a vision for women's education, health and was inclusive of all races and pacifists.

The Moravian settlement in East Tytherton began through the ministry of John Cennick. Cennick had started preaching with John Wesley. He then joined George Whitefield before committing himself to the Moravians in 1745, having purchased a property in East Tytherton 'in Faith that hereafter that it might be a Fold for the flock to assemble in', 'tho at this it was far out of the way'.[491]

After Wesley and Whitefield, Cennick was one of the most committed evangelists of his era, tirelessly preaching in Wiltshire and the north of Ireland until his early death. He recounted how he was sprayed with ditch water, had a blunderbuss fired so near to him that his face was blackened, had the box on which he was standing to preach kicked away, and more. Already he had conducted his first burial at East Tytherton, of the twenty-seven-year-old single woman, Elizabeth Pinnel, which had been made 'before my own Door' (of the settlement) on 11 March 1744.[492]

Fig. 249: John Cennick committed to the Moravians in 1745.

Fig. 250: The Moravian church in 1787. On the left is the 'Sisters House' (now Kellaways House) where a school opened in 1794.

At the Moravian community, a school for girls was founded in 1794 out of missionary zeal by the pioneering founding headteacher, Ann Grigg. The notes (below) were written by Ann's friend, Anna-Mary Browne, after Ann's death:[493]

at the request of many friends, she ventured, in reliance upon the Lord, to begin a boarding school for girls. This undertaking, though it had to encounter many difficulties in the beginning, was evidently attended with blessing and prosperity; so much that in the following year, a house for this purpose was erected and on June 11th 1794, she entered the same with eight or nine boarders which number was increased to fourteen before the end of the year.

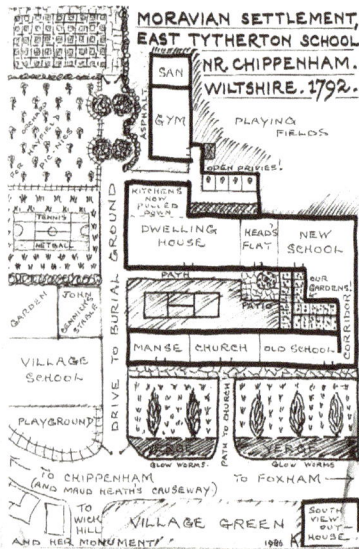

Fig. 251: Plan of the Moravian Settlement as it was in 1792.

The school had an ambitious curriculum, including music, geography, art, and languages. It was to be instrumental in the lives of many women, including Leonora Casey Carr.[494] Leonora was buried in the Moravian churchyard at East Tytherton and has one of very few gravestones of an enslaved (or ex-enslaved person) in the UK and the only known one in Wiltshire. Leonora joined the school at about twelve years old. She was to live in the Moravian settlement until her death at age twenty-eight (perhaps from tuberculosis) in 1837. When Leonora finished her education, she transferred to the single sisters' house, where she both worked (probably at needlework and lace-making) and enjoyed the support of the Moravians. She was evidently a committed Moravian, being formally 'received'. There was a feisty, rebellious or easily led streak there too, as she and others were hauled before the Moravian authorities for stealing provisions from the larder. Or perhaps they were just plain hungry, as life could be very frugal in the settlement. The minister's diary recorded that Leonora was suitably repentant.

Another student was Harriet Maynard, born in Paramaribo, the capital of Surinam. Her mother was Magdalena Martha Mijnhard, an enslaved woman, and her father an English cotton plantation manager and Amsterdam bank representative by the name of William Maynard.[495] Martha was a member of the Moravian church in Paramaribo.

This is what may have led to Harriet's journey to England, and eventually to East Tytherton, where she later became a student at the school. Sometime before 1854, Harriet was put on a boat for England, possibly travelling together with the Rev. Charles Lewis Schwartz, his wife, Maria Cornelia, and his sister Henrietta Mary, who were Moravians serving in Paramaribo, all of whom are buried in East Tytherton.

Harriet became a student at the prestigious Royal Female School of Art. She was listed as winning a prize for her work and later exhibited at a major exhibition (of 360 paintings, including the 'masters') in Hampshire, displaying her painting, *Chrysanthemums*, in 1882. Harriet left London and died in Launceston, Cornwall, from ovarian cancer, in 1906, possibly the first black female artist of slave origins in Cornwall.

In the twentieth century, one notable local Moravian was Rev. Walter Asboe, minister in East Tytherton from 1948–52. Three things exemplified his ministry: his pacifism, his missionary commitment, and less favourably, his well-intentioned destruction of the Moravian burial ground in East Tytherton. One resident of East Tytherton who knew the Rev. Asboe well was the late Joan Archard (née Bull), who had warm memories of him. However, it was clear that Rev. Asboe had entertained his plan of 'tidying up' for some time since it was reported that the groundsman, Edwin Bull, was completely hostile to the idea and that Rev. Asboe apparently dared not implement his intentions while Mr Bull was alive.[496] It is unlikely that Mr Bull would have been alone in feeling this way. What was Rev. Absoe's greatest strength may have proved his greatest weakness in the matter of the gravestones' removal.

He had a quite outstanding record as a missionary and was clearly strongly driven, single-minded, intelligent, and with lots of initiative and ideas. He was not a man to hang about if he could help it. Walter Asboe was nineteen years old when he started work as a stretcher-bearer on the Somme. When he arrived at Tytherton he was fifty-three. In this time, he must have seen a huge range of human suffering, trauma, and struggles in the face of major difficulties. At the same time, Walter was a man of powerful convictions that enabled him to persevere for twenty-seven years in Tibet.

Fig. 252: The gravestone of Leonora Casey Carr, the only known enslaved person to be buried in Wiltshire.

Fig. 253: Landscape painting attributed to Harriet Maynard.

CHAPTER EIGHT

Wars, Change
& The Parish Today

8.1 The Dawn of a New Age

Two years before Queen Victoria's Diamond Jubilee in 1897, the first meeting of the Bremhill parish council took place in January 1895, with the miller, Charles Pavy, installed as its chairman.[497] Symptomatic of the changing times, the new parish council had fewer powers than its predecessor, which were instead given to the more distant district council. Nonetheless, as it had for hundreds of years, discussion at the parish local government meetings reflected the worries and anxieties of the moment: the provision and upkeep of locks, bridges and roads, delivery of water supplies and the management of Maud Heath's Trust.[498]

However, probably the most pressing problem faced by the parish of the early twentieth century was insufficient housing for local people. The situation had led to delayed marriages and individuals and families moving away. As a further consequence, some cottages had become overcrowded.[499]

In 1910, the Bowood estate of the Marquess of Lansdowne, which still owned most of the modern parish of Bremhill, sold over 1,000 acres of land, farms and cottages in Foxham.[500] Lord Lansdowne had, according to newspaper reports, decided on the sale in order to increase the number of local landowners. Auction lots were intentionally of varying sizes; the stated hope was to encourage sitting tenants to purchase the property.[501] It was a considerable change; of the forty-seven cottages within Foxham village, thirty-five changed hands.[502] However, the sale appeared to do nothing to improve the supply of local housing stock, described as a 'public scandal' in a letter to the *Wiltshire Times*. Evictions began soon after the sale.[503]

Yet, the parish council, dominated by farmers, overruled the minority of councillors who were labourers and declared there was no necessity for further housing. Indeed, its chairman was worried that with the provision of more houses, 'they would have people coming from Chippenham and elsewhere'. Efforts by local labourers to circumvent the parish council and expedite a process to get more homes built came to nought.[504] The topic was widely discussed in the press. In November 1911, it was the subject of a local government board enquiry at Foxham School, possibly the result of intervention by the National Land and Home League. The League was a campaigning organisation concerned about the decline of traditional rural life as it saw it. At the meeting, the issue of the impending evictions of local men Robert Grimshaw and Alfred Fortune was discussed and drew the focus of attention.[505] Both had lived in their cottages many years, were good tenants, worked locally and had raised families, but both were being evicted to make way for new tenants by the new owner of the farm, Wiltshire County Council who had divided the property into smallholdings. Neither man could find alternative local accommodation.

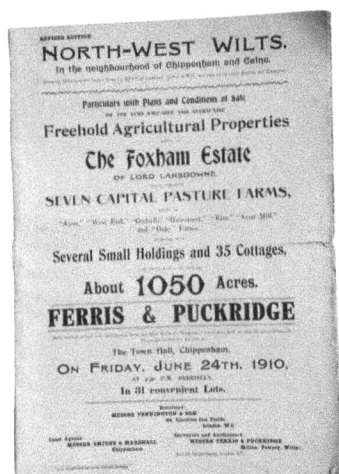

Fig. 254: The sale brochure of 'The Foxham Estate', 24 June 1910.

Fig. 255: (Previous page) Lady Lansdowne lays a wreath at the memorial dedication in November 1920 to the members of the community who lost their lives in The Great War.

Lord Fitzmaurice, brother of the Marquess of Lansdowne presented the circumstances at the enquiry as unfortunate, an unintended consequence of an otherwise successful move to broaden landownership. However, he also suggested that the county council could consider rehousing the men in newly built properties.[506] Local feeling ran high against both the rural district council and the parish council, undoubtedly helped by the testimony from twenty local labourers, all members of the National Land and Home League.[507] The subject brought to the fore centuries' old frustrations with low agricultural wages, rising rents and access to land.[508]

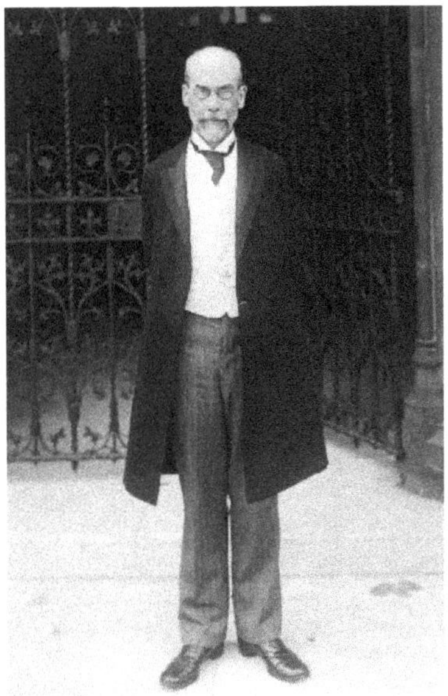

Fig. 256: Lord Fitzmaurice. brother of the Marquess of Lansdowne.

On 21 January 1912, as snow lay on the ground, and while Robert Grimshaw and Alfred Fortune were at work, their families were evicted from their cottages attended by five police officers, a bailiff and a council representative. Later a newspaper reporter arrived who described in detail the condition of the weeping women and distraught children. He candidly wrote 'pressmen at the many points at which they touch life are accustomed to witness strange scenes, but here was one indeed calculated to stir the feelings of anger against those who were the cause of it, and to move the heart to pity for the poor victims.' *The Wiltshire Times* pictures appeared under the headline 'Houseless and Homeless on a Cold Winter's Day'.[509]

However, despite the huge interest at the time, aside from the repair of a few cottages, the Grimshaw and Fortune families moving away and the judicious restoration of the Foxham reading room by Lord Fitzmaurice, the longer-term effects of the evictions, were muted.[510] Nonetheless, with two years remaining before the outbreak of World War I, it perhaps presaged the major changes which were to come.

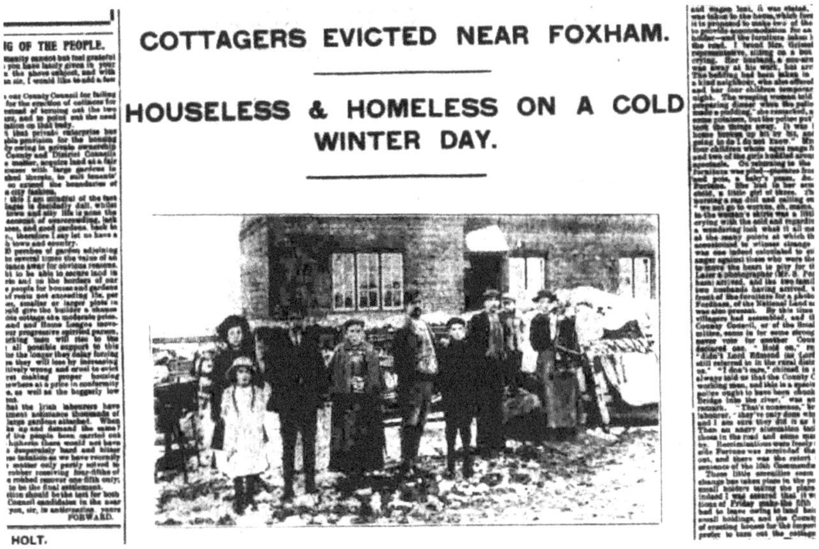

COTTAGERS EVICTED NEAR FOXHAM.

HOUSELESS & HOMELESS ON A COLD WINTER DAY.

HOLT.

Fig. 257: *Wiltshire Times and Trowbridge Advertiser*, January 1912.

Fig. 258: St Nicholas' Church, Tytherton Lucas.

8.2 Parish at War: World War I

The Heath Family at War and Peace

On 2 February 1890, Sidney Heath, a farm labourer from Sutton Benger, married Kate Knight from Tytherton Lucas at her local church, St Nicholas'.[511] Both were the children of farm labourers. On their marriage, they moved into a cottage in the village and their first child, a son named Frank, was born and baptised in October.

More children: Fred, John, Maurice and Charlie followed. Between the birth of Frank in 1890 and Charlie in 1900, the family lost one child. This may have been a pregnancy which ended in a miscarriage as there was no baptism or burial recorded at Tytherton Lucas, where the family celebrated baptisms and mourned the death of another baby, Edward Septimus. Edward lived just seven weeks and was interred 30 March 1901. Unusually it was marked in the parish register as a 'private' burial. The reason for Edward's death is unclear. The family may have been particularly religious, their last children were named for two of the three great Christian virtues: faith and hope.

The children would have attended school, probably at East Tytherton. There were complaints locally that children were taken out of education by their parents to help at harvest time or planting and it may have been the case with the Heath children. Certainly, as soon as the boys could earn a living, they joined their father in the fields. By 1911, four of them were working as farm labourers, including Maurice, aged fourteen. This brought more money into the household after lean years as the family had grown. We cannot know the Heath boys' aspirations or hopes for the future, but in 1914 the start of hostilities in Europe was to change the course of their lives.

Fig. 259: Hay making was a family affair.

Like many with a flush of excitement and optimism it would be over by Christmas, the Heath boys quickly joined up. Maurice was only seventeen when he enlisted with older brother Fred. The boys journeyed to Bristol and joined the Navy, on the same day, 9 September 1914. Their younger sister, Hope, aged just nine, also helped in the war effort. From 1914, she knitted garments for the British Red Cross, part of the Red Cross work party based in East Tytherton.

The enlistment papers of the Heath boys reveal they were both fresh-faced with hazel eyes and brown hair. Both gave their father, Sidney, as their next-of-kin. Tragically, they both perished during the hostilities. After serving on HMS *Venerable* on the Dardanelles and the Mediterranean, in 1915 and 1916, Maurice was reassigned to join the frontline in Flanders. He was killed on the first day of the 2nd Battle of Passchendaele. His name is on the Tyne Cot Memorial to the Missing, in Belgium, along with many thousands of others. Fred saw action on HMS *Britannia* which served in the Adriatic and Atlantic, he survived almost the whole war unscathed but died two days before the Armistice in 1918 when *Britannia* was sunk by a German torpedo off Cape Trafalgar.

Fig. 260: British Red Cross Society enamel brooch.

Fig. 261: HMS *Venerable*. London class. Pre-dreadnought battleship, built 1904-5.

Fig. 262: HMS *Britannia*. King Edward VII class, pre-dreadnought battleship, built 1904-6.

Maurice and Fred died with millions of that generation in World War I. After the war, John and Frank resumed their lives working on the land as farm carters until at least the late 1930s. The use of horses on local farms persisting at least until the 1940s. Frank stayed in Tytherton and married a local girl. The girls, Faith and Hope, married and moved to Chippenham. They became housewives, raised families, and remained in Chippenham until their deaths. Charlie became a labourer and lived with his sister, Hope, and her husband a painter and decorator. Their mother died in the 1930s and father, Sidney, married five years later in Swindon, where he retired.

While the role of men, such as Maurice and Fred Heath, who left their homes to join the military and made the ultimate sacrifice during World War I is better known, there were many ways in which the people of Bremhill parish supported the war effort. Local farmers were ordered to plough up and cultivate some grasslands and sow crops. In this way, by September 1917, Francis Freegard at Bencroft had ploughed over six of his 113 acres to help raise food production.[512] Householders followed, so that a month later the parish council were able to inform the county council there were no uncultivated gardens or allotments within the parish.[513]

Concerts and fundraising took place to support the work of the local Red Cross. In February 1916, the 'class of sewing girls' at Foxham School organised a concert that raised £4.[514] In April at the Moravian Girls School, another audience enjoyed performances that included 'Land of Hope and Glory', several pianoforte duets, a dialogue from Shakespeare's *Henry V* and 'a display of dumb-bell exercises to music by five girls'.[515] There were food collections at Foxham, East Tytherton and Tytherton Lucas, possibly weekly, to provide fresh produce to the Red Cross Hospital at Chippenham. Many contributions were made by women, some of whom like Myra and Fanny Ferris, who also volunteered locally for the Red Cross.[516] Minnie Shipp of Cadenham Manor, a head cook at the Chippenham hospital, often donated food items. These included poultry, greens and asparagus, although her contributions also included newspapers and dishes.[517] Minnie made the Red Cross roll of honourable service at the end of the war and was mentioned twice in dispatches (working 5,088 hours for no pay throughout the war). Minnie's daughters, Ivy and Vera, also worked in the hospital kitchen, although Vera later became a nurse. Husband, Edgar, as the representative of the Board of Agriculture, was active in local politics and often at the tribunals to decide the cases of men who appealed against conscription into the army.[518]

Fig. 263: British Red Cross War Service medal, 1914-18.

Fig. 264: Interior of Chippenham Town Hall War Hospital 1915.

The men of Bremhill parish were predominately employed in agriculture, so once men began to be mobilised into military service, their scarcity was quickly felt in the sector. Unsurprisingly, in some cases, families and employers appealed for a military exemption to keep individuals at home to help maintain the highly important task of feeding the nation. These included James Eyles of Bremhill who in 1916 appealed for a military exemption for his son who was a ploughman and milkman.[519]

Fig. 265: Sarah Pegler with family in the early 1900s.

In April 1916, Robert Pegler was granted an absolute military exemption as the only able-bodied man working on the 240-acre family-owned Elm Farm.[520] His mother, 'Widow' Sarah, purchased the farm in 1910 from the Bowood estate. Sarah was a formidable woman, disqualified due to her sex from bidding at the estate auction in 1910; she had used Edgar Shipp from Cadenham Manor as a proxy bidder to help her secure the property.[521]

Perhaps coincidentally, Edgar was among those officiating at the tribunal which granted the exemption to her son, Robert, despite the fact three other men were working on the farm (but who, due to sciatica, fits and having only one hand, were not deemed at the time able-bodied). However, Robert's exemption was given only temporarily as the military later appealed it on the grounds 'that Mrs Pegler is a most capable woman and that this man can well be spared'.[522]

It was not just farmers' sons who were the subject of appeals against going to war. Thomas Broomfield, whose father was a baker at East Tytherton, was not given an exemption. His father was deemed to be able to carry on the trade without Thomas's assistance.[523]

Fig. 266: Elm Farm, Foxham in the early 1900s.

Fig. 267: Elsie Minty c.1916.

Fig. 268: John Minty, farmer at East Tytherton.

Fig. 269: The Minty family's farmhouse at Friday Street, East Tytherton.

Fig. 270: Caricature of William Palmer, 2nd Earl of Selborne (1859-1942).

Other groups in the community were encouraged to fill gaps in the workforce left by working-age men. John Pointing of the Dumb Post Inn was told at a military tribunal that he was not exempt from the army because his wife could take over their smallholding.[524] The vicar Rev. G. E. Long was told to find a woman to drive his short-sighted curate to services after he tried to appeal against his groom's military mobilisation.[525] At her son's tribunal, Sarah Pegler, aged sixty-one, had clearly been expected to get more involved working on the family farm but had responded by saying, 'you cannot expect me to do so much as I used to do' and suggesting she might have to sell the farm as a result. Instead, the tribunal proposed her son could be replaced by 'an older man'.[526] Charles Smith, of Hazeland Farm, was advised to employ a boy to replace his carter after he was unable to find a suitable replacement. The implications of a labour shortfall for agriculture were serious during a period when the country needed to increase production. Worryingly, farmers such as Charles sometimes complained they were behind on work.[527]

However, the mobilisation of women into the agricultural labour force proved difficult. In December 1916, farmer's daughter Elsie Minty, milked the cows and looked after the poultry on her father's farm at East Tytherton, but with her brothers joining the army, Elsie's father, John, could not get other local women to work for him.[528] (He was, tragically, to lose a son, and another was wounded.)[529] There was undoubtedly some ambivalence over women working. In 1916, Lord Selborne, President of the Board of Agriculture, visited Devizes and probably reflected the views of many by both encouraging women to work in food production while adding he 'had no wish that women should compete with men'. He would 'regard such competition as social calamity'.[530]

Women's Work in Wartime

From August 1914, when Britain declared war on Germany, the patriotic women of Bremhill were quick to mobilise in support of the war effort.[531] At Barn Bridge in East Tytherton, Alice Collett set up a British Red Cross hospital homework party (no. 4933) from November 1914. Alice had been a nurse herself but had lost her leg after a bad infection. She supervised ladies to support the Red Cross not by nursing, but by knitting and making garments for the auxiliary hospitals either at Bowood House or Chippenham; where a hospital was established in the Neeld and Town Halls.

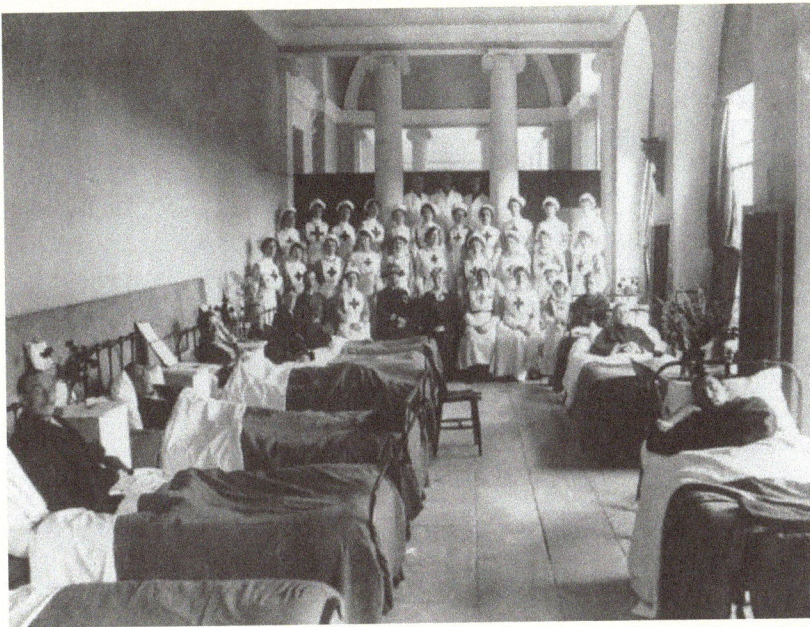

Fig. 271: Lady Lansdowne with nursing staff in the auxillary hospital at Bowood.

Alice was supported by her female relatives, Olive and Lucie, and many other community residents, mainly from East Tytherton and Tytherton Lucas. The women included farmer's wife, Emma Brewer, in her seventies who knitted part-time and Isabel Flora Whittle, a labourer's wife in her forties, who made garments alongside her mother-in-law Mary Ann. Another helper was Emily Strange in her twenties and likely to have been locally employed as a domestic servant. Lily Brewer and Edith Newman were only about eleven when they first provided part-time support by knitting for the war effort. Edith worked alongside her mother.

The no. 4933 homework party was not the only way local women worked to support the war effort. Fanny (or Annie) Ferris of Bosmere Farm joined the Red Cross at sixteen in 1913; she later became a probationer nurse at the hospital created by Lady Lansdowne at Bowood House. In 1915, Fanny transferred to the Chippenham hospital at its opening.

Fig. 272: Maud Petty - Fitzmaurice, Marchioness of Lansdowne, 1904.

She later became a staff nurse, tending men who were convalescing from injuries which had been treated at the military hospitals, such as Bristol Royal Infirmary and Southmead Hospital. She worked 5,184 hours over five years and received an award for honourable service from the division's vice-president, Lady Margaret Spicer.[532]

Fanny worked alongside other parish residents at Chippenham including: Clara, Eva May and Lily Rose Bryant of the Beeches, Tytherton Lucas, who worked as mess room workers and East Tytherton girl, Frances Marion Jefferys who cleaned the wards.[533] Towards the end of the war, the group were joined by Bertha Lewis of Jays Farm at Stanley whose duties were 'mending'.

Despite Fanny working at Bowood Hospital, there was surprisingly no significant presence of local women either among the volunteers or paid staff there. Nor were local collections of food or fundraising efforts directed towards the hospital. The Lansdowne family of Bowood House still owned much of Bremhill parish. The hospital's organisation was largely down to Lady Lansdowne, and its operation stood slightly outside the organisation of the other local hospitals of the Red Cross. Whether the connection to the Lansdowne family put off local women or the opportunity to work or support its operation was not available to them is difficult to say.

The local women of the Red Cross generally did not receive any payment for their services.[534] However, there were also opportunities for women to do paid war work. Once men began to be mobilised, women were increasingly encouraged to work on the land. In support of this there was planning for a women's 'land army'.

By the end of the war, the Wiltshire Agriculture Executive Committee reckoned 600 women had been mobilised into the land army within the county.[535] There were also several thousand more 'village women workers on the land'. [536] Unfortunately, there is no central list of those who joined the World War I land army or of those locally recruited. However, it is credible, especially given the considerable work done voluntarily by women in support of the Red Cross that many also worked on local farms through the war.

There was other paid war work available to women. The most significant was at the railway signalling works of Saxby and Farmer (later Westinghouse) at Chippenham, which was given over to munitions production during the war.

Fig. 273: Saxby & Farmer publicity card in 1911.

The research already undertaken suggests that the women employed at the factory came from Chippenham; thus, there is currently little evidence that the women of Bremhill parish were involved in munitions work. However, the children of Bremhill School were used during the war to gather acorns to produce cordite for munitions manufacture.

The war ended in November 1918. At a ceremony to mark the end of hostilities, one of the Red Cross medical officers in Chippenham, Dr Wilson, paid homage to the volunteers who had supported the hospital. 'The work in the early days of the war might have been regarded by some as mainly an amusement, but for four and half years it had involved continuous hard work, often carried out at great sacrifice, and those who performed this strenuous hard work were deserving of their most hearty thanks.'[537]

Many of the women who supported the war effort continued to do so for months after the war ended. Nurse (Gertrude) Ellen Griffin had been a dressmaker at Stanley before the outbreak of hostilities. She became a Red Cross nurse and served at Bath War Hospital from 1917 until February 1919.[538]

Lily-Rose Bryant worked at the hospital in Chippenham until April 1919. There, the hospital had continued to operate to look after returning soldiers, much to the reluctance of Chippenham Borough Council who wanted their town hall back. Even later, in July 1919, Bremhill resident Elizabeth Smith was still working as a charwoman in another military hospital at Calne.

However, there was an expectation that women would resume their more traditional roles at the end of hostilities and many local women seem to have acquiesced. Nurses Fanny Ferris and Ellen Griffin married soon after the war. In 1939, both were undertaking 'unpaid domestic duties'. Ellen's husband was Robert Broomfield, a grocer in East Tytherton.

Nonetheless, a few women who volunteered in the Red Cross's local division developed their medical training, and some decided to emigrate. Vera Shipp of Cadenham Manor had been a nurse at the Red Cross hospital in Chippenham until April 1919. In September, Vera boarded a ship bound for Singapore. On the passenger list were several other seemingly unaccompanied single women, who, like Vera, had recently been working at Red Cross hospitals across the country and were headed to the same destination, Malaya. It is possible that Vera was thus continuing her journey begun with her war work and starting a role nursing abroad.

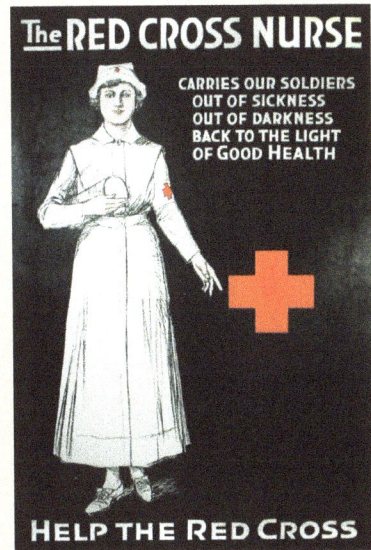

Fig. 274: British Red Cross advertising poster, WWI.

Fig. 275: Nursing staff at the Bath War Hospital, 1917.

Fig. 276: Red Cross nurses posed in front of the original fountain at the recreational ground, Calne.

8.3 The Interwar Years

Celebrations to mark peace at the end of World War I took place in August 1919. Many of the returning soldiers had brought home war trophies.[539] In December 1919, there were plans to display them, but one month later, the parish council, possibly concerned by the danger many of these items posed, instead sought how to dispose of them safely.[540]

Another urgent concern for the parish council was housing provision (again) for the working class.[541] Despite problems the lack of housing had caused in Foxham before the war, only five cottages had been erected between 1911 and 1917. A further nine had been demolished.[542] In 1919, the parish council suggested twenty-two new properties were required across the villages of Bremhill, but the following year, possibly influenced by a major sell-off by the Bowood estate, the council scaled back its assessment.[543] The Bowood sale benefited some local families. Alfie Holder recalls how his grandparents, Alfred and Emily Salter, bought 54 Wick Hill in the sell-off for £200. They raised ten children there, and after 100 years, it remains in the family's ownership.[544] However, during the interwar period the local population continued to shrink, and the housing issue remained, to be broached again and again through the 1920s and 30s, albeit not with the ferocity that the issue had raised at pre-war Foxham.[545]

While the population was contracting, community life was rich. Retail was thriving. The Fry family bakery had been established in Bremhill in 1875, but there was now another bakery in East Tytherton, and further grocers, shops and even a bootmaker throughout the parish.[546]

Fig. 277: Cartoon entitled *Un-perfect peace* by Fred Buchanan.

Fig. 278: Provis Grocery and Drapery Store pre-1920.

Fig. 279: Fry family bakery established in 1875, Bremhill.

It was an era of great social change nationally. While insulated from some of the effects, probably due to its rural location, these changes had repercussions locally. A new village hall was erected at East Tytherton in 1924, not due to the largesse of the Lansdowne estate, but rather the efforts of local people over a number of years.[547] By contrast, the membership of local reading rooms (which had been built and sponsored by the Lansdowne family) was falling. There were new organisations, such as the Women's Institute, a social club and a working men's and women's club.[548] Some of these had a political edge, possibly reflecting the extension of the voting franchise after the war. The temperance movement was popular for a while too.[549] But, the influence of religion was loosening with diminishing chapel and church attendance.[550]

Fig. 280: East Tytherton Village Hall built on the site of the old village pond in 1924.

Fig. 281: Mothers Union outing to Cliveden on the River Thames.

Fig. 282: Hatts Coach outing to Southsea in 1938.

Fig. 283: Dancing display at a Foxham fete.

Local farming was beginning to be more mechanised. The Peglers, at Elm Farm, were early adopters of the latest technological advances. The family bought their first tractor in 1917 or 1918, the newly introduced Fordson Model F, although horses were still used on the farm up to the late 1950s. The family also had an early Chevrolet car with wooden wheel spokes. The main produce of the farm was livestock and cheese, while the milk from their Dairy Shorthorns was taken to Dauntsey train station or Wootton Bassett to go to London.[551] Dairy farming remained important across the parish, and reflecting the possibilities of the time, one East Tytherton resident, Walter Pocock, was to become influential during the interwar period in its organisation nationwide through his association with United Dairies.[552]

Walter Pocock started life as a farm boy. He then became a milkman, courting his future wife, Emily, in Kellaways, while on his rounds. Walter was later a founder of the dairy business Long and Pocock, which became incorporated with United Dairies during World War I. He became the managing director of United Dairies, a highly successful distributor and manufacturer of dairy products that pioneered the sale of pasteurised milk.[553]

Fig. 284: Fordson Model F, the first tractor at Elm Farm.

Fig. 285: Wiltshire United Dairies milk float.

Fig. 286: Walter Dunsdon Pocock (1879-1939) with his wife and three of his children.

Fig. 287: Exhibition stand promoting the quality of Wiltshire milk.

The company later became Unigate and, more recently, Dairy Crest. Walter died in 1939 and is interred at the Moravian churchyard at East Tytherton. The minister described him in his eulogy: 'God made his physique big, and this was symbolic of his big faith, his big heart, his big generosity, and his great service.' Walter's great nephew, Nigel, describes how his uncle enjoyed driving through the village in a selection of luxury cars, one of which, his Bentley had to have its floor reinforced.[554] However, while the interwar period suggested change and opportunity, by the mid-1930s the possibility of another war was increasingly apparent.

8.4 The Parish at War: World War II

Planning for the outbreak of hostilities of World War II started early in Bremhill. In February 1937, the parish council made enquiries about the air raid warning system at Calne and Chippenham and a speaker was sought 'to give an address to a general meeting at the hall in East Tytherton on air raid and gas defence'. Later in the month, Mr R. L. Baker was elected to form a committee to further gas and air raid precautions.[555] Efforts redoubled in the early days of the war. The threat from air raids and even invasion meant one of the first concerns locally was how to accommodate fatal casualties. After the use of the forge or village hall at East Tytherton was initially discussed, the vicar, Rev. Payne, agreed to become superintendent of a mortuary and to use the vicarage stables as a temporary morgue (utilising Mr Vines's barn if required). When Rev. Payne retired in 1942, his replacement agreed to do the same.[556]

In 1939, local school managers were informed that, in the event of a national emergency arising, various measures would at once come into force, such as the immediate closure of all schools pending further instructions, the suspension of the use of lights in the schools, or alternatively the provision of effective screening arrangements.[557] Furthermore, in the event of the arrival of evacuated children in Wiltshire, schools were asked to cooperate with the Local Education Committee to use their premises as receiving centres and make arrangements for their schools to be used to continue the education of evacuees, perhaps by a double-shift system. It was also suggested that steps were needed to be taken to find shelter for the children in the event of air raids

By September 1939, four evacuees were on the school roll at Bremhill, although none under the Government Evacuation Scheme. The following year, five further evacuees were admitted during June, with three more during July from London. Around twenty-five attended the school over the duration of the war, but most children only stayed for a period of months. Indeed, of the first four evacuees, two, Leonard Williams and Patricia Blythe went home the month after they had arrived. Children stayed with local families such as at Hazeland Farm, the Dumb Post and even at the Bremhill schoolhouse, presumably with headteacher Daisy Pickett.

School holidays were adapted to allow children to work on the land. Land Cultivation Orders were in place as they had been during the previous war and much local pasture was ploughed up and planted with winter wheat and other cereals. Rex Grimshaw whose family moved to the parish just before the war recalled how several bombs were dropped nearby by bomber planes flying back from raids over Bristol and dumping their payload on the way home.[558] Four of them never exploded, including one near the road in his current [2013] front garden at Catbrook House.

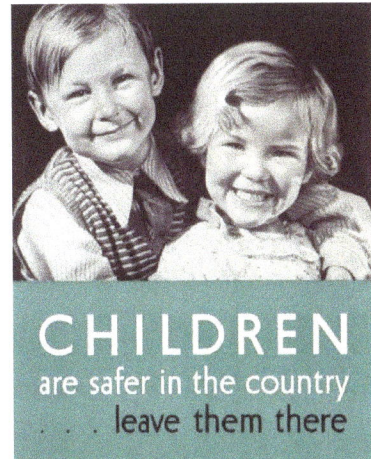

Fig. 288: In January 1940 bombing raids had not materialised so some children were brought home from the countryside resulting in reactionary publicity.

Fig. 289: Evacuee poster 1940 issued by the Ministry of Health.

Fig. 290: Rex Grimshaw outside Catbrook House, Tytherton Lucas.

An oil bomb landed in the lake at what is now Cherry Tree Farm. One day coming back from school, Rex remembered how he and his friends had to take cover in a ditch as a bomber flew low overhead. Later, he heard that it had been shot down near Salisbury. There was a searchlight and half a dozen soldiers stationed in his father's field at Tytherton Lucas. The searchlight was used to look for enemy planes, and Rex remembered how he and his friends played at swinging it around.

Despite the excitement of local children, in some senses, community life continued as it had before with whist drives, summer fêtes and garden parties at the vicarage. However, these now raised funds to help with the war effort. In June 1943, the vicar was able to report that all the money for blacking out the school had been raised from the proceeds of whist drives.

Fig. 291: Mobile searchlight looking for enemy planes at night.

Fig. 292: Garden party at the Old Vicarage (Bremhill Court).

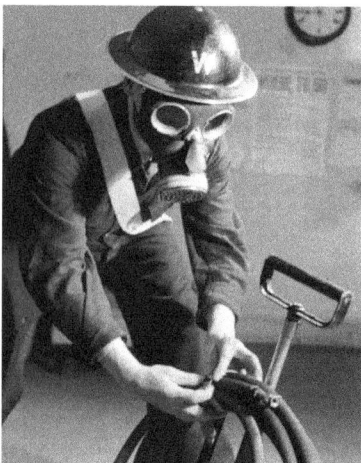

Fig. 293: Fire drill in the event of an invasion or an air-raid.

By 1941, invasion committees were being set up across Wiltshire, encouraged by the Ministry of Home Security, to provide local plans on what to do in the event of an invasion. In Bremhill, the plan's organisation was centred on East Tytherton.[559] It was here that the main depots of food and clothes and rest house were to be kept. The position of the settlement within the parish may have facilitated the decision - it was easier to transport goods and people on the main road from Chippenham than to tackle the hill up to Bremhill. There was also the bonus of having a Moravian church and East Tytherton school and village hall, which all provided readily available accommodation. In addition, there was also a police station with a police constable situated at the settlement. The constable had the only priority phone in the area that would be kept operative in the moment of invasion or indeed other crisis. All others were planned to be switched off at the exchange to prevent misuse of information. Possibly reflected by the need to join up efforts, parish council meetings were also increasingly held at East Tytherton, although they were made difficult by blackout arrangements.

The involvement of the Moravian church was emphasised as the chairman of the invasion committee was C. H. Shawe, a Moravian church bishop. A distinct gender division of labour persisted in the distribution of the tasks. Women were allocated food, clothes, rest centre, salvage collection and first aid while the men were messengers, wardens, Home Guards and fire watchers. The local plan contained little indication of the age of the men, but it would be reasonable to suppose thirty years plus, as many of those younger may well have enlisted. One comment under the heading of emergency labour suggested that some volunteers 'maybe old offering limited services, so less can be expected of them'.

There were allocated first-aid contact points, situated in the East Tytherton church room, the Charlcutt Institute [reading room], the Foxham reading room and the Bremhill vicarage, staffed by women and with a named person in charge, plus a doctor-on-call who came from Seagry. These were basic treatment points with two stretchers, blankets and a small amount of medicine, disinfectant and dressings. The instructions stated to treat those with minor injuries, but for anything more serious, the casualty had to be sent to hospital. Those in Tytherton and Foxham went to Chippenham and those from Bremhill were taken to Calne. Transport was to be by summoning an ambulance, but if unavailable then by car and, as a last resort, cart 'with straw litter'.

The main food depot was in East Tytherton, but with subsidiary ones in Bremhill, Foxham and Charlcutt and Spirthill. Control of the depots was under a food organiser, but each area was responsible for local distribution. The rest centre was based around the Moravian church and was open to anyone needing some form of sustenance. However, its main objective was to house any 'stragglers' who arrived in the village and to accommodate refugees who, the instruction stated 'are not meant to exist'. The local plan also stipulated, 'Our own people should be prevented from leaving – less likely if they are well occupied', although no indication is given as to how they should be so 'occupied'.

In the rest centre, there was strict segregation of the sexes, with men and boys in the village school, women and girls in the Moravian school gymnasium. The East Tytherton village hall was the (mixed) dining room. There was total provision for seventy people. If the need arose for the billeting of troops, however, East Tytherton offered to receive fifteen and Foxham a further twelve.

In the event of an invasion, the plan instructed people in the parish not to be openly aggressive: 'Do not have a shot at the enemy. Leave it to the Home Guard and the Military.' The advice continued, 'If asked by the enemy to provide labour or information, give as little as possible. Hide some, but not all, of your food.' Despite the recommendation not to shoot at the enemy, the plan also suggested 'each house is responsible for its own protection.'

Fig. 294: Chairman of the invasion committee at East Tytherton, Clarence Shaw.

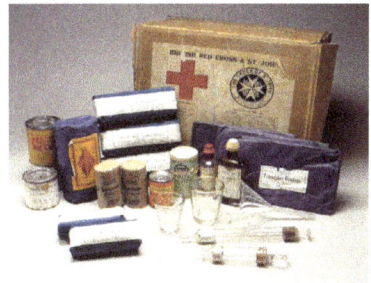

Fig. 295: British Red Cross medical kit.

The Home Guard

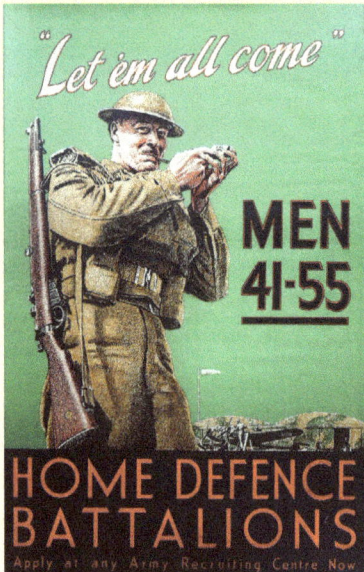

Fig. 296: Home defence volunteer poster appealing for part-time soldiers.

Fig. 297: The badge of the 1st Battalion Wiltshire Regiment, Bremhill.

On 14 May 1940, Secretary of State for War Anthony Eden, made an urgent appeal on the Home Service radio to all men aged between seventeen and sixty-five.[560] He wanted all those not already serving in the armed forces to become part-time soldiers, called Local Defence Volunteers (LDV). In Bremhill parish, men were quick to volunteer in all of the villages. Nationally within twenty-four hours of the radio broadcast, a quarter of a million men had volunteered. In the summer of 1940, Prime Minister Winston Churchill gave a speech where he suggested the name of the LDV be changed to the Home Guard. His speech was instrumental in encouraging more men to join. By the end of July, the number who had volunteered had risen to over 1.4 million, far more than ever anticipated by the government. These local volunteers came from all walks of life. In the parish, there were those already in full-time work, mainly farm workers but others such as clerks and machinists. Some had already volunteered to become air raid wardens or first aiders.

After the fall of Dunkirk on 5 June 1940, the German Blitzkrieg turned south and swept across France. Less than three weeks later, on 22 June 1940, France surrendered. Great Britain then stood alone. The British Army had sustained huge losses. Although over 350,000 men of the British Expeditionary Force escaped back to the British Isles, they left enough equipment behind on the beaches to equip ten divisions of the army. It was one of the reasons the British Army was in no condition to defend the country from the inevitable German invasion. The newly formed local defence force (Home Guard) was now seen as a vital part of the defence of the British Isles.

A meeting was held at the offices of Wood and Awdry in Chippenham attended by many retired military personnel, and a structure was agreed for the local volunteers. As a result, the parish became a part of the H Company of the 1st Battalion Wiltshire Regiment. H Company consisted of five platoons: Bremhill; Tytherton and Spirthill; Foxham; Christian Malford and Sutton Benger and Draycot. H Company was under the control of Major M. S. D. Day and supported at HQ level by Captain Gold and Captain Dr W. G. Ayes, a local GP, as a medical officer.

The three platoons in the Bremhill parish (Bremhill, Tytherton and Foxham) were led by platoon commanders generally with previous military experience. It exceeded 120 men. In Bremhill, the platoon commander was Lt. Clive Hillier – a local farmer who had seen service in World War I. The platoon leadership in Tytherton was initially under Lt. Sancroft Baker and later Lt. Fuller Birtill, again an ex-World War I soldier.

Fig. 298: Bremhill platoon at Field Farm, Bremhill, home of the platoon commander Lt. Clive Hillier.

Fig. 299: Tytherton platoon under the command of ex- army officer Lt. Sancroft Baker.

Fig. 300: Lt. Fuller Escourt Birthill, 2nd platoon leader (post 1942) of the Foxham HG.

Fig. 301: Lt. Clive Hillier holding the cup for best platoon using a Smith gun.

Fig. 302: Vivian Pegler, local farmer and Foxham platoon leader.

Fig. 303: The Smith gun designed as an anti-tank weapon that could be pulled behind a car.

Fig. 304: Matthew (Tat) Portch in Foxham, dressed ready for action.

Fig. 305: Spent .303 cartridge cases found at Spirthill.

Fuller Birtill had spent much of his youth at East Tytherton, where his father had been the Moravian minister, so he knew the parish well. At the outbreak of war, Fuller, by now a Moravian minister, was in Canada but quickly returned to England. Early in the war, there was concern that the archives of the Moravian church held in the church offices in Muswell Hill, London, would be in danger of being destroyed by enemy action. The Moravian school in Tytherton had closed in 1938, and Fuller was put in charge of arranging for the archives to be moved from London to Tytherton and held in safety in the old school.

After Dunkirk, there were only sufficient weapons and ammunition in the country to equip two regular army divisions. As a result, weapons and ammunition for the Home Guard were in very short supply. Only 40 per cent of the men who joined were equipped with rifles. So, the Home Guard had to improvise. The message was simple – if you owned it and it could be used as an offensive weapon, it was accepted, from pitch forks to old Boer war rifles. Improvised weapons also became the norm. These ranged from petrol bombs, glass bottles filled with petrol and a piece of rag in the neck which was lit and thrown at the advancing enemy or inside a tank. Later weapons were made locally, such as the Smith Gun, a mobile gun that could be towed to its firing location by a domestic car and then turned on its side to fire small shells. The late Brigadier George Powell, who joined the Home Guard as a young man reported that the Smith Gun probably killed more Home Guard men than German soldiers as the barrel was likely to explode. Within eighteen months, most Home Guard men had a more modern weapon of some sort, and the old Boer war and American weapons were replaced.

With fears of invasion, there was concern that an advancing enemy might see Home Guard members as guerrilla forces, and so a uniform was conceived rather than the simple armband which was initially issued. The uniforms were of good quality, and a local farmer recollected that his father used his for many years to keep warm while ploughing in the cold.

Weapons continued to be more readily available. Competency and proficiency standards were introduced with regular weekend training at local farms such as Elm Farm, Naish Farm and Home Farm. A rifle range was in use just outside Naish farmhouse. Local resident John Harris has reported several finds of cartridge cases at Spirthill. At Elm Farm, Robert Pegler, the grandson of the platoon commander for Foxham, has described an event in the 1960s when a stack of sticky bombs (grenades with an adhesive designed to stick on an advancing enemy tank) were found inside a farm outbuilding. The bomb squad was called and moved the bombs to a pond where they were blown up. The pond is now much larger than it was.

These volunteer amateur soldiers needed to be trained into an efficient fighting unit. Many local men with World War I experience stepped into the training role. Initially, training was a local responsibility longer term the war office issued training material and in 1944 also introduced proficiency standards. There were also many privately printed pocketbooks.

In the proficiency tests, the Bremhill platoon won the cup for operating the Smith Gun in the autumn of 1944. A photograph of the winning platoon with Clive Hillier holding the cup is on display in St Martin's Church, as is the actual cup.

Following advances by the Allies towards Germany, H Company of the Home Guard was stood down in December 1944 after a march past through Chippenham and a parade in John Coles Park. Upon completing service in the Home Guard, each member was given a certificate and medal to record their service.

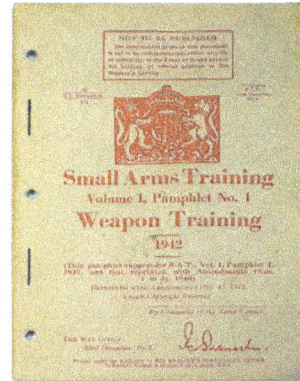

Fig. 306: Small Arms Training Manual.

Fig. 307: The entire Home Guard Battalion photographed at Elm Farm, Foxham.

Wheels of Change
in the Parish during the 1900s

Fig. 308: Three members of the Fry family pose by the delivery cart in the Bakery rick-yard.

School Life in the 1940s: The Memories of Jim Scott

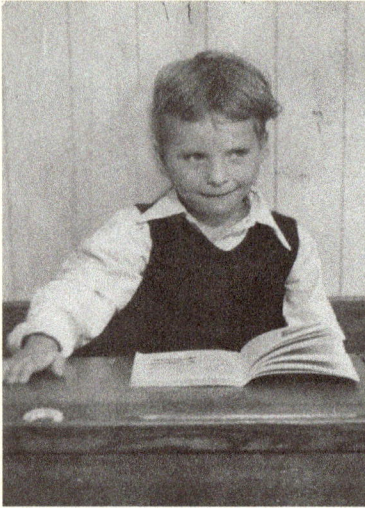

Fig. 309: Jim Scott at Bremhill School.

In September 1944, I began my formal education. I was five years old, a big lad, but nevertheless rather shy (I think I have outgrown that tendency now – seventy years later).[561] By any standard, Bremhill School was not a very large building, but to me, this timid little boy from the hamlet of Stanley (about two miles away), it seemed enormous, imposing in fact. I was one of several children of my age beginning my schooling at Bremhill that autumn day in 1944. We were warmly welcomed by the headteacher Mrs Jones and her assistant, Miss Woodford. In spite of my earlier fears, the years that I spent in that little school were both beneficial and pleasant, full of good memories.

In the course of my years at the school, I made many friends, lifelong friends in many cases. The fact that most of my adult life has been spent in the area made keeping in touch relatively easy. Some names? The Pocock children: Brian, Martin, Christabel and Robin; Nancy Bull and sisters; Ray Wicks; John Summers. Just a few. It was at Bremhill School that I developed my great love of reading with my friend Ray Wicks. We would race each other to grab the latest book on the library shelves. It was a busy little school in those days. The teachers, Mrs Jones and Miss Woodford, were great communicators, firm but fair. The head, Mrs Jones, lived in the schoolhouse next to the school.

Fig. 310: Modern photograph of the schoolhouse next to the village hall.

Pupils came from all around the parish, many having walked from home. Getting to school for myself and my brother was a simple matter, we walked. We lived in Stanley at the bottom of Bencroft Hill, two miles from school – no school bus. It was a good school, and any ex-pupils that you come across will speak highly of their time at 'Bremhill University'.

8.5 Post-War Bremhill

After World War II, the parish council was increasingly concerned with local modernising of the parish infrastructure. They pressed for improvements in the water and electricity supply, the provision of bus services and the condition of roads. Alongside the parish's suggestions for sites available for council house development, eventually provided in Foxham and Charlcutt, were polite recommendations to the rural district council that utilities could be improved in the surrounding area at the same time. There was frustration that certain parts of the parish were better served. While Tytherton had 'electric light' in 1947, the same was not available in Bremhill, Foxham and Charlcutt, precipitating a letter to the local MP. However, improvement was slow, and with plans to connect one part of the parish to the electricity supply in 1948, the parish council again wrote to the district council to ask about plans for the rest. Foxham residents felt particularly disadvantaged and petitioned for better buses and road improvements (one reason why bus services proved challenging).

The situation precipitated some householders to make their own arrangements. In Spirthill residents got water from wells situated at every property.[562] These were hand dug and stone lined. Some were traditional winched bucket systems while others, particularly those on the top of the hill, where the wells were deeper, utilised a manual pump system. This was the case when the Satchell family moved from Somerset to the village in 1939, the family of nine took over the tenancy of two run down farms adjacent to each other, Leeks Hedge Farm and Naish House Farm. Four years later, the family took a decision to access the spring water in a new way using a hydraulic ram mechanism. The nearest flowing spring to Naish House Farm is over a quarter of a mile away. The new mechanism lifted the water uphill to a height of 100 feet to reach the farmhouse attic via a two-inch galvanised metal pipe which was hand dug into trenches through the fields. Replenishment tanks holding 1,500 gallons supported by rolled steel joists in the roof space supplied the water on demand by a conventional pipe and tap system. It was the first piped water in Spirthill until the mains water was installed in 1951.

Alongside efforts to bring utilities and improve transport, there were new worries, particularly about the threat of nuclear war, so much so, the parish council discussed civil defence planning. Lectures on the topic were considered, as were plans for carrying out a drill.

Along with improvements and new threats, the centuries-old influence of big landowners such as the Lansdownes of Bowood continued to wane. In 1919, the estate sold off 1,900 acres across the parish.[563] In 1947, it sold off most of the remaining land and property within Bremhill, including eight farms and the Dumb Post Inn.[564]

Fig. 311: Post-war council houses at Lodowicks, Bremhill.

Fig. 312: Advert for Blakes Hydram, a self-perpetuating water pump.

Fig. 313: 'Duck and cover' was recommended practice in the event of a nuclear attack.

Fig. 314: Modern photo of Curricomb Farm, East Tytherton.

This provided new opportunities but resulted in the consolidation of land holdings into larger tracts. Farming was changing too. At Combe Farm (later Curricomb) at Tytherton Lucas, Alfie Holder remembers the first tractor being acquired in 1948: 'Before that, we had horses. The first time Auntie Bren went down the field with the tractor and shouted "Whoa!" the tractor didn't stop. She was a character.'[565] Today's farm is double the size it was during the 1950s and 1960s. Mechanisation and consolidation contributed to fewer residents being employed within agriculture.

Fig. 315: Bremhill School showing the playground.

At Bremhill School, the end of World War II also brought the prospect of change. As early as March 1945, the Local Education Authority announced that, under a proposed reorganisation resulting from the 1944 Education Act, the old Victorian school would in all probability have to be rebuilt, unless land already available at the back 'for the emptying of buckets' could be used for an extension. On the positive side, the LEA chairman told the school managers that he 'had it on good authority' that no action was likely to be taken for seven to ten years since the most pressing need after the war would be for housing.

In the background, rural life continued. The parochial preoccupations of the council persisted: complaints were made about roadmen coming to repair the road at Tytherton 'but not doing anything but drink tea' and there was frustration that a bridleway was being obstructed by pigs. The pace of improvements remained frustratingly slow through the 1950s. Christopher Kent of Tytherton Lucas recalls his mother-in-law had no electricity at The Laurels until the late 1950s.[566] Indeed, it took the Bremhill parish council seven years of discussion and pressure before a telephone box was finally provided at Charlcutt in 1961.[567] In 1960, new plans by the rural district council to improve local sewers still left properties unconnected to the mains. The parish council complained, but the rural district council wrote back to say that the connection of the additional buildings was not economical.[568]

Fig. 316: The much loved red telephone box.

End of an Era: The Closure of Bremhill School 1969

Despite post-war plans to rebuild Bremhill School, no new school ever materialised. It may have been an early indication of what was to follow when, in 1958, the parish council expressed concerns that, despite the obvious need, the county council had decided to shelve planned improvements to school sanitation.[570]

On 17 April 1967 an extraordinary meeting of school managers was held, at which two county education department officials were present. The impending retirement of Mrs Wroe, the headteacher, had acted as a catalyst, and the education department informed the managers of their intention to press for the closure of the school at the end of the summer term in 1968. Reasons given for this decision included inadequate and out of date buildings with no room for expansion, the uneconomical staffing of the school with its present number of pupils, and too wide an age range in each class for modern methods of teaching. Concentration of children in larger units with a consequently lower cost per pupil per annum was the government's policy at the time. After closure, Bremhill children would be transported to Calne each day for their schooling and Charlcutt children to East Tytherton School, which was to be expanded.

Following this meeting, the chairman of the managers, Rev. Jackson, submitted to the education department a written record of their objections to the closure. This was a lengthy document, running to twelve paragraphs. It began with a moving statement, that 'the school was originally provided by progressive and philanthropic Christian folk for the education of local children with due attention to their spiritual development.' It stated that it had continued to provide a sound basic education according to the spirit of its founders for many generations. Much was made of the close ties between the school and the community and of the advantage of a headteacher who lived in the village and had personal knowledge not only of her pupils, but also their parents and home circumstances. A school with smaller numbers allowed for more individual attention, and the headteacher had taken steps to avoid any disadvantage caused by the range of age and ability in her class. Recent examination results were well up to expectations 'given the average IQ of the locality'.

Overcrowding in a small village school was surely preferable to the 'overcrowding in a modern glass-house' in Calne. Some practical suggestions followed. The house next door to the school, currently on the market, could be purchased, providing accommodation for the headteacher and enlargement of the playground. It would allow the existing teacher's house to be used to enlarge the teaching area.

Fig. 317: Children at Bremhill School playing a game.

Fig. 318: Plans were suggested in 1967-8 to utilise the teacher's house as part of the school.

A roofed walk could be built from the school building to the toilets to protect the pupils from rain and snow. Although a playing field was not felt to be so important for children in the country, there was a vacant plot of land, owned by the council at the bottom of the council estate in Bremhill, which could be used.

Fig. 319: Aerial view and map of land at Lodowicks, now a protected green space.

A modern heating system could be installed in the school and fluorescent strip lighting would solve the lighting problem. The staffing issues could be addressed by cooperation between the county council and the Salisbury Diocese, who could provide a school master or priest. The document ended with the commitment of the managers to help with the fundraising needed to implement the measures outlined.

Another year passed, and on 26 September 1968 a public meeting was held in Bremhill School to discuss the proposed closure. It was attended by a county councillor, the prospective Liberal candidate, a representative of the archdeaconry, a local press representative and twenty-four parents. The local MP had been invited but was unable to attend. The general tenor of the meeting was summed up in a letter in the form of a petition, which three ladies of the parish took to every household in Bremhill, Charlcutt and Ratford. A total of 160 signatures of parents and ratepayers had been collected.

The petitioners reiterated and supported the points put forward by the school managers. In addition, they argued that the school 'is an integral part of our rural community where many of us were educated, and our parents and even grandparents before us' and that its removal 'would tend to diminish the sense of community, not only in our children as they grow up, but also in the adult population too'.

As inhabitants of a rural community with a character of its own, they objected to 'the ever-increasing tendency to centre our lives and those of our children upon the town'. As ratepayers, they felt they received little enough return on their rates – no mains drainage or sewerage, no street-lighting, refuse collection only once a fortnight, no local policemen, two local railway stations recently closed and only a sparse bus service – and the removal of the school would even further reduce their amenities. They pointed out that the closure of the school would add to the difficulty of attracting people to the area, since their children would have to travel some distance to school, and that this would raise economic and social problems, such as obtaining sufficient agricultural labour, an ageing population and the loss of community interest in a population that looked upon the villages as mere dormitories.

Fig. 320: Bremhill School prior to closure.

The petition was sent to the Minister of State for Education and Science, the education department of County Hall and to the local press. All to no avail. The school, with twenty-eight pupils on roll, closed its doors on 10 July 1969. It was the end of an era.

Fig. 321: The last cohort of pupils and their teachers.

School photographs from the past...

Can you spot a family member?

Fig. 322: Bremhill School 1935

Fig. 323: Bremhill School 1939

Fig. 324: Foxham School 1917

Fig. 325: East Tytherton School 1949

Recollections of Tytherton Lucas and Stanley: An Interview with Verina Vanzillotti

Fig. 326: The Vanzillotti Family.

My father, Emilio Vanzillotti, was born in southern Italy in 1921.[571] He trained as an electrician but was called up when he was eighteen to do National Service in the army and was then involved in World War II. My father spoke very little about the war. It must have been very harrowing. We know he went with the army to Tripoli and was involved in repairing the telephone communications. He was captured by the English after the battle of El Alamein and taken to a POW [Prisoner of War] camp in Scotland. The prisoners were treated well, and he was able to use his electrical skills and was encouraged to do woodwork and metalwork. He was transferred to work at an American camp in Devizes and helped in a factory as an engineer. Then they were asked if anyone wanted to work outside on the farms. He agreed to do that in preference to working inside. He was based at Easton Grey camp and Mr Cottle from Bosmere Farm came to collect him every day. He worked tending the dairy herd.

One day Mr Cottle asked Emilio if he would like to stay at Bosmere, and, of course, he agreed. Mr Cottle had to write to the Home Office to get permission which was granted. So, Emilio moved into no. 2 Bosmere Cottages. Mr and Mrs Cottle had no children and were like parents to him. My mum was born in northern Italy, and because there was no work in Italy after the war, she came over here to work as a chef. Initially, she worked at a place in Sandy Lane (three miles south of Bremhill). On a night off, she went to the fish and chip shop in Chippenham and met my dad. But they immediately recognised each other because they had met before in Italy. My dad had driven his car from the south to the north of Italy before the war. He had broken down and needed water, and her father had helped him.

Everyone knew her as Tina, although her real name was Clementina. Dad had an Italian friend, mum had a friend who cooked with her, and the four of them decided to go out together for an evening, and that's how it happened.

When Mr Cottle died, Emilio ran the farm with Mrs Cottle helping a bit. But she became unwell, and when she couldn't look after herself, she moved in with us. We started at no. 2 Bosmere Cottages, and she moved into the downstairs at no. 1, which had become empty. We knocked the wall down inside, and we had the use of the extra bedrooms upstairs because she couldn't go up the stairs. Bosmere farmhouse was left empty for several years until she died.

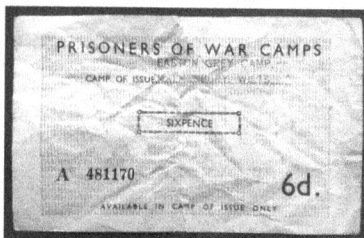

Fig. 327: Prisoner of War camp vouchers were used in place of actual currency.

Fig. 328: Tina (Clementina) and Emilio Vanzillotti on their wedding day.

My father was always grateful that the Cottles had given him a roof over his head and treated him like a son, but he refused to be adopted because he had a mother in Italy. He did the milking and haymaking and never took a holiday, except once when his mother was ill, and he went back to Italy for a week. We all had to muck in with the haymaking. I have two older sisters: Patrizia and Raffaella. My mum helped with the milking as well as looking after us and old Mrs Cottle. It was instilled into all of us as children, we were all workers. From the age of six, every school holiday, I used to go potato picking for Mr Davies at Manor Farm and was paid 6d per crate. It was all done by hand, walking behind the tractor ploughing them up. Then Mr Davies went into asparagus in a big way. We used to cut and bundle them each evening, and then Mr Davies would take them to market in Bristol early the following morning.

Mrs Cottle had always said to my dad that she would see he was 'OK'. She asked him whether he wanted Bosmere or Stanley where there was a bit of an old house, but he could build his own. He chose Stanley because he'd done all those years of milking.

He felt like a king to have his own plot and build a house. So that was all in her will when she died. She left him a brand-new Massey Ferguson 165 tractor, £1,000, Stanley Farm with twenty-two acres and no. 1 and no. 2 Bosmere Cottages. He was in his element, although he was very sad to leave Bosmere as it held very good memories and sad to leave his friends in West Tytherton [Tytherton Lucas] because the whole village was so friendly. My dad (Emilio Vanzillotti) died in 1997, at the age of seventy-six years, and is buried in the churchyard at Tytherton Lucas.

Fig. 329: Modern photograph of Riverside Farm built on the site of the old Stanley Farm.

Fig. 330: Emilio and Tina's gravestone in St Nicholas' churchyard, Tytherton Lucas.

8.6 Modern Bremhill

Fig. 331: Friesian cows on winter rations.

For many centuries the rural parish of Bremhill has been defined by agriculture. However, changes to farming have been seismic since the last war. Many of the oral history interviews mentioned how some farms had moved away from dairy farming as it was increasingly hard for farmers to make a living.[572] Sarah Grimshaw recounts how at Pound Farm, Stanley, 'When milk quotas came in, the farm made less money, the number of cows were reduced and some of the land was sold, reducing it to just seventy-two acres. This was barely profitable, and we couldn't afford to invest in modern equipment.'[573]

Farmers in Bremhill parish have had to adapt to survive. Locally it has led to many changes, such as the consolidation of landholdings, fewer people working on the land, and farmhouses converted to purely residential use, or with a few acres attached for recreational purposes.

Fig. 332: Robert Pegler on his tractor.

Sarah's family no longer farms Pound Farm. Robert Pegler took over the family farm at Foxham from his father in the late 1980s.[574] Robert enlarged the dairy herd before selling it; he then went into organic farming to get a better price for his livestock and arable. Now the farm grows oats. They also have an Aberdeen Angus beef cattle suckler herd and a flock of pedigree Lleyn sheep. Contractors are now used for much of the mechanised work as they can afford the better equipment.

The changes have sometimes been difficult. Pam Sawyer recalls 'we had to finish with the dairy herd in '98 which was a very sad day after all those years of dairying. We had to pen the cows up before they went. Then we went away for the weekend and we looked at the milk served and wondered "is this milk or white water?" as ours was so rich straight from the herd.' It is not to say that life was not hard. She also recalls, 'When it was holiday times, people used to say "Great, it's Christmas Day", but we had to get up an hour earlier because the tanker would come early. We never had a day off. Before we had a milk tank, the milk went straight into churns and the churns had to be taken down the lane and put on a stand for the lorry to go to the factory.'[575]

Fig. 333: Milk churns on a stand ready for collection.

With the loosening of the economic reliance of the parish upon agriculture, the socio-economic make-up of the local population has changed too. In his interview, Christopher Kent described the house owners of Tytherton Lucas as people largely from 'professional backgrounds'.[576] Many new people have moved in and embraced village life. Harvest suppers, fetes, dog shows and produce competitions are well attended, and the village halls provide venues for a wide range of events. The inhabitants of East Tytherton have recently begun building a new village hall.

Fig. 334: Bremhill Produce Show in the village hall, 2014.

Fig. 335: Produce marquee at the Foxham Show, 2017.

Fig. 336: Foxham Spring Dinner/Dance in the village hall in 2010.

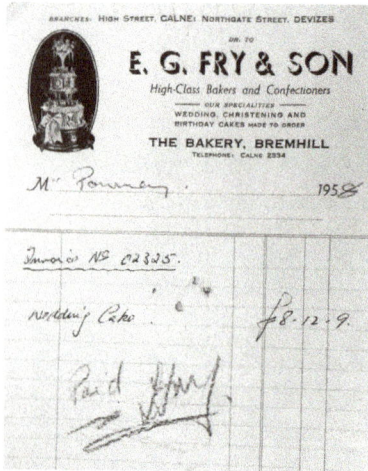

Fig. 337: Wedding cake invoice for Dennis Powney, the Bremhill postman.

Fig. 338: Tytherton Ride drinks stop at Ratford, 2015.

The parish over the last few decades has become much more connected to the broader region. It has become much easier to travel out of the community for work and recreation. Sometimes, there has been no choice. After the closure of the primary school at East Tytherton in the early 2000s, there has been no school in the parish. There are no longer any shops within the parish. Indeed, it has been many decades since Les Fry employed four at the Bremhill bakery and made a wedding cake for the local postman.[577] And, until recently, limited work opportunities often required travel beyond the bounds of the parish too. However, the possibilities provided by the internet mean that once again an increasing number of people are able to work from home or within the parish, as several farms have converted farm buildings into work units for small businesses.

Communication with the outside has been two-way, also bringing people into the parish, particularly for recreation. The East Tytherton Women's Institute is a vibrant community group, but most of its membership is now drawn from outside the village. The area is popular with equestrians - the Foxham Horse Show and the Tytherton Ride pull people annually from the broader region - as well as the many local people who keep and ride horses.

Fig. 339: One of the many jumps in the main ring at Foxham Horse Show in 2015.

The extensive network of footpaths and cycle tracks appeals to cyclists and walkers. Residents and visitors participate in a range of country sports - there are several shoots in existence, the Beaufort Hunt meet regularly on a Thursday in the parish during the winter months, and the rivers Avon and Marden are in demand for angling.

More visitors come throughout the year as an increasing number of farms have converted buildings to provide holiday or short-stay accommodation, and the Dumb Post Inn and Foxham Inn are popular with people of the parish and further afield.

Although there has been much change in the parish over the last fifty or so years, there has been much continuity. So, while certain aesthetic elements have changed – the thatched roofs have all but disappeared – looking at a Victorian photograph of East Tytherton village, the picture has hardly altered. Indeed, throughout the villages of Bremhill the buildings provide a constant visual reminder of the past, the surrounding countryside seemingly eternal too. It is not just the visual picture. Some of the families have been here for well over 100 years, such as the Peglers, Pococks, Mintys, Vines and Gingells. There remains a reverence for the history and traditions of the village, as anyone who has heard Rev. Jim Scott describe the history of the St. Martin's Church or David Wood talk about the parish at war will attest. Symptomatic of this, although the Dumb Post Friendly Society was founded in the eighteenth century, a framed copy of its orders (articles) are still displayed on the wall of the inn which perpetuates its name. The fund provided members with sickness benefits, one way in which the community looked after its own.

The Dumb Post Society was dissolved in the late nineteenth century, but in 1979 the Friends of St Martin's was formed, reawakening the spirit of the original friendly society. It holds local events to raise money (over £150,000 to date) to help support the fabric of St Martin's and, also, to support worthwhile projects and groups in the parish.[578]

Fig. 340: East Tytherton Common in the early 1900s.

Fig. 341: 'Caribbean themed night' fund raiser in the marquee by the Friends of St Martin's, 2005.

Fig. 342: The Bremhill Neighbourhood Plan was adopted in February 2018.

The parish has also proved effective in recent years at coming together to resist perceived threats – there was a vigorous (and successful) campaign in 2016 against a planned large solar farm and a five year process culminated in 2018 with the publication of the Bremhill Parish Neighbourhood Plan. This aimed 'to maintain the character of Bremhill Parish as a place with a sense of community and history' by maintaining the essential rural characteristics of the parish and guarding against inappropriate encroachment by the towns of Calne and Chippenham. The campaign is ongoing.

Also in 2018, the Bremhill Parish History Project was launched to explore the heritage of the community, tapping into the considerable interest of residents, bringing to life many of the stories of those who lived in the parish, reaffirming the ties of the present community with those of the past, and looking to record the history for future residents. The next fifty years will, no doubt, bring further change. However, if the history of Bremhill has taught us anything, it is as the first parish historian Rev. William Lisle Bowles said we should 'ne'er forget', but it is also that the parish will continue to adapt and thrive as it has for the last 1,000 years of its existence, shaped by its people and their shared heritage.

'ne'er forget'
Rev. William Lisle Bowles

Fig. 343: View from the ridge at Spirthill looking due west across the Avon valley in the parish.

Bremhill Parish

Designated Neighbourhood Plan Area

Approved by Wiltshire Council - April 2014

References

Chapter 1

1. W.L. Bowles, A Parochial History of Bremhill in the County of Wiltshire (London, 1828), 1.

2. OS 1:25,000, sheet 156 (1999 edn).

3. G. Brown, Stanley Abbey and its Estates 1151–c.1640: A Cistercian Monastery and its Impact on the Landscape (Oxford, 2012), 17.

4. Bowles, Parochial History, 77–8.

5. A geophysical survey was conducted in 2019 on a field belonging to Elm Farm, Foxham, as Roman material had been previously discovered. However, no evidence of Roman habitation was found. Wiltshire Archaeological Field Group Report, No. 2019.02 (Aug. 2019).

6. Reg. Malm. I, 307–9. The year 935 is suggested as its original year of creation; C. Plummer, Two of the Saxon Chronicles Parallel (Oxford, 1892–9), II, 132; S. Keynes, 'The Diplomas of King Æthelred 'the Unready' 978–1016: A Study in their Use as Historical Evidence' in Cambridge Studies in Medieval Life and Thought, 3rd ser. (Cambridge, 1980).

7. WAM 96, 82. S.E. Kelly (ed.), Charters of Malmesbury Abbey (Oxford, 2005), 220–2.

8. Reg. Malm. I, 321–4. Disputed e.g. D.N. Dumville, Wessex and England from Alfred to Edgar: Six Essays in Political, Cultural and Ecclesiastical Revival (Woodbridge, 1992), 41 n.57, 43; H.P.R. Finberg, The Early Charters of the West Midlands (2nd edn, Leicester, 1972), no. 180; Kelly, S.E. (ed.) Charters of Malmesbury Abbey, 246–9.

9. http://www.esawyer.org.uk, no. S1575 (Accessed 29 July 2021).

10. W.H. Jones, Domesday for Wiltshire (London, 1865), 61; C. & F. Thorn, Domesday Book: Wiltshire (Chichester, 1979), 22, 5.

11. J.E.B. Gover, Place Names of Wiltshire (Cambridge, 1970), 87; Brown, Stanley Abbey, 14.

12. Figures taken from Domesday Book: Wiltshire, 22, 5; 8,12.

13. Gover, Place Names of Wiltshire, 86–7.

14. VCH Wilts. II, 126.

15. A. Williams and G.H. Martin (eds), Domesday Book: A Complete Translation (London, 2002), 186.

16. V.C.M. London (ed.), Cart. Bradenstoke Priory (WRS 35), 184 (no. 619).

17. Brown, Stanley Abbey, 32.

18. Thorn, Domesday Book, 37, 6.

19. M. Gelling, Place-names in the Landscape (London, 1984).

20. Brown, Stanley Abbey, 32.

21. https://services.wiltshire.gov.uk/HistoryEnvRecord/Home/ViewHERItem?HER=MWI5217 (Accessed 29 July 2021).

22. R. Coates, 'Tyther- as a Place Name Element', Jnl of the English Place Name Society 43 (2011), 35–42.

23. M. T. Clanchy (ed.), Civil Pleas of the Wiltshire Eyre, 1249 (WRS 26), 89.

24. Gover, Place Names of Wiltshire, 87. The origins of the name were also discussed at a lecture given by Dr Simon Draper to the Bremhill Parish History Group in September 2020.

25. H.P.R. Finberg, Lucerna (London, 1964), 158; M. Gelling, Signposts to the Past (3rd edn, Chichester, 1997), 184–5.

26. Gover, Place Names of Wiltshire, 87, 88.

27. WAM 96, 82.

28. Ibid.

29. From a talk given by Dr Simon Draper to the Bremhill Parish History Group in September 2020.

30. E.g. see J. Chandler (ed.), Printed Maps of Wiltshire, 1787-1844 (WRS 52), 55.

31. Wiltshire Archaeological Field Group Report (Feb. 2020); Wiltshire Archaeological Field Group Report (Mar. 2020).

32. WAM 35, 546.

33. https://historicengland.org.uk/listing/the-list/list-entry/1363795 (Accessed 29 July 2021).

34. Department of the Environment, List of Buildings of Special Architectural or Historic Interest: District of North Wiltshire: Parishes of Bremhill, Cherhill, Christian Malford, Compton Bassett, Dauntsey, Great Somerford, Hilmarton and Little Somerford (London, 1988), 20.

35. North Wiltshire District Council letter from the Chief Planning Officer to O.R. Cleg of The Old Vicarage, Bremhill, dated 30 Jan. 1986. John Harris kindly provided a copy of the letter.

36. J. Aubrey & J.E. Jackson (eds), Wiltshire: the Topographical Collections of John Aubrey (Devizes, 1862), 60.

37. M. Hurford, et al., Bremhill Court, Bremhill, Wiltshire: Tree Ring Analysis of Timbers, Historic England Report: 77-2010 (Swindon, 2010); North Wiltshire District Council letter from the Chief Planning Officer to O.R. Cleg of The Old Vicarage, Bremhill, dated 30 Jan. 1986. John Harris kindly provided a copy of the letter.

38. VCH Wilts. III, 269–75; W.L. Bowles, Annals of Lacock Abbey (London, 1835), 9.

39. Brown, Stanley Abbey, 32.

40. Aubrey, Topog. Colln. ed. Jackson, 112.

41. G. Brown, Stanley Abbey & its Estates 1151-c1640 (Oxford: Archaeopress, 2012), 22.

42. Brown, Stanley Abbey, 51.

43. H. Brakspear, 'The Cistercian Abbey of Stanley, Wiltshire', Archaelogia 60 (1907), 494.

44. Brown, Stanley Abbey, 27.

45. Ibid.

46. VCH Wilts. III, 269–75; Brown, Stanley Abbey, 67.

47. Brown, Stanley Abbey, 57–8.

48. Brown, Stanley Abbey, 151–3.

49. Brown, Stanley Abbey, 52.

50. Bowles, Parochial History, 86.

51. As highlighted by Dr Graham Brown at a talk given to the Bremhill Parish History Group in December 2020.

52. WAM 35, 546, and as quoted in E. Hutton, Highways and Byways in Wiltshire (London, 1917), 388.

53. Brown, Stanley Abbey, 27. Brown states that they did not go to an abbey at Beaulieu as has been noted elsewhere.

54. Bowles, Parochial History, 122.

55. As highlighted by Dr Graham Brown at a talk given to the Bremhill Parish History Group in December 2020.

56. For example, the 1612 survey of the manor records that their properties were tiled and not thatched (as was usual) and suggests tiles from the abbey were being re-purposed.

57. As highlighted by Dr Graham Brown at a talk given to the Bremhill Parish History Group in December 2020.

58. Aubrey, Topog. Colln. ed. Jackson, 113.

59. https://historicengland.org.uk/listing/the-list/list-entry/1001619 (Accessed 29 July 2021).

60. C.A.F. Meekings (ed.), Crown Pleas of the Wiltshire Eyre, 1249 (WRS 16), 183, 188, 193, 260.

61. D.A. Crowley (ed.), The Wiltshire Tax List of 1332 (WRS 45), 97–8.

62. VCH Wilts. IV, 307.

63. A. Whiteman (ed.), Compton Census (London, 1986), 129.

64. Cal. SP Dom., 1654, 43.

65. https://www.historyofparliamentonline.org/volume/1604-1629/member/bayntun-sir-edward-1593-1657.

66. Quoted by Aubrey, Topog. Colln. ed. Jackson, 63.

67. See DOE, List of Buildings, 51.

68. Historic England HER, Research Report Series 38-2016.

69. Wilts. Pedigrees (Harl. Soc. cv/cvi), 190; TNA, PROB 11/171/417.

70. TNA, PROB/11/530/281.

71. Wilts. N&Q, VI, 99–107.

72. Wilts. N&Q, VI, 171–6; Hist. Parl. Commons, 1715–54, I, 414.

73. https://historicengland.org.uk/listing/the-list/list-entry/1199069 (Accessed 29 July 2021); N. Pevsner, Wiltshire (2nd edn, New Haven and London, 2002), 140–1.

74. VCH Wilts. III, 218; Aubrey, Topog. Colln. ed. Jackson, 60.

75. https://historicengland.org.uk/listing/the-list/list-entry/1022442 (Accessed 29 July 2021).

76. See ch. 3 for further information on the local cloth trade. K.H. Rogers, Wiltshire and Somerset Woollen Mills (Edington, 1976), 89.

77. DOE, List of Buildings, 42.

78. J. Freeman (ed.), Commonplace Book of Sir Edward Bayntun (WRS 43), 44, 50; WSA, P1/S/633; P1/3Reg/160–162.

79. OS Map 1:2500, Wilts. 26.4 (1924 edn).

80. Rogers, Wilts. and Som. Woollen Mills, 90.

81. DOE, List of Buildings, 46; WSA 1409/15/176; Rogers, Wilts. and Som. Woollen Mills, 90.

82. Historic England HER, Bremhill, Hazeland Mill, 1022431 [OS: ST 97190 72328].

83. TNA, PROB 11/191/381.

84. Hazeland Mill was acquired along with other property in Bremhill by the Bowood estate in whose possession it remained until the twentieth century. After the demise of the cloth trade, the building was used solely as a grist mill until 1965.

85. DOE, List of Buildings, 31.

86. DOE, List of Buildings, 31.

87. See also, ch. 7.

88. DOE, List of Buildings, 31, 24.

89. G.L Gomme (ed.), Topographical History of Warwickshire, Westmoreland and Wiltshire (London, 1901), 211.

90. VCH Wilts. IV, 342; Census, 1961–2011.

91. VCH Wilts. IV, 319, 342. See also, ch. 2.

92. See ch. 2.

93. Bowles, Parochial History, 21.

94. Bowles, Parochial History, 249.

95. Pevsner, Wilts., 141.

96. See ch. 7.

97. See ch. 4.

98. DOE, List of Buildings, 34, 41. Harden's is dated 1781.

99. DOE, List of Buildings, 31, 3-6, 38.

100. VCH Wilts. IV, 342.

Chapter 2

101. G.B. Grundy, 'The Ancient Highways and Tracks of Wiltshire, Berkshire, and Hampshire, and the Saxon Battlefields of Wiltshire', Archaeol. Jnl 75, 1918, 82–3.

102. J. Ogilby, Britannia, 1 (1675), plate II.

103. J. Ogilby, Britannia, 1 (1675), plate II.

104. VCH Wilts. IV, 446–7.

105. As revealed in various editions of Kelly's Directory of Wiltshire throughout the century.

106. W.L. Bowles, A Parochial History of Bremhill in the County of Wiltshire (London, 1828), 254.

107. H. Lewis, The Church Rambler (London, 1878), II, 408–9.

108. The following sources have been used in this article: Wiltshire Gazette Archive; www.chippenham.gov.uk/chippenham-museum (Accessed 29 July 2021); K. Taylor, Dry Shod to Chippenham: A History of Maud Heath's Ancient Causeway in North Wiltshire (Bradford-on-Avon, 2012); Wiltshire History Centre, Chippenham; J.A. Chamberlain, Maud Heath's Causeway (Chippenham, 1974).

109. Toft: a word of Saxon origin meaning homestead.

110. Royal cartographer, John Ogilby (1600–76). J. Ogilby, Britannia, (1698).

111. Langley riots occurred in the aftermath of the Kington Langley Revel 1822. Chamberlain, Maud Heath's Causeway, 20.

112. The poem, 'A lamentation over the state of Maud Heath's Causeway' was addressed to the Maud Heath Trustees and was published in Devizes and Wilts. Gaz., 6 Apr. 1876.

113. L.J. Dalby, The Wilts & Berks Canal (Usk, 2000); D. Small, Wilts & Berks Canal Revisited (Cheltenham, 2010); A.J. Lewery, Narrow Boat Painting (Exeter, 2016); www.canaljunction.com (Accessed 29 July 2021); www.auntiemabel.org (Accessed 29 July 2021); Wilts & Berks Canal Trust.

114. J. Tanner, The Calne Branch (Oxford, 1972); C. Maggs, The Calne Branch (Bath, 1990).

115. Devizes and Wilts. Gaz., 27 Oct. 1859.

116. Wilts. Ind., 17 Nov. 1859.

117. Devizes and Wilts. Gaz., 24 Nov. 1859.

118. Wilts. Times and Trowbridge Ad., 28 Jan. 1905.

Chapter 3

119. Abstract of Answers and Returns under Act for taking Account of Population of Great Britain (Parl. Papers 1822 (502), xv), 357.

120. Sussex Ad., 19 Feb. 1827.

121. VCH Wilts. XX (forthcoming).

122. WSA, 122/1.

123. T. Davis, General View of the Agriculture of Wiltshire (London, 1811), 211.

124. The story of John Harding has been reconstructed from the following list of sources and Bremhill parish registers. The account given by Mrs Bowles, in particular, is used with caution as the level of detail and extravagant language suggest heavy poetic licence. WSA, P3/H/1395, 1171/21, P1/1835/32; Devizes and Wilts. Gaz., 27 Dec. 1832; Salisbury & Winchester Jnl, 31 Dec. 1832, 30 Mar. 1835; Mrs Bowles, John Harding: A Tale of a Church Going Christian (London, 1833); W. Parker, 'A Tale of a Humble Life,' The Saturday Mag., 8 Mar. 1834, 94; Gent. Mag., May 1835.

125. Salisbury and Winchester Jnl, 30 Mar. 1835.

126. Salisbury and Winchester Jnl, 31 Dec. 1832.

127. TNA, MAF32/30/12.

128. W. Marshall, The Rural Economy of Gloucestershire including its Dairy Together with the Dairy Management of North Wilts II (London, 1796), 161.

129. Marshall, Rural Economy, 156.

130. Marshall, Rural Economy, 185.

131. Reports of Special Assistant Poor Law Commissioners on Employment of Women and Children in Agriculture (Parl. Papers 1843 [510], xii), 61.

132. VCH Wilts. IV, 224.

133. Marshall, Rural Economy, 157.

134. A. Wilson, Forgotten Harvest: The Story of Cheese Making in Wiltshire (Calne, 1995), 74–5.

135. Communications to the Board of Agriculture on Subjects Relative to the Husbandry and Internal Improvements of the Country I (London, 1797), 35.

136. WSA, P3/B/1077.

137. WSA, P1/M/390.

138. Salisbury and Winchester Jnl, 15 July 1826.

139. Marshall, Rural Economy, 179.

140. Marshall, Rural Economy, 146.

141. WSA, P3/B/1077.

142. WSA, 1154/80 (13 Dec. 1816).

143. WSA, 1154/80.

144. T.H. Barker, Record of Seasons of Prices and Phenomena (London, 1911), 250–1.

145. WSA, 1154/80 (4 Jan. 1828).

146. T. Davis, General View of the Agriculture of Wiltshire (London, 1811), 213.

147. In 1776, c.10% of the amount spent on welfare had been on rents. Reports from the Committee Appointed to Inspect and Consider the Returns Made by the Overseers of the Poor (Parl. Papers 31 Oct. 1776 – 6 June 1777, ix), 484.

148. The cost of relief was covered by a local tax called the 'poor rates' paid by the occupiers of property on a sliding scale depending on the value of the property. Barker, Record of Seasons, 271–5; WSA, 1154/40.

149. WSA, 1154/80.

150. Bath Chron. and Weekly Gaz., 20 Jan. 1820.

151. WSA, 1171/21.

152. Marshall, Rural Economy, 145.

153. W.L. Bowles, A Parochial History of Bremhill in the County of Wiltshire (London, 1828), 21.

154. J.W. Parker, 'A Tale of a Humble Life,' The Saturday Mag., 8 Mar. 1834, 94; When John Harding died, Bowles composed an epitaph in his honour which was published by the Gentleman's Magazine.

155. Bowles, Parochial History, 21.

156. Commission of Inquiry into Charities in England and Wales: Twenty-Ninth Report (Parl. Papers 1835 (216)).

157. Even though local people were supposed to have access to almshouses in Calne under Dr Tounson's Charity, it had been withdrawn by 1785, if not much earlier.

158. E.g. 15 Geo. III c. 72.

159. Morning Ad., 26 Feb. 1846.

160. Bowles, Parochial History, 22–3.

161. Bowles, Parochial History, 22.

162. Bowles, Parochial History, 199. Interestingly, the parish overseers in 1830, thereby those responsible for making up wages, were all local farmers. They were also among those who later in the year tried to bring in a minimum wage. WSA, 1154/40 (25 Mar. 1830); WSA, 1171/21.

163. WSA, 1154/80 (21 Apr. 1836), 24 Mar. 1842.

164. Reports of Special Assistant Poor Law Commissioners on Employment of Women and Children in Agriculture (Parl. Papers 1843 [510], xii), 62.

165. Morning Chron., 12 Feb. 1846.

166. D. Roberts, 'Charles Dickens and the "Daily News": Editorials and Editorial Writers', Victorian Periodicals Review 22(2) 1989, 51–63.

167. Wilts. Ind., 12 Feb. 1846.

168. Ibid.

169. Morning Post, 12 Feb. 1846.

170. Wilts. Ind., 26 Feb. 1846.

171. Morning Chron., 12 Feb. 1846.

172. Ibid.

173. Wilts. Ind., 12 Feb. 1846.

174. Morning Chron., 12 Feb. 1846.

175. Wilts. Ind., 12 Feb. 1846.

176. Ibid.

177. Morning Post, 12 Feb. 1846.

178. J.C. Hotten, Charles Dickens: The Story of His Life (New York, 1870), 52.

179. D. Roberts, 'Charles Dickens and the "Daily News": Editorials and Editorial Writers', Victorian Periodicals Review 22(2) 1989, 51–63; D. Birch (ed.), The Oxford Companion to English Literature (Oxford, 2009).

180. Daily News, 14 Feb. 1846.

181. J.H. Berard, Dickens and Landscape Discourse (New York, 2007), 88.

182. Kelly's Dir. Hants., Wilts. and Dors. (1855 edn), 19; Wilts. Ind., 12 Feb. 1846.

183. It was raised in the debate on 17 and 20 Feb. 1846. 83 Parl. Deb. 3rd ser. 86. 1048-1144, 1254-1347.

184. WSA, P3/D/116.

185. WSA, P3/B/1294.

186. G.D. Ramsay, The Wiltshire Woollen Industry in the Sixteenth and Seventeenth Centuries (Oxford, 1965).

187. K.H. Rogers, Wiltshire and Somerset Woollen Mills (Edington, 1976), 89.

188. WSA, P1/H/672.

189. Rogers, Wilts. and and Som. Woollen Mills, 9.

190. J. Freeman (ed.), Commonplace Book of Sir Edward Bayntun (WRS 43), 44.

191. WSA, P3/H/468.

192. WSA, A1/525.

193. J. De L. Mann, The Cloth Industry in the West of England 1640–1880 (Oxford, 1971), 141.

194. Mann, Cloth Industry, 168

195. Wilts. Ind., 4 Jan. 1838; Devizes and Wilts. Gaz., 18 Jan. 1838.

196. Historic England HER, Bremhill, Hazeland Mill, 1022431 [OS: ST 97190 72328].

197. WSA, P1/12Reg/217A; P1/10Reg/420A.

198. WSA, P3/R/490.

199. E.g. bees were kept by the labourer Thomas Eatall in 1677. WSA, P1/E/111 and serge maker, Zachariah Bradbury in 1730, WSA, P3/B/1294. Beer was brewed among others by yeoman Richard Bayley in 1709, WSA, P3/B/699.

200. Bowles, Parochial History, 18.

201. WSA, P3/W/288. Not only does his will inventory contain a pig and a few cows but an abundant stockpile of wheat and beans.

202. WSA, P3/W/711.

203. WSA, 451/24.

204. Kelly's Dir. Hant., Wilts. and Dors. (1855 edn), 19; Kelly's Dir. Wilts. (1859 edn), 391; Kelly's Dir. Wilts. (1867 edn), 228.

205. This is revealed in the probate inventories of local widows, e.g. WSA, P3/K/70.

206. T. Davis, General View of the Agriculture of Wiltshire (London, 1811), 213–9.

207. Freeman, Commonplace Book of Sir Edward Bayntun (WRS 43); WSA, 122/1.

208. WSA, 1171/21.

209. Devizes and Wilts. Gaz., 20 Jan. 1853.

210. WSA, 1171/21.

211. Occasionally, a woman inherited a farm. Mary Mansell was baptised in Bremhill in 1693. In 1712, her father left her his farm (after debts had been paid off). There is no other record of her in the parish registers after her father's death, WSA, P1/M/390.

212. WSA, P3/R/583.

213. Paul's will mentions his son-in-law, William Reeves, by name, although he does not mention by name his four daughters, just their spouses. He left William a useful set of 'patty pans', WSA, P3/N/300.

214. E.g. WSA, P1/1845/8.

215. WSA, 84/36.

216. WSA, P3/R/188.

217. http://www.histparl.ac.uk/volume/1690-1715/member/pinnell-henry-1670-1721 (Accessed 29 July 2021).

218. Bowles, Parochial History, 23–4.

219. Reports of Special Assistant Poor Law Commissioners on Employment of Women and Children in Agriculture (Parl. Papers 1843 [Cd 510], xii), 61.

220. Entry is listed Register of Duties Paid for Apprentices' Indentures, 1710–1811 available at: https://Ancestry.co.uk.

221. Kelly's Dir. Hant., Wilts., and Dors. (1855 edn), 19.

222. WSA, P3/1811/24.

223. WSA, 141/6 and H/4/110/1 (E.g. 10 May 1836, 17 May 1836).

224. Select Committee on Petition of Persons Concerned in Woollen Trade and Manufactories in Somerset, Wiltshire and Gloucestershire: Report (Parl. Papers 1802–3 (30), v), 8.

225. N.J. Williams (ed.), Tradesmen in Early Stuart Wiltshire (WRS 15), 61.

226. WSA, P1/T/92.

227. WSA, P3/C/101.

228. WSA, P1/H/672.

229. WSA, P3/W/711.

230. WSA, P3/H/468.

231. Salisbury and Winchester Jnl, 15 May 1769.

232. WSA, 141/2.

233. WSA, 141/4.

234. WSA, P3/R/490.

235. WSA, 1154/80 (28 Feb. 1839).

236. Much of the information for this section comes from Admiralty records at the TNA, with Covid-19 restrictions in place (9 June 2020) only those sources available for download were used. TNA, ADM-159-82-10960; ADM-158-62-25; ADM-158-93-6; ADM-158-193-3; ADM-139-896-9556; ADM-188-29-54604; ADM-158-134-1; ADM-158-132-5; ADM-158-122-14; ADM-158-94-12; ADM-158-128-21; ADM-158-94-13; ADM-158-49-17; ADM-158-94-11; ADM-158-45-11; ADM-188-503-308496; ADM-158-131-6; ADM-158-126-15; ADM-158-200-19; ADM-158-98-10. Apart from these sources, census returns and parish registers were also utilised.

237. Military recruitment parties were not always well behaved. In 1828, after having 'interfered with the amusements of labourers', at Potterne Feast, at least one of the recruitment party had drawn his bayonet. A row ensued, and the party was overpowered and driven from the village, leaving their drum and accoutrements behind. Devizes and Wilts. Gaz., 25 Sept. 1828.

238. These parties are sometimes mentioned in news reports of the time, e.g. in 1840, a recruitment party was sent from Portsmouth under the command of Captain Evans. Salisbury and Winchester Jnl, 19 Oct. 1840.

239. Wilts. Ind., 22 July 1847.

240. Devizes and Wilts. Gaz., 23 Dec. 1841.

241. The detail about the ship is mostly taken from R. Winfield, British Warships in the Age of Sail 1793–1817 (Barnsley, 2014).

242. A letter, to the Right Honourable the Lords of the Admiralty; setting forth the inconveniences and hardships, the marine officers are subject to, who serve on board the fleet (London, 1757), 4.

243. Salisbury and Winchester Jnl, 26 Dec. 1836.

244. E. Kole_nik (ed.), Conway's All the World's Fighting Ships (New York, 1979), 64.

245. There was one anomaly in Foxham 1901. It was likely the result of the tiny number of people employed (14) and designation of some as 'general labourers', but may have been principally employed on local farms.

Chapter 4

246. See also, Kelly's Dir. Wilts. (1915 edn), 46–7.

247. P. Slack, The English Poor Law, 1531–1782 (Cambridge, 1995), 18.

248. Slack, English Poor Law, 18.

249. I. Slocombe (ed.), Wiltshire Quarter Sessions Order Book 1642–1654 (WRS 67), 170–1, 191, 203, 213.

250. WSA, 141/2, 141/3.

251. WSA, 84/36 (26 Jan. 1783).

252. It appears that the parish occasionally paid for apprenticeships, one of which is recorded within the parish register and dated 1662. W.L. Bowles, A Parochial History of Bremhill in the County of Wiltshire (London, 1828), 199; S. Hobbs (ed.), Gleanings from Wiltshire Parish Registers (WRS 63), 26, 293.

253. Poor Law Abstract, 1776, p. 188.

254. WSA, 84/36.

255. WSA, 84/36 (23 July 1775, 20 Apr. 1783).

256. WSA, 84/36 (4 Jan. 1774).

257. WSA, 84/36.

258. Ibid.

259. This was possibly the same church house in Foxham which had been gifted by Andrew Hungerford for the use of Foxham chapel in 1712 or one attached to the church in Bremhill. Bowles, Parochial History, 263–6; WSA, 1154/26; WSA, 84/36.

260. He was not assessed to pay local land-tax in 1780. WSA, A1/345.

261. WSA, 84/36 (16 May 1786).

262. WSA, 84/36.

263. There is no parish listing for another Sarah Newman living at the same time. It was an unusual local surname, and Paul himself had moved into the village. Evidence for Sarah being a serge maker comes from the fact she had an apprentice in 1790. She died in Jan. 1792, and Paul died later that same year in May. Entry is listed Register of Duties Paid for Apprentices' Indentures, 1710–1811 available at: ancestry.co.uk.

264. Paul had initially been in the clothing business in Melksham in partnership with his father, Paul senior, and brothers Dennis and John. However, Paul seems to have fallen out with his father as, despite being mentioned in his father's will, Paul the elder left his son nothing. The argument may have centred on religion as Paul senior was a Quaker while Paul seems to have been Church of England. The disagreement cost Paul dearly as his father had a large estate comprising of substantial property holdings and was able to leave individual monetary gifts of up to £1,000. WSA, P2/N/341.

265. Abstract of Answers and Return Under Act for Procuring Relative to Expense and Maintenance of Poor in England (Parl. Papers 1803-4 (175), xiii), 561.

266. WSA, H/4/110/1 (15 Apr. 1835, 4 Nov. 1835, 29 Mar. 1836).

267. WSA, H/4/110/1 (14 June 1836).

268. WSA, H/4/110/1 (31 May 1836).

269. I. Slocombe, Wiltshire Village Reading Rooms (Salisbury, 2012), 59.

270. I. Slocombe, Wiltshire Village Reading Rooms (Salisbury, 2012), 59, 61–2, 68; Kelly's Dir. Wilts. (1915 edn), 47; Kelly's Dir. Wilts. (1939 edn), 46.

271. WSA, 1154/51.

272. WSA, 1154/51 (17 Oct. 1921).

273. Coms. Of Inquiry into Charities in England and Wales: Twenty-Eighth Report (Parl. Papers 1834 (606), xxii), 307.

274. Endowed Charities (County of Wilts) Report (Parl. Papers 1908 (273), lxxx), 138.

275. WSA, 1154/28.

276. Endowed Charities (County of Wilts) Report (Parl. Papers 1908 (273), lxxx), 138; Coms. Of Inquiry into Charities in England and Wales: Twenty-Eighth Report (Parl. Papers 1834 (606), xxii), 307.

277. For further information see http://www.calnewelfarecharities.org/ (Accessed 29 July 2021).

278. Abstract of Answers and Return Under Act for Procuring Relative to Expense and Maintenance of Poor in England (Parl. Papers 1803-4 (175), xiii), 560–1; Abridgement of Answers and Returns for Procuring Relative to Expense and Maintenance of Poor in and Wales, (Parl. Papers 1818 (82), xix), 494–5; Registrar of Friendly Societies in England: Annual Report (Parl. Papers 1864 (498), xxxii), 159.

279. Wilts. Ind., 24 Dec. 1863.

280. Registrar of Friendly Societies in England: Annual Report (Parl. Papers 1866 (406), xxxix), 10.180

281. Coms. Of Inquiry into Charities in England and Wales: Twenty-Eighth Report (Parl. Papers 1834 (606), xxii), 307–9; Endowed Charities (County of Wilts) Report (Parl. Papers 1908 (273), lxxx), 267–9. See also, K. Taylor, Dry Shod to Chippenham: A History of Maud Heath's Ancient Causeway in North Wiltshire (Bradford-on-Avon, 2012).

282. Bowles, Parochial History, 159.

283. As specified in the oldest deed associated with the trust. Coms. Of Inquiry into Charities in England and Wales: Twenty-Eighth Report (Parl. Papers 1834 (606), xxii), 307–9.

284. WSA, 1195/28

285. Ibid.

286. The Universal British Directory (London, 1790), II 595; New Monthly Magazine (London, 1816), V, 276; The Penny Cyclopaedia of the Society for the Diffusion of Useful Knowledge (London, 1836), 168.

287. WSA, 1195/28.

288. WSA, 84/36 (19 May 1781 and 16 June 1782).

289. WSA, 84/36.

290. WSA, F8/500/37/1/1 (20 Feb. 1865).

291. WSA, 811/216.

292. WSA, D1/42/20.

293. WSA, 84/36. For example: 19 May 1782, 14 July 1782, 26 Dec. 1784, 16 May 1784.

294. Abstract of Answers and Returns under Act for Procuring Returns Relative to Expense and Maintenance of Poor in England (Parl. Papers 1803–4 (175), xiii), 560–1.

295. Select Committee on the Education of the Poor (1818). Digest of Parochial Returns. Vol. I, II, and III (Parl. Papers, 1819 (224), ix), 1020.

296. Abstract of Answers and Returns on State of Education in England and Wales, Volumes I., II., III (Parl. Papers 1835 (62), xli-xliii), 1030.

297. Committee of Council on Education: Minutes, Correspondence, Financial Statements, and Reports of H.M. Inspectors of Schools, 1854–55 (Parl. Papers 1854–5 [Cd 1926], xlii), 234. 298 WSA, 782/14.

299. Account of Schools for Children of Labouring Classes in County of Wiltshire, by Rev. W. Warburton (Parl. Papers 1859 Session 1 (27)), 10.

300. WSA, F8/500/37/1/1.

301. WSA, F8/500/37/1/1 (e.g. 4 Nov. 1865).

302. Committee of Council on Education: Minutes, Correspondence, Financial Statements, and Reports of H.M. Inspectors of Schools, 1850–51, General Report for the Year 1850 on the Schools Inspected in Berks. And Wilts by Her Majesty's Inspector of Schools Etc. (Parl. Papers 1851 [Cd 1357, 1358], xxxxiv), 25.

303. Account of Schools for Children of Labouring Classes in County of Wiltshire, by Rev. W. Warburton (Parl. Papers 1859 Session 1 (27)), 10.

304. WSA, F8/500/37/1/1 (5 July 1864).

305. WSA, F8/500/37/1/1 (14 June 1865).

306. WSA, F8/500/37/1/1 (25 Aug 1868).

307. Committee of Council on Education: Report, Appendix, 1869–70 (Parl. Papers 1870 [Cd C.165], xxii), 660.

308. On 22 Apr. 1872 low attendance was down to 'potato planting and bird starving'. WSA, F8/500/37/1/1.

309. Return of Civil Parishes in England and Wales under Education Act, of Population, Rateable Value, Number of Schools and Scholars in Attendance (Parl. Papers 1871 (201), lv), 421.

310. Ibid.

311. Committee of Council on Education: Report, Appendix, 1875–76 (Bye-Laws of School Boards) (Parl. Papers 1876 [Cd C.1513-1 C.1513-II], xxiii), 647–8.

312. Numbers were sixty-five at Bremhill, twelve at Charlcutt, forty-five at Foxham and forty-four at East Tytherton. Statement of Schools in receipt of Parliamentary Grants, Grants paid to School Boards under Section 97, Elementary Education Act, School Board Accounts and List of Loans, 1895–96 (Parl. Papers 1896 [Cd C.8179], lxv), 244.

313. Statement of Schools in receipt of Parliamentary Grants, Grants paid to School Boards under Section 97, Elementary Education Act, School Board Accounts and List of Loans, 1899–1900 (Parl. Papers 1900 [Cd 332], lxiv), 255.

314. The parish council stopped electing school managers for Foxham school in 1928. WSA, 141/9.

315. All dates of enrolment at the school are taken from the Bremhill School Admission Registers 1887–1969. WSA, F8/600/37/1/6/1.

316. All information on the teachers and conditions at the school is taken from the Bremhill School Logbooks 1911–67 and the Bremhill School Managers' Minutes 1903–1968. WSA, F8/500/37/1/3, F8/600/37/1/3/1.

317. All of Herbert's words are taken from an 'Account by FH Freegard of his time at Bremhill School'. WSA, F8/600/37/1/3/1.

318. C. Figes, 1743–1993: 250 Years of the Moravian Settlement at East Tytherton (London, 1993); N. Pocock, Wiser than We Deserve (London, 2009).

319. Select Committee on the Education of the Poor (1818). Digest of Parochial Returns. Vol. I, II, and III (Parl. Papers, 1819 (224), ix), 1020.

320. Account of Schools for Children of Labouring Classes in County of Wiltshire, by Rev. W. Warburton (Parl. Papers 1859 Session 1 (27)), 15.

321. Pocock, Wiser than We Deserve, 125.

322. Report of the Committee of Council on Education (England and Wales); with appendix. 1881–82 (Parl. Papers 1882 [cd C.3312-I], xxiii), 285.

323. Return of Public Elementary Schools examined, showing Accommodation, Average Attendance, Income from Fees, Books etc, 1888–9 (Parl. Papers 1890 (403), lvi), 282.

324. Statement of Schools in receipt of Parliamentary Grants, Grants paid to School Boards under Section 97, Elementary Education Act, School Board Accounts and List of Loans, 1897–8 (Parl. Papers 1898 [Cd C.8989] lxix), 254; Board of Education. List of Public Elementary Schools and Certified Efficient Schools in England (excluding Monmouthshire), on 1st August 1906 (Parl. Papers 1907 [Cd 3510] lxiii), 666

325. Newbury Weekly News and General Ad., 11 Oct. 1906.

326. https://www.gazetteandherald.co.uk/news/7412011.ghost-school-set-to-be-closed/ (Accessed 29 July 2021).

327. WSA, 84/36.

328. Salisbury and Winchester Jnl, 14 Sept. 1835.

329. Bath Chron. and Weekly Gaz., 6 Jan. 1820.

330. Salisbury and Winchester Jnl, 10 Jan. 1820.

331. Hampshire Chron., 3 Jan. 1825.

332. Salisbury and Winchester Jnl, 4 Jan. 1836, 16 Jan. 1837.

333. The account is taken from a pamphlet by Magdalene Bowles, wife of the Bremhill vicar Rev. Bowles. M. Bowles, Summer Visits to Cottages in a Country Village (London, 1836).

334. WSA, D1/42/46 fol. 50.

335. WSA, H/4/110/1 (8 Apr. 1835, 30 Dec. 1835, 13 Jan. 1836, 23 Feb. 1836, 2 Mar. 1836). See also, WSA, 1154/40.

336. WSA, H/4/110/1(19 July 1836).

337. WSA, H/4/110/1 (30 Aug. 1836).

338. WSA, 473/52.

339. I am grateful to Steve Hobbs for bringing my attention to this case. WSA, D1/42/18, D1/42/19, D1/42/20.

Chapter 5

340. Thanks to Rev. Jim Scott for this story.

341. R. Whitlock, The Folklore of Wiltshire (London, 1976), 129.

342. Rev. E.P. Eddrup, 'Notes on some Wiltshire Superstitions', WAM 22, 330–4.

343. Eddrup, 'Notes on some Wiltshire Superstitions'.

344. Eddrup, 'Notes on some Wiltshire Superstitions'.

345. Andrew had inherited the Bayntun fortune from his father, the vice-chamberlain to five of the wives of Henry VIII. Andrew had also served at the Tudor court, not least in the household of Henry's chief minister, Thomas Cromwell, before Cromwell was beheaded in 1540.

346. Hist. Parl. Commons, 1509–58, I, 399–400; Hist. Parl. Commons, 1558–1603, I, 409–10. See also, Hist. Parl. Commons, 1509–58, I, 400–3; Hist. Parl. Commons, 1558–1603, I, 410.

347. As quoted in Hist. Parl. Commons, 1558–1603, I, 371. The court battle seems to have been resolved by 1566.

348. J. Burke, A Genealogical and Heraldic History of the Extinct and Dormant Baronetcies of England (London, 1841), 453. In the Wiltshire Visitation of 1565 and later in Burke's Commoners, Andrew Bayntun was listed but not recorded as having inherited the estate before brother Edward; W. Harvey, Visitation of Wiltshire, 1565 (Exeter, 1897), 4; J. Burke, A Genealogical and Heraldic History of the Landed Gentry; or Commoners of Great Britain and Ireland, IV (London, 1838), 685.

349. The primary sources for the witchcraft trial are TNA, C3/8/113. See also, Wilts. N&Q, IV, 72–4.

350. Dorothy is likely the youngest child of Sir Walter Mantell. Burke, Genealogical and Heraldic History, 452–3; TNA, 11/23/158.

351. D.R. Dean, Gideon Mantell and the Discovery of Dinosaurs (Cambridge, 1999), 6; Hist. Parl. Commons, 1558–1603, I, 1–14. For an account of the misadventures of Dorothy's brother, John Mantell http://theesotericcuriosa.blogspot.com/2010/06/of-reckless-youth-thomas-fiennes-9th.html (Accessed 29 July 2021). The execution of the two Mantell's is mentioned in Foxes Book of Martyrs.

352. Agnes's affair was with Sir William Stourton. The case over Stourton's legacy was only finally resolved positively when the other Stourton heir was executed for murder in 1557. Agnes's father was Rhys Ap Gruffydd or anglicised Sir Griffith Rhys.

353. Hist. Parl. Commons, 1558–1603, I, 410. Agnes Bayntun's mother was Katherine Howard see https://thehistoryofengland.co.uk/resource/katherine-howard-countess-of-bridgewater/ (Accessed 29 July 2021). For William Stourton, see Hist. Parl. Commons, 1509–58, III, 391.

354. This information is provided by the tomb inscription of Sir Edward Bayntun in St Nicolas' Church, Bromham.

355. https://thehistoryofparliament.wordpress.com/2019/11/05/parliaments-politics-and-people-seminar-the-political-andreligious-origins-of-the-1563-witchcraft-act/ (Accessed 29 July 2021).

356. 5 Eliz. I, c. 16. For the text of the Act see: http://statutes.org.uk/site/the-statutes/sixteenth-century/1563-5-elizabeth-1-c-16-an-act-against-conjurations-inchantments-and-witchcraft/ (Accessed 29 July 2021).

357. M. Gaskill, 'Witchcraft trials, England', in New Oxford Companion to the Law https://www-oxfordreferencecom.libezproxy.open.ac.uk/view/ 10.1093/acref/9780199290543.001.0001/acref-9780199290543 (Accessed 29 July 2021). However, figures vary. According to figures quoted by K. Edwards, between 1560–1706 in England, 2,000 cases were convicted, with 300 executed (15%). K. Edwards, 'Witchcraft in Tudor England and Scotland', in A Companion to Tudor Literature (Oxford, 2010), 32; M. Gaskill, 'Witchcraft and Evidence in Early Modern England', Past and Present 198 (2008), 33–70.

358. M. Gaskill, 'Witchcraft Politics and Memory in Seventeenth Century England', Hist. Jnl, 50 (2007), 290. Another historian also asserts that the accusation against Agnes came originally from Edward and Agnes Bayntun themselves. K.J. Kesselring, 'Bodies of Evidence: Sex and Murder (or Gender and Homicide) in Early Modern England, c.1500–1680', Gender & History 27 (2015), p. 245–62.

359. Edwards, 'Witchcraft in Tudor England and Scotland', 35.

360. W.L. Bowles, A Parochial History of Bremhill in the County of Wiltshire (London, 1828), 264.

361. However, Andrew probably died at Rowden, Chippenham where his final will had been made and he was buried.

362. Anne Bodenham was the only other witch convicted and sentenced to death at the county gaol. Her case is much better known because it was the subject of pamphlets printed immediately after her trial. E.g. E. Bower Doctor Lamb Revived (London, 1653); Anon, Doctor Lamb's Darling (London, 1653). See also, Gaskill, 'Witchcraft Politics and Memory in Seventeenth Century England', 289–308.

363. Not all those who were accused of being witches were elderly and impoverished, Anne Bodenham was in her 80s, but she was a literate middle-class married woman.

364. Jewel was an active magistrate. S.A. Wenig, Scott, 'John Jewel and the Reformation of the Diocese of Salisbury, 1560–1571', Anglican and Episcopal Hist. 73 (2004), 141–68.

365. The bishop's friendship with Sharington is outlined in J. Britton, The Beauties of Wiltshire (London, 1825), III, 236. Also stated in Aubrey, Topog. Colln. ed. Jackson. For Sharington, Hist. Parl. Commons, 1558–1603, I, 371–2. This is also related to Sharington's friendship with Andrew Bayntun, with whom Edward is likely to have had strained relations. Hist. Parl. Commons, 1558–1603, I, 409–10; Hist. Parl. Commons, 1509–58, I, 399–400; Hist. Parl. Commons, 1558–1603, I, 409–10.

366. The two named justices she confessed to were George Penruddock and John Hooper. A social climber, Pendruddock had been facilitated in his aspirations in no small part by the acquisition of a half-manor, unsurprisingly, from the easily manipulated Sir Andrew Bayntun. Hist. Parl. Commons, 1558–1603, I, 409–10; Hist. Parl. Commons, 1558–1603, I, 198–200.

367. Edward Bayntun's half-brother, another Henry Bayntun, did feature. As William Harvey probably visited Edward Bayntun to record the information, it is likely Edward consciously neglected to provide it, or William Harvey, mindful of the ongoing court case between the two, did not ask. Harvey, Visitation of Wiltshire, 1565, 4.

368. E.g. VCH Wilts. VI, on Fisherton Anger (published in 1962).

369. For further information on this pamphlet, see ch. 1. M. Gibson, Early Modern Witches: Witchcraft Cases in Contemporary Writing (London and New York, 2000).

370. J. Gibson, Hanged for Witchcraft: Elizabeth Lowys and her Successors (Canberra, 1998).

Chapter 6

371. VCH Wilts. XX (forthcoming).

372. VCH Wilts. XX (forthcoming).

373. VCH Wilts. XX (forthcoming).

374. WSA, D1/42/18.

375. WSA, 473/52.

376. WSA, 473/52.

377. Stockham Marsh was enclosed during the late eighteenth century.

378. VCH Wilts. XX (forthcoming).

379. WSA, 473/53.

380. D.A. Speath, The Church in an Age of Danger: Parsons and Parishioners, 1660–1740 (Cambridge, 2000), 88.

381. The source material comes from: TNA, STAC 8/164/18; WSA, P3/H/278.

382. WSA, 473/61.

383. E.g. Kelly's Dir. Wilts. (1939 edn), 46–7.

384. Charmian Mansell and Mark Hailwood (eds). Court Depositions of South West England, 1500–1700, University of Exeter: http://human-ities-research.exeter.ac.uk/womenswork/courtdepositions (Accessed 29 July 2021).

385. WSA, 209/1.

386. WSA, 209/1, 209/3-209/6.

387. WSA, 1154/80 (3 Nov. 1842).

388. Wilts. Ind., 23 July 1846.

389. Morning Chron., 12 Feb. 1846.

390. WSA, 1154/80 (13 Oct. and 3 Nov. 1842).

391. WSA, TA Bremhill (1848).

392. Vines is listed in several trade directories of the 1850s. See also, census returns.

393. Salisbury and Winchester Jnl, 9 Apr. 1853.

394. He died without leaving a will, WSA, P3/1854/62.

395. Devizes and Wilts. Gaz., 2 Feb. 1837.

396. Devizes and Wilts. Gaz., 11 May 1826.

397. WSA, 118/162.

398. C.A.F. Meekings (ed.), Crown Pleas of the Wiltshire Eyres 1249 (WRS 16), 193, 188.

399. Devizes and Wilts. Gaz., 5 Aug. 1824.

400. Wilts. Times and Trowbridge Ad., 25 May 1895.

401. WSA, 1154/29 (25 Mar. 1869).

Chapter 7

402. VCH Wilts. III, 215; WAM 96, 82; S. Draper, 'Landscape, Settlement and Society: Wiltshire in the First Millennium AD' (Durham Univ. PhD thesis, 2004), 113.

403. I am grateful to Dr Simon Draper who spoke on this subject at the Bremhill Parish History Festival 2020.

404. VCH Wilts. III, 219; VCH Wilts. VII, 197–8; J. Aubrey, The Topographical Collections of John Aubrey, ed. J.E. Jackson (Devizes, 1862), 60.

405. T. Phillips, Institutiones Clericorum in Comitatu Wiltoniae, Ab Anno 1297, Ad Annum 1810 (Worcestershire, 1825), 1, 2.

406. W.L. Bowles, A Parochial History of Bremhill in the County of Wiltshire (London, 1828), 142.

407. Bowles gives a very convoluted version of Tounson's tenure as vicar with great sympathy for his treatment over the sequestration of the benefice. See Bowles, Parochial History, 172–94.

408. ODNB, s.v. Townson, Robert, bishop of Salisbury, accessed 29 July 2021.

409. ODNB, s.v. Davenant, John, bishop of Salisbury, accessed 29 July 2021.

410. WSA, D1/41/4/38.

411. D.A. Spaeth, The Church in an Age of Danger: Parsons and Parishioners, 1660–1740 (Cambridge, 2000), 40.

412. S. Hobbs (ed.), Wiltshire Glebe Terriers 1588–1827 (WRS 56), 53–4.

413. WSA, D/1/54/6/3/30.

414. Spaeth, Church in an Age of Danger, 87, 144.

415. Rowde Parish Registers 1606–61.

416. Bremhill Parish Registers 1591–1726; England & Wales, Quaker Birth, Marriage and Death Register 1578–1837.

417. WSA, 1699/18. Wiltshire Friends Sufferings Books 1653–1756, 2.

418. J. Bese, A Collection of the Sufferings of the People Called Quakers, (London, 1753), II, 41

419. Wilts. N&Q, II, 168.

420. N. Pocock, The Quakers in East Tytherton from Wilts. N&Q, V, 6, 7.

421. Bese, Sufferings, 42.

422. Bese, Sufferings, 47.

423. WSA, 1699/18. Wiltshire Friends Sufferings Books 1653–1756, 62.

424. WSA, D/1/54/6/3/30.

425. These included Humphrey Tuggwell and his wife, Alice Danvers, Robert Brooks and his wife and Henry Hayward and Richard Broome who were reported to the bishop in 1674 and Tounson reported they were back to the fold in 1675. WSA, D/1/54/6/3/30; D/1/14/1/3/45-7; D/1/14/1/3/34.

426. Spaeth, Church in an Age of Danger, 86–7, 92–3.

427. Aubrey, Topog. Colln ed. Jackson, 63; Bowles, Parochial History, 158, 264; S. Hobbs (ed.), Gleanings from Wiltshire Parish Registers (WRS 63), 26. See also, WSA, 1154/26, 1154/91.

428. WSA, 1154/28.

429. C.C. Southey (ed.), The Life and Correspondence of Robert Southey (New York, 1851), 544.

430. G. Garland (ed.), A Wiltshire Parson and his Friends: The Correspondence of William Lisle Bowles (Boston and New York, 1926), 7.

431. J. Russell (ed.), Memoirs, Journals & Correspondence of Thomas Moore, vii (London, 1860).

432. J. Russell (ed.), The Diary of Thomas Moore, ii (London, 1853–6), 153

433. J. Britton, Autobiography, i (London, 1851), 372.

434. C.C. Southey (ed.), Life and Correspondence, 544.

435. J. Britton, Autobiography, i (London, 1851), 372.

436. Bath Chron. and Weekly Gaz., 5 May 1836. This fact was also reported by papers across Britain and Ireland, e.g. Limerick Chron., 18 May 1836; Gloucester Chron., 7 May 1836; Hampshire Chron., 2 May 1836.

437. Rev. G. Gilfillan, The Poetical Works of William Lisle Bowles: With Memoir, Critical Dissertation and Explanatory Notes (Edinburgh, 1855), II, p. xv–xvi. See J.J. van Rennes, Bowles, Byron and the Pope Controversy (New York, 1966) and R. Moody, The Life and Letters of William Lisle Bowles: Poet and Parson (Salisbury, 2009), 118–33.

438. Bowles, Parochial History, 266.

439. Bowles, Parochial History, 202; R. Moody, Life and Letters, 181–2.

440. Devizes and Wilts. Gaz., 17 Apr. 1834.

441. Devizes and Wilts. Gaz., 24 Apr. 1834.

442. Ibid.

443. Salisbury and Winchester Jnl, 21 Apr. 1834; Devizes and Wilts. Gaz., 17 Apr. 1834.

444. https://historicengland.org.uk/listing/the-list/list-entry/1283495 (Accessed 29 July 2021); Kelly's Dir. Wilts. (1915 edn), 46; Wilts. Times & Trowbridge Ad., 22 May 1880. See also, WSA, 1154/58.

445. Devizes and Wilts. Gaz., 5 Feb. 1883.

446. WSA, 1154/66.

447. Ibid.

448. N. Pevsner, Wiltshire (2nd ed. New Haven and London, 2002), 268; For a history of St Peters at Highway see VCH Wilts. VII, 197–8.

449. WSA, 1154/65.

450. https://www.mardenvale.org.uk/ (Accessed 29 July 2021). See also, 'The Benefice of Marden Vale, Comprising Bremhill, Calne and Blackland, Derry Hill, and Foxham' in Crockford's Clerical Directory. Church House Publishing <https://www.crockford.org.uk/places/19792/the-benefice-of-marden-vale%2c-comprising-bremhill%2c-calne-andblackland% 2c-derry-hill%2c-and-foxham> (Accessed 29 July 2021).

451. VCH Wilts. II, 138, 143.

452. E.J. Bodington, 'The Church Survey in Wilts.', WAM 41.

453. Pevsner, Wilts., 541; Historic England HER, Tytherton Lucas, Church of St Nicholas, 1022442 [ST 94664 74288].

454. WANS 22, 368

455. Tablet on wall of north aisle, St Nicholas' Church.

456. Hobbs, Wiltshire Glebe Terriers 1588–1827 (WRS 56), 89, no. 163.

457. N. Penney (ed.), The Journal of George Fox (New York, 1924). Ch. 9.

458. WMA, MSS.438.

459. Bese, Sufferings, 41–2. See also, VCH Wilts. III, 116; Wilts. N&Q, II, 168–9; WSA, 1699/18.

460. WSA, 1699/18.

461. VCH Wilts. III, 120.

462. J. Chandler (ed.), Wiltshire Dissenters Meeting House Certificates (WRS 40), 3.

463. WSA, 1699/115, 1699/75-78; K. Taylor, 'Society, Schism and Sufferings: the first 70 years of Quakerism in Wiltshire' (Univ. of the West of England PhD thesis, 2006).

464. The preacher at Foxham, John Cennick, was originally a Wesleyan but later became a Moravian. He established the Moravian church at East Tytherton. J. Cennick, The Life of Mr J. Cennick (Bristol, 1745), 38; VCH Wilts. III, 130–1.

465. M. Ransome (ed.), Wiltshire Returns to the Bishops Visitation Queries (WRS 27), 44.

466. John Cennick preached in Foxham during July 1740. The Baptist Magazine, lvii (London, 1865), 30.

467. The Weekly-History or An Account of the Most Remarkable Particulars Relating to the Present Progress of the Gospel, 46 (Glasgow, 1743), 6.

468. John Cennick preached in Foxham during July 1740. The Baptist Magazine, lvii (London, 1865), 89.

469. The Baptist Magazine, lvii (London, 1865), 93.

470. Chandler, Wiltshire Dissenters, 121; https://historicengland.org.uk/listing/the-list/list-entry/1199325 (Accessed 29 July 2021).

471. Wilts. Ind., 26 Sept. 1844.

472. Dumfries and Galloway Standard, 16 Oct. 1844.

473. This account is largely drawn from Bowles's own account. WSA, BRE.922.

474. It is likely that this was the Strict Baptist minister, John Warburton who, although based in Trowbridge, also preached in local chapels.

475. Bowles's attitude to the Moravians at East Tytherton was very different. He stated they provided 'no officious intrusion' and could be considered subsidiary to the Church of England. He was also friends with the Moravian minister, Lewis West. Bowles, Parochial History, 153–7; G. Greever, A Wiltshire Parson and his Friends (Boston & New York,

1926), II, 10.

476. Wilts. Times and Trowbridge Ad., 5 June 1880.

477. WSA, 2053/42.

478. Chandler, Wiltshire Dissenters, 161, 165,

479. Devizes and Wilts. Gaz., 29 May 1845.

480. WMA, MSS.438.

481. Spirthill Chapel: WSA, 2783/10. Foxham Chapel: WSA, 3083187.

482. WSA, 3083/188. For Stanley chapel: WSA, 1907/143; Wilts. Times and Trowbridge Ad., 15 May 1897.

483. Wilts. Times and Trowbridge Ad., 12 Mar. 1904.

484. WSA, 3083/187 (18 Feb. 1958).

485. WSA, 3083/187 (13 Mar. 1963).

486. WSA, 2783/10 (29 Sept. 1977).

487. WSA, 3083/187. All meetings between 1948 and 1970 are listed as taking place at Monkton Hill.

488. WSA, 2783/10 (29 Sept. 1978).

489. WSA, 2783/10 (23 Oct. 1982). There is some confusion over dates with the date noted of the next annual meeting on 13 Oct. 1983.

490. WSA, 2783/10 (13 Oct. 1983). See note above.

491. J. Cennick, Journal. Entry for 4 Sept. 1742. The actual purchase was on 25 Oct. 1742.

492. Ibid, 11 Mar. 1744.

493. This manuscript is in the Moravian archives in Muswell Hill, London. It is annotated Manuscript in the notebook of Miss Anna-Mary Browne, friend of Ann Grigg. Some accounts are of the life of the single sister, Ann Grigg who departed at Tytherton Dec. 11th, 1814. Written by herself.

494. Leonora's gravestone was unfortunately removed in the 1950s. It has been replaced in the second row from the top, next to that of Diana Ormond, who died just before her.

495. I am enormously grateful to Jean-Jacques Vrij of the Surinam Genealogy Society for all the findings from the Dutch/Surinam records.

496. Inf. from Joan Archard, 2009.

497. Wilts. Times and Trowbridge Ad., 12 Jan. 1895.

Chapter 8

498. WSA, 141/9.

499. E.E. Green, The Tyranny of the Countryside (London, 1913); Wilts. Times and Trowbridge Ad., 5 Aug. 1911.

500. These included West End Farm, Avon Farm, Avon Mill, Elm Farm, Godsell Farm, Gate Farm and Harestreet Farm. Information provided by Dr Cathryn Spence, archivist, Bowood.

501. Wilts. Times and Trowbridge Ad., 2 July 1910.

502. Green, Tyranny, 145 (this publication was biased, perhaps understandably, in favour of local labourers but was selective in its portrayal of events); Wilts. Times and Trowbridge Ad., 5 June 1910.

503. Wilts. Times and Trowbridge Ad., 5 Aug. 1911.

504. Green, Tyranny, 31, 145–6; Wilts. Times and Trowbridge Ad., 26 Aug. 1911, 21 Oct. 1911, 16 Dec. 1911.

505. Wilts. Times and Trowbridge Ad., 18 Nov. 1911, 2 Dec. 1911.

506. Salisbury and Winchester Jnl, 18 Nov. 1911; Wilts. Times and Trowbridge Ad., 18 Nov. 1911, 2 Dec. 1911; North Wilts Herald, 1 Dec. 1911.

507. Wilts. Times and Trowbridge Ad., 16 Dec. 1911.

508. For example, see correspondence Wilts. Times and Trowbridge Ad., 30 Dec. 1911.

509. Wilts. Times and Trowbridge Ad., 27 Jan. 1912.

510. Evidently fifty newspapers across the country reported the affair. Wilts. Times and Trowbridge Ad., 2 Mar. 1912, 9 Mar. 1912, 16 Mar. 1912.

511. For this piece I have used parish registers, census and military records and other records available at: https://Ancestry.co.uk. For further information on the local casualties of WWI see D. Wood, The Great War 1914–18: A Remembrance (Bremhill, 2018).

512. North Wilts. Herald, 21 Sept. 1917.

513. WSA, 141/9 (17 Oct. 1917).

514. North Wilts. Herald, 11 Feb. 1916.

515. Wilts. Times and Trowbridge Ad., 15 Apr. 1916.

516. E.g. North Wilts. Herald, 29 Dec. 1916, 16 Feb. 1917, 21 June 1918, 26 July 1918, 20 Dec. 1918. Contributions by women included Minnie Shipp of Cadenham, who sent various items poultry, greens, asparagus, e.g. North Wilts. Herald, 24 Dec. 1915, 7 Jan. 1916, 7 July 1916, 21 July 1918, 26 July 1918 (includes contributions by Miss and Mrs Ferris).

517. Ibid. Collections included those for East and West Tytherton (Tytherton Lucas), North Wilts. Herald, 29 Dec. 1916, etc.

518. Edgar was a significant contributor to the Red Cross. E.g. Wilts. Times and Trowbridge Ad., 25 Aug. 1917. Other local contributors included C. Cleverley W.J. Collett and H.J. Pocock. Mrs Pegler, C. Amore. Contributors of livestock included W. Ferris (e.g. North Wilts. Herald, 7 Sept. 1917). His appearance at tribunals includes North Wilts. Herald, 26 Oct. 1917.

519. Wilts. Times and Trowbridge Ad., 1 July 1916.

520. Wilts. Times and Trowbridge Ad., 8 Apr. 1916.

521. Inf. from Lynne and Robert Pegler, May 2021.

522. North Wilts. Herald, 7 Apr. 1916, 21 July 1916.

523. Wilts. Times and Trowbridge Ad., 1 July 1916.

524. Wilts. Times and Trowbridge Ad., 29 July 1916.

525. Wilts. Times and Trowbridge Ad., 17 June 1916.

526. North Wilts. Herald, 7 Apr 1916, 21 July 1916.

527. Wilts. Times and Trowbridge Ad., 22 July 1916.

528. Wilts. Times and Trowbridge Ad., 16 Dec. 1916.

529. Wilts. Times and Trowbridge Ad., 9 Mar. 1918.

530. As reported by Wilts. Times and Trowbridge Ad., 15 Apr. 1916.

531. Inf. provided by David Wood, Ray Alder, Nigel Pocock and Dr Cathryn Spence. Much of the material on the contribution of local women to the British Red Cross was initially gathered from https://vad.redcross.org.uk/ (Accessed 29 July 2021). I have also used parish registers, tax returns and census records on https://Ancestry.co.uk (Accessed 29 July 2021). Much information is found in R. Alder, Unity and Loyalty (Gloucester, 2021).

532. North Wilts. Herald, 27 Dec. 1918.

533. Although she was the daughter of local farmer James Jeffreys, Frances Marion Jeffreys gave her address as 'Girls School Tytherton'. [She may have been the teacher, Miss M. Jeffreys, at the Girls School mentioned in the work of Nigel Pocock].

534. However, rumours circulated in 1917 that they were paid, which the chair of the finance committee of the Red Cross Hospital Chippenham, Clare Garnett, had to scotch in the Wilts. Times. Wilts. Times and Trowbridge Ad., 13 Oct. 1917.

535. Wilts. Times and Trowbridge Ad., 28 June 1919.

536. According to the Wiltshire Women's War Agricultural Committee, North Wilts. Herald, 31 May 1918. Some other figures published in the war were higher, e.g. 3,023 women were reported as employed on farms in Wiltshire in Aug. 1916. Som. Standard, 18 Aug. 1916.

537. North Wilts. Herald, 27 Dec. 1918.

538. Shortly after she married local boy Robert Stanley Broomfield.

539. While these war trophies were not listed they are likely to include weaponry, such as guns, mortars and even machine guns.

540. WSA, 141/9 (11 Sept. 1919, 19 Dec. 1919, 14 Jan. 1920).

541. WSA, 141/9 (e.g. 6 Sept. 1919, 19 Dec. 1919, 6 Sept. 1946).

542. WSA, 141/9 (6 Sept. 1917). For information about the Foxham housing problems see ch. 8.1.

543. WSA, 141/9 (e.g. 19 Dec. 1919, 14 Jan. 1920).

544. Inf. from Alfie Holder, Jan. 2021.

545. WSA, 141/9 (e.g. 5 Oct. 1936).

546. Kelly's Dir. Wilts. (1939 edn), 46–7. My thanks to John Harris who provided details of the Fry family.

547. North Wilts. Herald, 5 Sept. 1924.

548. See ch. 4.2. Kelly's Dir. Wilts. (1939 edn), 46–7; WSA, 2276/8. See also, 2276/9-13, 23.

549. See ch. 7.3.2.

550. See ch. 7.

551. Inf. from Lynne and Robert Pegler, May 2021.

552. Inf. from Nigel Pocock, Nov. 2020.

553. Western Daily Press, 14 Dec. 1939. The North Wilts. Herald stated in its obituary, United Diaries Ltd 'was formed from that firm [Long and Pocock]'. North Wilts. Herald, 15 Dec. 1939. See also, Middx County Times, 9 Dec. 1939.

554. Inf. from Nigel Pocock, Nov. 2020.

555. WSA, 141/9.

556. WSA, 141/9.

557. The information on Bremhill school during WWII is taken from Bremhill School Managers' Minutes 1903–1968 at the Wiltshire and Swindon History Centre unless otherwise referenced. WSA, F8/600/37/1/3/1.

558. Rex Grimshaw was interviewed in Mar. 2013 by Helen Stuckey and Dr Christopher Kent. Notes were taken, read back and agreed with Rex for inclusion in a village history book. Rex sadly died 21 May 2018.

559. The Bremhill plan is contained in the 'parish war book' at the Wiltshire and Swindon History Centre, WSA, F2/851/3/13.

560. The following sources are used by David Wood is this account: Maj. E.A. Mackay, The History of the Wiltshire Home Guard (1946), 25–46; WSA, 1710/53.

561. Inf. from Rev. Jim Scott, Dec 2020.

562. Inf. from Terry Satchell and John Harris, July 2021.

563. WMA, SC.9.5.

564. This comprised the farms of: Hazelwood, Charlcote, Bencroft, Monument, Bremhill Wick, Bremhill Field, Ash Hill. Wilts. Times and Trowbridge Ad., 18 Oct. 1947.

565. Inf. from Alfie Holder, Jan. 2021..

566. Inf. from Dr Christopher Kent, Mar. 2014.

567. WSA, 141/9.

568. WSA, 141/9.

569. All information in this account is taken from Bremhill School Managers' Minutes 1903–1968 unless otherwise referenced, WSA, F8/600/37/1/3/1.

570. WSA, 141/9 (30 June 1958).

571. Inf. from Verina Vanzillotti, Feb. 2021.

572. Inf. from Alfie Holder, Jan. 2021.

573. Inf. from Sarah Grimshaw, in Dec. 2020.

574. Inf. from Lynne and Robert Pegler, May 2021.

575. Inf. from Pam Sawyer, Jan. 2021.

576. Inf. from Dr Christopher Kent, Mar. 2014.

577. Inf. from Nigel Pocock, Mar. 2021.

578. Inf. from John Harris, June 2020 and Martin Nye, Aug. 2021.

Image Credits

The Bremhill Parish History Group is a not-for-profit organisation for those interested in researching the history of Bremhill Parish and share their interests by gathering, archiving and publishing the information in order to help advance education in schools and of the public. We would like to thank the following for permission to reproduce the images in this book. Every care has been taken to contact or trace all copyright owners where possible. We would be pleased to correct any errors or omissions in future editions brought to our attention.

Chapter 1

Fig. 1: Drawing of a carpentum in a Roman frieze. Eon images.

Fig. 2: Reconstruction of the Iron Age Gateway and ramparts on Blewburton Hill. Artist Richard Hook, first published in "A view from a Hill" by Cockrell and Kay for Sustainable Blewbury.

Fig. 3: Roman coins. Wiltshire Museum collections.

Fig. 4: thepostgradchronicles.org. A case of clerical fraud-King Athelstan and Malmesbury Abbey.

Fig. 5: Illustration by John Harris.

Fig. 6: thepostgradchronicles.org.

Fig. 7: Unknown engraver. Public Domain via Wikipedia Commons.

Fig. 8: National Archives UK.

Fig. 9: Detail see Fig. 2

Fig. 10: Illustration by John Harris.

Fig. 11: Bookplate from 'The parochial history of Bremhill'.

Fig. 12: Illustration by John Harris.

Fig. 13: Photograph by John Harris.

Fig. 14: Photograph by John Harris.

Fig. 15: Photograph by John Harris.

Fig. 15a: Engraving of Bremhill Court. Alamy DDECX4.

Fig. 16: Cistercian monk. F.A.Gasquet. Public Domain. Wikipedia Commons.

Fig. 17: Harold Brakspear FCA.

Fig. 18: saintedmondscalne.org.

Fig. 19: Photograph by John Harris.

Fig. 20. Dr Graham Brown.

Fig. 21: Airborne survey. J.K. Joseph. Cambridge University.

Fig. 21a: Photograph. Bremhill Exhibition 1990.

Fig. 21b: Charter. W&SHC.

Fig. 21c: saintedmundscalne.org

Fig. 22: The Gateway, Spye Park by Maurice Pullin, CC BY-SA 2.0, via Wikimedia Commons.

Fig. 24: Photograph by Martin Nye.

Fig. 25: Photograph by Martin Nye.

Fig. 26 Spye House. Unknown author. Public Domain via Wikipedia Commons.

Fig. 27: Photograph by Helen Stuckey.

Fig. 28: Postcard from Bremhill Exhibition 1990.

Fig. 29: Photograph by John Harris.

Fig. 30: Image. David Wood.

Fig. 31: Photograph. W&SHC.

Fig. 32: Evan Butterfield, www.ebutterfieldphotography.com.

Fig. 33: Photography by Helen Stuckey.

Fig. 34: Photography by Helen Stuckey.

Fig. 35: Photography by Helen Stuckey.

Fig. 36: Photography by Helen Stuckey.

Fig. 37: Photography by Martin Nye.

Fig. 38: Photograph. W&SHC.

Fig. 39: Photography by John Harris.

Fig. 40: Photograph from Bremhill Exhibition 1990.

Fig. 41: Illustration by John Harris.

Fig. 42: Philanthropy of Rev Bowles, talk by Louise Ryland Epton. bremhillparishhistory.com.

Fig. 43: No paradise CC BY-SA 4.0 Wikipedia Commons.

Fig. 44: 'Beauties of Wiltshire'. W L Bowles.

Fig. 45: Photograph by John Harris.

Fig. 46: Vintage postcard.

Fig. 47: W&SHC archive.

Fig. 48: Image. Helen Stuckey.

Fig. 49: Bremhill Exhibition 1990.

Fig. 50: Photograph by Helen Stuckey.

Fig. 51: Image, Helen Stuckey.

Fig. 52: Image from Sale Brochure of Foxham Estate courtesy of Chris Minty.

Chapter 2

Fig. 53: etc.usf.edu.Roman Army on the March.

Fig. 54: clipground.co (amended).

Fig. 55: John Speed. Public Domain via Wikipedia Commons.

Fig. 56: John Ogilby map. John Chandler.

Fig. 57: Wiltshire Museum archive.

Fig. 58: The History Scroll Blog.

Fig. 59: W&SHC archive.

Fig. 60: Photograph courtesy of Maud Heath Trust.

Fig. 61: Illustration by John Harris.

Fig. 61a: Map and case study illustrations by John Harris, courtesy of Maud Heath Trust.

Fig. 62: (main) Bryan Matthews, L-R. Craig Gingell, Rummings family, Fry family, Foxham Village Hall archive, Nicol Jordon, Helen Stuckey.

Fig. 63: Illustrations by John Harris.

Fig. 64: Illustration by John Harris.

Fig. 65: Photograph by John Harris.

Fig. 66: Photograph by Helen Stuckey.

Fig. 67: Photograph. Wilts & Berks Canal Trust.

Fig. 67a: Photograph. Calne Heritage Centre

Fig. 68: Photograph. Calne Heritage Centre.

Fig. 69: Photograph. Calne Town Council.

Fig. 70: Photograph courtesy of the Lovelock family.

Fig. 71: Photograph courtesy of the Lovelock family.

Fig. 72. Photograph by D. Pritchard.

Fig. 73: Photograph courtesy of the Lovelock family.

Fig. 74: Photograph courtesy of Christopher Kent.

Chapter 3

Fig. 75: Haymaking by John James Wilson. Public Domain via Wikipedia Commons.

Fig. 76: Diarama of Medieval Ploughing 14th century. Science Museum. Creative Commons license. Attribution 4.0 International (CC by 4.0)

Fig. 77: Stories for the household, 1889.

Fig. 78: Wellcome Collection. V0038716.

Fig. 79: Spinning wheel. Public Domain via Wikipedia Commons.

Fig. 80: Photograph by John Harris. Wiltshire Museum DZSWS:1990:89

Fig. 81: The story of cheese- making in Britain. Val Cheke. 1959.

Fig. 82: Engraving, men working in a field.

Fig. 83: Collecting firewood. London Illustrated News.

Fig. 84. Henry Petty-Fitzmaurice. Wikipedia.

Fig. 85: Bookplate. Fourteen Sonnets, 1786.

Fig. 86: Detail of The Plan of THE MANOR and Parish of BREMHILL in the county of WILTSHIRE, map. Wiltshire Museum.

Fig. 87: A drunkard stands before his family and swears by the Holy Bible, after George Cruikshank (detail). Wellcome Collection V0019432.

Fig. 88: Poor Law Union. Wiltshire Museum.

Fig. 89: British History Online. Parochial government.

Fig. 90: Postcard. Bremhill Village Cross.

Fig. 91: oll:libertyfund.org. 2337.8 Voter registration.

Fig. 92: Night meeting of workers DP9W33. Alamy.

Fig. 93: opc.org.uk Sudden death of Henry Drury, Archdeacon of Wiltshire 1863.

Fig. 94: Charles Dickens. Woodberrytype. Public Domain via Wikipedia Commons.

Fig. 95: Sir Robert Peel by Henry Pickersgill. Public Domain via Wikipedia Commons.

Fig. 96: oll:libertyfund.org. Illustration 11. Images of freedom and liberty.

Fig. 97: Labours of the field. Woman spinning (Millet) Public Domain via Wikipedia Commons.

Fig. 98: A weaver's cunning hand. istock 890027990.

Fig. 99: Fulling stocks by Clem Rutter. CC. By 3.0.

Fig. 100: Hazeland Mill interior. LOWE 0857.141.

Fig. 101: William Fox Talbot via Calne Heritage Centre.

Fig. 102: Photograph courtesy of Kim Stuckey.

Fig. 103: Ale next door. Painting by Henry Singleton.

Fig. 104: Print by George Morland.

Fig. 105: Photograph by John Harris.

Fig. 106: Spinning frame. Author unknown. Public Domain via Wikipedia Commons.

Fig. 107: Woman beside two cows. Popular Graphic Arts. Public Domain via Wikipedia Commons.

Fig. 108: Engraving 19th century baker.

Fig. 109: Scullery maid MET53.600.588. Anne Claude de Caylus CC0 via Wikipedia Commons.

Fig. 110: Photograph by John Harris.

Fig. 111: Apprenticeship by Emile Adam (1839-1937) Public Domain by Wikipedia Commons.

Fig. 112: 17th century bond. Nottingham University UK. Manuscripts and special collections.

Fig. 113: Postcard of Devizes Gaol. Wiltshire Museum.

Fig. 114: Covered waggon. Alamy AA48W9

Fig. 115: Arch St. Ferry. Author unknown. Public Domain via Wikipedia Commons.

Fig. 116: The King's Shilling, 1871, by James Campbell. Public Domain via Wikipedia Commons.

Fig. 117: Original Engraving. Royal Marine Barracks in Woolwich.

Fig. 118: Capture of Curacao, 1807 by Thomas Whitcombe. Public Domain via Wikipedia Commons.

Fig. 119: Photograph of Hammock on the Grand Turk.

Fig. 120: HMS Inconstant built 1868. Public Domain via Wikipedia Commons.

Fig. 121: HMS Boadicea by Henry Morgan. Public Domain via Wikipedia Commons.

Fig. 122: HMS Northampton, 1876. Public Domain via Wikipedia Commons.

Fig. 123: Photograph from Bremhill Exhibition 1990.

Fig. 124: Photograph from Bremhill Exhibition 1990.

Fig. 125: Photograph from Bremhill Exhibition 1990.

Fig. 126: East Tytherton. Alexander Anderson (1775-1870}, engraver Paul Abraham. Public Domain via Wikipedia Commons.

Fig. 127: Photograph from Bremhill Exhibition 1990.

Chapter 4

Fig. 128: Two tax collectors by Marinus van Reymerswaele. Public Domain via Wikipedia Commons.

Fig. 129: nationalarchives.gov.uk.

Fig. 130: Edward Jenner vaccinating his young child held by Mrs. Jenn. Wellcome L0011550. Creative Commons by 4.0 via Wikimedia.org.

Fig. 131: 18th century untitled engraving.

Fig. 132: Children of the poor. Alamy D95RA4.

Fig. 133: workhouses.com

Fig. 134: The sewing class. iStock 873330734.

Fig. 135: Visiting the poor, 1844 by Karl Girardet.

Fig. 136: 5th Marquess of Lansdowne by George Fiddes Watt.

Fig. 137: Sir George Hungerford. Cadenham Manor library.

Fig. 138: Calne Almshouses. Photographs, Calne Heritage Centre.

Fig. 139: Photograph. From original print by John Harris.

Fig. 140: First day cover 1927 from Chippenham Museum.

Fig. 141: Large bottles of medicine. Image by Jenny Odonnel.

Fig. 142: Surgeon lancing an abscess of the forearm. Canstock photo 7928271.

Fig. 143: An enquiry into the cause and effect of variolllae vaccinae. Edward Jenner.

Fig. 144: Vaccination by Ernest Board. Public Domain by Wikipedia Commons.

Fig. 145: bioedge.org

Fig. 146: Medical cures, engraving 1898. Punch.

Fig. 147: Images from Thomas Gardiner's remedy book W&S H C.

Fig. 148: Photograph by John Harris.

Fig. 149: Photograph from the Bremhill Exhibition 1990.

Fig. 150: PB works.com. Colonial School/ School Masters.

Fig. 151: George Clausen. Public Domain via Wikipedia Commons.

Fig. 152: Photograph from Bremhill Exhibition 1990.

Fig. 153: JLL Childhood Collection - school desks 2737 photo by Clem Rutter CC by SA 3.0 via Wikimedia Commons.

Fig. 154: Photograph by John Harris.

Fig. 155: Bremhill School pageant c.1917. Courtesy of Kate Clark.

Fig. 156: Photograph courtesy of Nigel Pocock.

Fig. 157: Photograph. W&SHC.

Fig. 158: Photograph courtesy of Chris Minty.

Fig. 159: Lager Beer Riot, 1855. Wikipedia.

Fig. 160: Photograph by John Harris from an original at Wiltshire Museum.

Fig. 161: Detail from 'The Bottle' after George Cruikshank. Wellcome Collection. International (CC by 4.0).

Fig. 162: Poor family, poor home. 19th century. Adobe Stock1587 049907.

Fig. 163: Women gossiping around a fire. Alamy HHEM18.

Fig. 164, 165, 166: Images by permission of the Public Record Office, London.

Fig. 167: Peasant woman by James Ward. Public Domain via Wikipedia Commons.

Fig. 168: Engraving. Imprisoned 1800.

Fig. 169; Lawyers and villagers in court. Alamy DMN7N5.

Fig. 170: Photograph. Calne Heritage Centre.

Fig. 171: Photograph. Calne Heritage Centre.

Fig. 172: Engraving (detail) A rakes progress. William Hogarth Public Domain Wikipedia Commons.

Fig. 173: Photograph by John Harris.

Chapter 5

Fig. 174: Crown post. Photograph by John Harris.

Fig. 175: Photograph by John Harris.

Fig. 176: Woodcut. Wellcome Collection. Ref. 33295i. Public Domain mark.

Fig. 177: Original woodcut print.

Fig. 178: Photograph by John Harris.

Fig. 179: Lithograph. Wiltshire Museum.

Fig. 180: Lithograph. Wiltshire Museum.

Fig. 181: Engraving. Execution of a criminal. Froissarts Chronicles. Public Domain via Wikipedia Commons.

Fig. 182: Copperplate engraving.

Fig. 183: Thumbscrew. Anagoria via Wikipedia Commons.

Fig. 184: Woodcut 1598. Witch trial. Public Domain via Wikipedia Commons.

Fig. 185: The History of Witches. No copyright. Wellcome Collection.

Fig. 186: Matthew Hopkins. Witchfinder General. Etching. Wellcome Collection V00258871.

Fig. 187: Execution. Original woodcut.

Fig. 188: Photograph by John Chandler.

Fig. 189: Agnes Waterhouse: woodcut. Public Domain via Wikipedia Commons.

Chapter 6

Fig. 190: Manor court book W&SHC.

Fig. 191: The bottle after George Cruikshank. Wellcome Collection. International (CC by 4.0).

Fig. 192: The parish constable. Postcard . Thomas Rowlandson, 1770.

Fig. 193: Manor commonplace book. W&SHC.

Fig. 194: Landscape with shepherd by Willhelm von Kobell (1766-1853).

Fig. 195: The County Courts, Devizes. Wiltshire Museum.

Fig. 196: Engraving, church court. iStock 614720966.

Fig. 197: Painting. Sir George Hungerford. Cadenham Manor library.

Fig. 198: Unknown 18th century artist.

Fig. 199: The cuckhold departs for the hunt. C1800. PBS Learning Media.

Fig. 200: Lovers in a Hayfield by A. Altdorfer. Public Domain via WikiArt. Org.

Fig. 201: Market place, Devizes. Wiltshire Museum.

Fig. 202: Photograph from Bremhill Exhibition 1990.

Fig. 203: Caricature. Sir Gabriel Goldney by Delfico. Public Domain via Wikipedia Commons.

Fig. 204: Illustration by Emma Brownlow. The Foundling Hospital.

Fig. 205: The Outcast by Richard Redgrave. Public Domain via Wikipedia Commons.

Fig. 206: Kitchen maid (detail) by Anthony Oberman.

Fig. 207: Peasants in a Tavern by A. C. Ostade. Public Domain via Wikipedia Commons.

Fig. 208: Sparrows by A. Brahms 1797. Public Domain via Wikipedia Commons.

Fig. 209: Paul Sansby. British Museum. Public Domain via Wikipedia Commons.

Fig. 210: Reaping Corn using a scythe. CC by 4.0. Staedel Museum.

Fig. 211: Bremhill, Dumb Post Inn. Unknown.

Fig. 212: Engraving by Charles Whymper (1858-1951).

Fig. 213: Engraving haystack with pitchfork.

Fig. 214: Wiltshire County Police. Mid- 19th century. Wiltshire Museum. By Charles Whymper.

Chapter 7

Fig. 215: Bremhill Church Yard, Engraving in display case at St. Martin's Church, Bremhill.

Fig. 216: Water colour of former chapel in Foxham.

Fig. 217: Photograph of St. Peters Church in Highway. Unknown.

Fig. 218: Watercolour by William Bartlett 1824. Wiltshire Museum.

Fig. 219: Victorian Photograph of Bremhill Court. Bremhill Exhibition, 1990.

Fig. 220: Satirical Engraving. British Museum. Public Domain via Wikipedia Commons.

Fig. 221: Original print of Quaker meeting.

Fig. 222: Photograph of Quaker Burial Ground courtesy of Nigel Pocock.

Fig. 223: Photograph of Quaker Burial Ground courtesy of Nigel Pocock.

Chapter 8

Fig. 264: Red Cross War Hospital, Chippenham. Courtesy of Wiltshire Council.

Fig. 265: Photograph courtesy of Lynne Pegler.

Fig. 266: Photograph courtesy of Lynne Pegler.

Fig. 267: Photograph courtesy of Chris Minty.

Fig. 268: Photograph courtesy of Chris Minty.

Fig. 269: Photograph courtesy of Chris Minty

Fig. 270: Caricature. NPG. Public domain.

Fig. 271: Bowood House War Hospital. Photograph courtesy of Bowood archive.

Fig. 272: Photograph. Lafayette portrait 1904. Share- alike. Creative Commons.

Fig. 273: Publicity Card 1911.

Fig. 274: Original poster. Artist unknown.

Fig. 275: bathwarhospital.org.

Fig. 276: Red Cross nurses. Calne Heritage centre.

Fig. 277: Fred Buchanan. Public Domain via Wikipedia Commons.

Fig. 278: Fry bakery, Bremhill from Bremhill Exhibition 1990.

Fig. 279: Photograph courtesy of Foxham Village Hall archive.

Fig. 280: Bremhill Parish Neighbourhood Plan.

Fig. 281: Mothers Union outing. Photograph from Bremhill Exhibition 1990.

Fig. 282: Photograph courtesy of Foxham Village Hall archive.

Fig. 283: Photograph courtesy of Foxham Village Hall archive.

Fig. 284: Fordson tractor courtesy of Lynne Pegler.

Fig. 285: Delivery waggon image courtesy of Nigel Pocock.

Fig. 286: Walter Pocock image courtesy of Nigel Pocock.

Fig. 287: Exhibition stand image courtesy of Nigel Pocock.

Fig. 288: IWM.org Art.IWM.PST8235.

Fig. 289: IWM.org Art.IWM PST15095.

Fig. 290: Rex Grimshaw. Photograph by Helen Stuckey.

Fig. 291: Taylor (Lt) War Office official photographer. Public Domain via Wikipedia Commons.

Fig. 292: Garden party. Photography from Bremhill Exhibition 1990.

Fig. 293: Air Raid Precautions on British Home Front. c1941. D3940. Public Domain via AWC.

Fig. 294: C .H. Shaw. moravian.org.uk

Fig. 295: museumandarchives.redcross.org.uk.

Fig. 296: IWM. Art.IWM PST 6230.

Fig. 297: Photograph, unknown author, courtesy of Bremhill Exhibition 1990.

Fig. 298: Bremhill Home Guard. Photograph from Bremhill Exhibition 1990.

Fig. 299: Tytherton Home Guard courtesy of David Wood.

Fig. 300: Photograph courtesy of David Wood.

Fig. 301: Photograph courtesy of David Wood.

Fig. 302: Photograph courtesy of David Wood.

Fig. 303: Smith gun. Photograph courtesy of the late Brigadier George Powell.

Fig. 304: Photograph courtesy of Foxham Village Hall archive.

Fig. 305: Photograph by John Harris.

Fig. 306: Photograph by John Harris.

Acknowledgements

This book would not have been possible without the support of many people and organisations. I wish to acknowledge the contributions of the following: -

The steering committee and volunteers of the Bremhill Parish History Group, for all the many ways they participated in this project, particularly Ewen Bird, John Harris, Dr Christopher Kent, Isobel Moore, Jim Scott, Helen Stuckey and David Wood for their contributions to the text;

Members of the Bremhill community who kindly consented to be interviewed, contributed to research or provided information to the project;

The Wiltshire Victoria County History Trust, particularly the support of James Holden, Chris Caswill and Dr Ros Johnson;

Dr John Chandler for his patient and diplomatic editing and mentorship;

Staff at the Wiltshire and Swindon History Centre, especially Helen Taylor and Julie Davies;

Jenny Pope and the volunteers of the Wiltshire Family History Society for the fantastic transcription of Bremhill Manor court record WSA, 473/52;

David Dawson and staff of the Wiltshire Museum in Devizes;

Lord Lansdowne, Lord Simon Kerry and Dr Cathryn Spence in relation to the Bowood archive and other information about the involvement of the Lansdowne family with the parish;

Trustees of Maud Heath's Trust for permission to reproduce the images of the Causeway;

Richard Broadhead, Dr Graham Brown, Dr Simon Draper, Dr Christopher Kent, Nigel Pocock and David Wood who all generously allowed access to their previous research and publications;

Staff at the Calne Heritage Centre, especially Sue Boddington;

Eleo Carson for her infectious enthusiasm, responsive and supportive comments and edits of the text;

Steve Harris for his skill in bringing bygone photographs and images back to life and his support for the project;

Dr Christopher Kent for kindly helping with the indexing;

Ray Alder for information and suggestions about the Red Cross voluntary effort in World War I;

Steve Hobbs for pointing out some exciting Bremhill cases from the church courts;

Finally, I wish to thank the Bremhill parish community, the three years of this project have been an absolute privilege and a pleasure.

Thank you.

Dr Louise Ryland-Epton
December 2021

Index

Chapel Bridge

Lenthams Fm.

Lenthams Br.

Bathing Pl.

Tytherton Calloways.

Currycombs.

Tytherton Lucas.

Wilts and Berk

River Marden

Bremhill Wick.

Scots Mill

Barsmore

Wick Hill

Jeffreys House

Bencroft.

Stanley

Catland Pond

Bremhill.

Fm.

Stanley Abbey

Hazeland Farm

Studley Fm.

Derry Hill

Studley.

Lanaway Fm.

Hill

Chil

Stockham

Goat Acre

Beacon Hill

Sperthill

Charlcot

Nath House Farm

Beacon Fm

Witcombs Mill

Manger

New Farm

Hillmarton

Cowage

Taps Br.

Whitley Fm

Upper Beversbrook

Middle Beversbrook

Penn

Penn Hill

Lower Beversbrook

Calne Marsh

Penn Fm

Frith Fm

Cherhill Common

Map dated 1813

Milton Keynes UK
Ingram Content Group UK Ltd.
UKHW050253091223
433878UK00006B/44

9 781914 407581